Praise for
Dr. Thompson's Straight Talk on Autism

"What sets [Thompson] apart from other brilliant and well-informed authors . . . is his positive attitude, his compassion, and his incredible ability to make complex information seem simple and clear to the average reader."

—Susan Moreno, M.A., A.B.S.
Founder and President, MAAP Services for the Autism Spectrum
Editor, *The MAAP*
Parent of a woman with autism

"A refreshing resource! Dr. Thompson cuts to the chase, highlighting the most relevant facts, stats, and *straight talk* for spectrum issues to date."

—Karen Simmons
Founder and CEO, Autism Today
Co-author, *Chicken Soup for the Soul, Children with Special Needs*

"With this book, Travis Thompson wins the "triple crown" for knowledge translation—best available research, state-of-the-art clinical practice, and family wisdom (as the grandfather of a youngster with autism). His triple crown expertise permeating this book is sure to make quality of life enhancements for children with autism spectrum disorders and their families."

—Ann Turnbull, Ed.D.
Beach Center on Disability, University of Kansas

"This book provides easily accessible information about autism that is factually accurate and evidence based. A must have for anyone who knows a person with autism."

—Craig H. Kennedy, Ph.D., BCBA
Chair, Special Education Department, Vanderbilt University

"An easy-to-follow road map for parents to actively and affordably become involved in bringing up emotionally healthy children with ASD … also provides teachers with the frameworks with which to better build inclusive teaching practices."

—Donna Williams, Dip Ed, BA Hons
Author, *Autism: An Inside Out Approach* and *The Jumbled Jigsaw*
Autism consultant and public speaker

Dr. Thompson's Straight Talk on Autism

Dr. Thompson's Straight Talk on Autism

by

Travis Thompson, Ph.D.
Department of Pediatrics
University of Minnesota School of Medicine
Minneapolis

Baltimore • London • Sydney

Paul H. Brookes Publishing Co.
Post Office Box 10624
Baltimore, Maryland 21285-0624
USA

www.brookespublishing.com

Typeset by Spearhead Global, Inc., Bear, Delaware.
Manufactured in the United States of America by
Versa Press, Inc., East Peoria, Illinois.

The individuals described in this book are composites or real people whose situations have been masked and are based on the authors' experiences. Names and identifying details have been changed to protect confidentiality.

The images that appear throughout the book are used by permission of the individuals depicted or their parents or guardians.

Library of Congress Cataloging-in-Publication Data

Thompson, Travis.
Dr. Thompson's straight talk on autism / by Travis Thompson.
p. cm.
Includes bibliographical references and index.
ISBN-13: 978-1-55766-945-2
ISBN-10: 1-55766-945-7
1. Autism. I. Title. 2007045701

British Library Cataloguing in Publication data are available from the British Library.

2012 2011 2010 2009 2008

10 9 7 6 5 4 3 2 1

Contents

About the Author

Travis Thompson, Ph.D., Professor, Department of Pediatrics, University of Minnesota School of Medicine, MMC 486 Mayo, 420 Delaware Street, Minneapolis, MN 55455

Travis Thompson is Professor of the Autism Program of the Department of Pediatrics at the University of Minnesota School of Medicine; a faculty affiliate of the University of Minnesota's Center on Neurobehavioral Development; and serves as Supervising Psychologist for the Minnesota Early Autism Project, a community-based treatment program for young children with autism spectrum disorders (ASDs). He completed his doctoral training in psychology at the University of Minnesota and completed both postdoctoral training at the University of Maryland and advanced studies at Cambridge University. He has been a professor of psychology, special education, psychiatry, and pharmacology at the University of Minnesota and Vanderbilt University and was Director of the John F. Kennedy Center on Human Development at Vanderbilt University and the Institute of Child Development at the University of Kansas School of Medicine.

He has been involved in research, teaching, and clinical activities related to developmental disabilities and related topics for many years, publishing more than 225 articles and chapters and 27 books. He served as advisor to 47 doctoral students. He has lectured in 41 states within the United States and 13 countries outside of the United States. In the past, he has been an advisor of the Twin Cities Society for Autistic Children (Minnesota) and the Davidson County Autism Society (Kansas). He has served on grant review panels of the Food and Drug Administration, National Research Council, and National Institute of Child Health and Human Development, including chairing the review of applications for Autism Centers of Excellence. Dr. Thompson has received numerous awards, including the Don Hake Award (American Psychological Association [APA] Division 25), for outstanding contributions in bridging basic and applied science; the Research Award, American Association on Mental Retardation; the Distinguished Research

Award, The Arc of the United States; the Academy of Mental Retardation Career Scientist Award; the Edgar Doll Award (APA Division 33), for contributions to improve the lives of people with developmental disabilities; and the Ernest R. Hilgard Award (APA), for distinguished contributions to integrating multiple areas of psychology.

Dr. Thompson's wife Anneke is a retired special education teacher, though she continues to tutor children with special needs, and his daughter Andrea is currently teaching children with ASDs. He also has three other adult children: Peter, Jennifer, and Rebecca. Rebecca's son, Michael Rodriguez, has an ASD.

Preface

Today I spend much of my time in other worlds, very unlike those which most of us occupy, for I share the province of individuals with autism spectrum disorders (ASDs). One can never fully understand another person's perspective, as psychologists, sociologists, and philosophers have long argued. But sometimes by placing one's shoes in the impression left by another's feet and looking out at the world as they have been doing, a remarkable thing can happen. For a moment or two, one begins to see the world through lenses that are utterly unlike one's own. It is a world without deceit, ulterior motives, or stealth. Facts and order reign supreme in this realm. It is a world in which you can trust those closest to you to do exactly what they say they are going to do, unfailingly without exception. But suddenly when another person approaches, the world abruptly becomes askew. People are speaking too rapidly to be understood, and things seem disturbingly out of order, except for bits and pieces here and there that intensely captivate one's attention. Nothing seems quite right. The heart races as apprehension takes hold of one's body. For a fleeting instant one truly grasps the unique perspective of that other person, one with an ASD.

The world of children with ASDs is a very far cry from where my career began as a basic behavioral scientist. During graduate school and postgraduate years, I conducted research on operant learning and behavioral effects of drugs. While my doctoral minor was in child psychology, most of my research was directed at understanding basic learning principles and how they were modified by biological factors. The field called *behavior modification*, application of basic learning principles to overcoming human behavior problems, was just emerging in the 1960s. The earliest clinical work was done in institutions and in special classrooms for children with intellectual disabilities or emotional disorders. I was aware of that work from a comfortable distance but had no plan to change the direction of my career, which was developing very well indeed. Publications based on our laboratory research were emerging at a disarming pace, and several research grants had been garnered. Academic life was good.

In the spring of 1968, I was contacted by administrators at Faribault State Hospital in South Central Minnesota to help develop treatment programs for their residents with intellectual disabilities to reduce their problem behavior and develop new skills based on operant learning principles. It seemed a daunting undertaking, but I agreed to visit the institution to see if I could be of assistance. I had no idea what lay ahead. In the preface to our book (Thompson & Grabowski, 1972) about the work that unfolded, I described my first visit to the institution. The language is outdated, but this excerpt conveys the powerful impression that I experienced that day.

> I was confronted with sights, sounds, and smells that I had never before experienced and hoped that I would never witness again. Seated in the middle of large ward area shackled to a chair was a young man in his twenties with the skin abraded from his knees and blood running down his shins. Along the seventy-foot wall of the ward were seated approximately fifteen men, huddled in fetal positions, with their heads between their knees. Most of them sat totally still, a few rocked from side to side, a few rocked forward and backward. Beneath half of the chairs were puddles of urine. The room reeked of urine and feces, and feces were smeared over the floor, over arms and legs, and on the trousers and shirts of numerous residents. Approximately half of the men were partially or totally unclad. Another twenty or so residents were walking, running, or twirling around the room. Some were rapidly twiddling their fingers in front of [their] faces, others were gnawing at their hands and forearms. Most residents were scarred or exhibited recent wounds, such as scratches, abrasions, or scabs. The noise level was unbelievable. The ward echoed with hoots, shrieks, and wails resembling those from the worst class B-horror movie.... It is impossible to pay a visit to this 'special inferno' without feeling that something must be done to help the retarded. They deserve the maximum human dignity which can be afforded them. (Thompson & Grabowski, 1972, p. viii)

As reported in our book, between 1968 and 1972, approximately 25% of the 1,800 residents of Faribault State Hospital were involved in the first large-scale behavior therapy program in the country for people with intellectual disabilities. My graduate students and I, in collaboration with Faribault State Hospital staff members, developed behavioral treatment programs. Staff training was critical, beginning with instilling in employees the conviction that doing what appeared to be impossible was indeed possible. As residents learned basic skills, their behavior problems plummeted. In one building, the use of locked seclusion because of violent behavior dropped from 2,400 hours per month to zero over 8 months. Psychotropic medication dosages were reduced by half. Dramatic improvements occurred in the residents' behavior and quality of life over the course of the program.

A class action right-to-treatment lawsuit was filed on behalf of the residents in several Minnesota institutions by two courageous young disability rights attorneys, Neil Mickenberg and Jeffrey Hartje (*Welsch v. Likins,* 1972). The lawsuit relied, in part for its evidentiary basis, on the improvements that were reported in our book. The legal team was later joined by attorney Luther Granquist, who oversaw implementation of the final ruling as Court Monitor. The Welsch case that was filed in 1972 included several state institutions, including Faribault and Cambridge state hospitals. The suit made two basic claims: that institutionalized mentally retarded persons are constitutionally entitled to habilitation services and that mentally retarded persons are entitled to live in the least restrictive setting. A key factual finding was made by U.S. District Court Judge Earl Larson in his first opinion in the case issued on February 15, 1974:

> The evidence in the instant case is overwhelming and convincing that a program of "habilitation" can work to improve the lives of Cambridge's residents. Testimony of experts and documentary evidence indicate that everyone, no matter the degree or severity of retardation, is capable of growth and development if given adequate and suitable treatment. (Granquist, 1982)

The consequences of the court's ruling included improvements in staffing and services within the existing institutions, but most importantly, over the succeeding years, it led to the transfer of most of the remaining residents with intellectual disabilities from institutions to community settings.

Our efforts on behalf of the people with intellectual disabilities in Minnesota's institutions, many of whom had autism, changed the course of my career. The interested reader can view a film based on that project made by Stephen Arhelger and me available on the web site of the Minnesota Governor's Council on Developmental Disabilities (see http://www.mncdd.org/parallels2/one/video/changes.html).

For nearly 4 decades I have worked as a clinician, teacher, and research scientist with children, adolescents, and adults with ASDs, as well as with their families, teachers, doctors, and therapists.

Gradually over many years I have gained a greater purchase on this world. In the early years, most of my work was with adults and adolescents in residential programs and public schools, mainly individuals with severe autistic disorder and behavioral challenges. I spent countless hours in residences that served individuals with autism and in their classrooms, working with their teachers. Adolescents and young adults with violently aggressive or self-injurious behavior who had severe tantrums and were occasionally responsible for property destruction were referred to me. We were often able to improve those individuals' behavior by rearranging the circumstances giving rise to their behavioral outbursts. Behavior therapy principles were very powerful, but with older adolescents and adults, often the gains were modest. Through that work I learned what happens to children with ASDs if they are deprived of appropriate early intervention and effective educational services.

For the past 5 years, I have worked primarily with preschool children in an attempt to prevent the emergence of severe autism symptoms like those I had seen in the past, through intensive early intervention. In the course of that work, I've spent hundreds of hours in homes of children with ASDs and their families. Some families had only recently learned of their child's diagnosis and others had cast about for several years looking for a remedy that would make their child whole again before seeking more effective therapy services for their child. They were all tormented. Through collaborating with them and working directly with their children, most parents eventually came to terms with their child's disability, investing themselves in a range of methods to promote their development and pleasure in life. Many of their children are successfully integrated into regular education settings with supplementary support; others are served in special education classrooms. These parents enjoy their child with autism as a member of their family, much as they revel in their other children's development and achievements.

Occasionally parents are unable to face the difficult reality that it is unlikely that their son or daughter is going to be the same as their other children or the neighbor child next door. Even with the best possible outcome after intensive early intervention, it is likely the youngster will persist in displaying residual limitations. For those parents, the search is relentless for a new diet, supplement, or other treatment that will make their child whole. Their frustration, disappointment, and anguish grows as one after another proposed therapy hasn't accomplished its claimed objective: recovery. Because they have yet to find the nostrum for which they are searching, one that will make their child with autism like their other children, such parents often find it difficult to fully incorporate that child as an integral part of their family's life. As they wait for the real child to emerge, they continue searching.

There is always a risk in drawing too heavily on personal family experiences in writing about a topic such as autism. But there may also be some advantages. My grandson, Michael Rodriguez, who is now 10 years old, has an ASD. He has been fortunate to grow up in a loving family with older brother Alex and sister Emma, who have taken him under their wing without being overly protective. They have treated him pretty much as siblings would treat any younger brother, while being tolerant of his quirky behavior. His mother, Rebecca, my oldest daughter, has been an understanding, loving mother, working closely with public school programs to maximize Michael's opportunities to succeed in regular education settings, and he is doing quite well indeed. His teachers are sincerely committed to providing him with opportunities many children with ASDs do not have, which is greatly appreciated. Miguel Rodriguez, Michael's dad, is remarried, and with his wife Stephanie, has provided a safe, supportive, structured home for Michael and his siblings, which is so important to any child with an ASD.

Having Michael in our family has been a pleasure and has provided a different kind of understanding of the life a child with an ASD, one with greater empathy for the daily dilemmas he faces. He does the best he can to cope with situations that continue to be unpleasant to him, and at times very disturbing. For Michael and other youngsters like him, most of their unusual behavior, like their hand flapping, twirling, lining up objects, repetitive speech, and tantrums are attempts to cope with a world that appears incomprehensible and often chaotic to them. It is their way of creating order and gaining control over a disorderly world. Michael seldom displays those symptoms any longer, but he occasionally lapses into earlier behavior patterns when he's especially tired, when he's experiencing stress, or occasionally when he's bored. Michael has come very far thanks to his family and dedicated teachers, but lingering remnants remain. They remind us that Michael's daily life continues to involve struggles from which the rest of us are spared.

When I started working in this field in the late 1960s, almost nothing was known about autism. Aside from Leo Kanner's (1943) classic description and a few very early studies using operant learning methods with small samples of children with severe autism, there was nearly no research on the subject. The first few parents of children with autism with whom I worked learned together. We developed interventions to deal with their children's behavioral challenges and teach new skills. Despite the naïveté of some of our efforts, we enjoyed considerable success, and their children's lives improved accordingly. I continue to be exceedingly grateful to the families I had the good fortune to know in those early days who served as my teachers as well as recipients of my services.

Over the past 20 years, knowledge within the field has mushroomed, so much so that it is difficult to keep abreast of the latest findings, especially in specialty fields distant from one's own. The National Institutes of Health PubMed database of scientific journal articles includes approximately 11,000 entries. In my earlier book *Making Sense of Autism* (2007), published by Paul H. Brookes Publishing Co., I attempted to capture the essence of this information, providing a framework for thinking about and understanding the puzzling world of individuals with autism. The book summarized evidence-based practices based on research and clinical experience and our growing understanding of autism. My primary goal in that book was not to suggest specific interventions that could be adopted by parents, teachers, and other therapists, but instead I wanted to help them understand their children, students, and patients.

Children, unlike computers, automobiles, and vacuum cleaners, do not come with owner instruction manuals. There is no step-by-step guide that explains how these unique living beings operate, nor is there a help line to call when problems arise. Parents are on their own. Where are parents and teachers to turn for information? Nearly as soon as *Making Sense of Autism* was published, I began being asked, "Now that I have a better understanding of what makes my child tick, what can I do to promote his development and overcome these shortcomings?" or "How can we reduce his behavior problems?" Parents, teachers, and therapists reasonably want specific suggestions for action steps they could take based on their new understanding of ASDs. "What can I do to teach him more appropriate social behavior in the classroom?" teachers have asked. That is the focus of the present book.

The content and writing style of this book reflects my best understanding of evidence-based practices, informed by my professional and personal experience working with individuals with ASDs. The book is intended to provide practical information that can be used at home and school in parenting children with ASDs and in providing educational and therapy services. While most of the procedures described have emerged from controlled research, some are logical extensions of those principles based on my own experience working with families, teachers, and therapists.

In the book, Chapters 1–3 provide descriptive information about the characteristics of ASDs; Chapters 4–6 focus on promoting communication, relationships, and social skills; Chapters 7 and 8 deal with the most common causes of behavioral challenges and possible interventions; and Chapters 9–11 deal with recreation and leisure and participation as a member of the family and community.

Throughout the book, many of the cases described involve children and families with whom I have worked. Names and, in some cases, ages have been changed to protect the privacy of those involved. Some of the cases are hypothetical examples similar to specific children with whom I have worked, but differing in gender, ethnicity, or age. Many of the visual illustrations throughout the book are sketches that I created based on photographs of children with whom I've worked. In several instances, I've included images of my grandson Michael and his sister Emma, illustrating ways children with ASDs can lead very ordinary lives. Several images are of children with ASDs whose parents kindly provided original photographs of their children that were converted to sketches, illustrating community and leisure activities. Several images are of children in a public school program. In one instance, a child who is participating in a home-based intensive early intervention is shown. In all cases, permissions have been obtained from anyone shown in these sketches.

I am grateful to the children with ASDs and their parents who have allowed me to participate in their lives. The teachers and therapists who have shared their experiences and permitted me to observe and learn from them deserve special thanks as well. Thanks to Ruth Elaine Hane and Kammy Kramer, who kindly shared their personal perspectives on the world of autism. I am especially indebted to Lisa Barsness and Meggan Kerkenbush of the Minnesota Early Autism Project. They are tireless advocates for children with ASDs and among the most skilled therapists I have known. It is a pleasure to observe them working their magic with children.

I am especially grateful to Dr. Teresa Estrem for her thoughtful comments on Chapter 4. To Paula Goldberg and Sue Pratt, whose kind comments were included in the foreword, I am enormously appreciative.

Finally, I would like to thank Rebecca Lazo, Senior Acquisitions Editor at Paul H. Brookes Publishing Co., for her support, and Marie Abate, Production Editor, for her skillful editorial work in improving the readability of the manuscript.

REFERENCES

Granquist, L.A. (1982). *A brief history of the Welsch case.* Paper presented at the 1982 meeting of American Association on Mental Retardation, Boston. Retrieved June 26, 2007, from http://www.mncdd.org/past/pdf/82-granquist-history-welsch.pdf

Kanner, L. (1943). Autistic disturbances of affective contact. *Nervous Child, 2,* 217–250.

Thompson, T. (2007). *Making sense of autism.* Baltimore: Paul H. Brookes Publishing Co.

Thompson, T., & Grabowski, J. (1972). *Behavior modification of the mentally retarded.* New York: Oxford University Press.

Welsch v. Likins, 373 F. Supp. 487, 495 (D. Minn. 1974).

What gift has Providence bestowed on man,
that is so dear to him as his children?

—Cicero

To my gifts:
Rebecca, Jennifer, Andrea, and Peter

1

A Road Less Traveled

Autism Spectrum Disorders

Maggie watches her 3-year-old daughter twirl a doll upside down by one leg so that the hair twirls around in circles. The child seems entranced by the doll's shimmering hair. Maggie is increasingly worried about her daughter's intense preoccupation with spinning objects. Brandon's father picks him up to comfort him when he bumps his knee, but Brandon cries and pulls away. The more Brandon's father attempts to console his son, the more the child screams and shoves him. The man finds his son's odd behavior disturbing. A preschool teacher notices that a 3-year-old child named Richard seldom plays with other children in her class. The teacher says he spends too much time "in his own world." Richard ignores play approaches from other children, and he seems to prefer sitting by himself lining up blocks on the floor. When another child inadvertently bumps into his row of blocks, Richard shrieks with displeasure. If parents and teachers scrutinize closely, they may see what they believe are other warning signs that confirm their worst fear, that these children have autism. Like most people, they don't really understand what autism is. But whatever it is, it isn't good.

In her poem "A Tale Begun," Nobel laureate Wislawa Szymborska wrote, "The world is never ready/ For the birth of a child" (1993). That is nowhere more the case than when a child with autism enters a family. The family embarks upon an entirely different road from the one on which they thought they had entered. As Robert Frost wrote, "Two roads diverged in the wood, and I / took the one less traveled by / and that has made all the difference" (1920).

All the difference indeed, for the family's life will never be the same. Autism strikes fear into the hearts of parents and causes alarm to many teachers who have had little or no training or experience in teaching youngsters with autism spectrum disorders (ASDs). But parenting a child with autism can also be filled with joy and discovery as you come to understand the unique way in which your child with an ASD sees the world.

Autism didn't exist in the daily lexicon of most Americans a generation ago. But *autism* has become a word of our times. Although autism is currently a popular topic for discussion, it appears that the disability has always been with us. More than 2 centuries ago, professionals were first made aware of this unusual disability (Itard, 1801) that is now affecting an estimated 1 in 150 children in the United States under 21 years of age (Rice, 2007). Today, autism is featured in television reports and newspaper headlines and is the subject of congressional hearings. Public school programs, medical practices, and entire service industries devoted to autism have emerged. *Autism* has become a household word that is very much on the American mind.

When a child's pediatrician first tells parents that their child may have autism, they experience two competing reactions: First is that it can't be true. It is impossible, absolutely unthinkable. "He is just a normal child who has been slow to talk and has some quirky behavior," they think. Although they are trying desperately to deny the possibility that the doctor's initial diagnostic hunch may be correct, the child's parents are simultaneously terrified. What if the doctor is right? What does this mean? Where can we turn for help, for answers? What should we do next?

This book is intended to be a practical guide for parents, teachers, and therapists who provide supports and services to children with ASDs. The first three chapters are devoted to defining autism, helping caregivers understand the nature of autism, and initializing steps on a new journey. The next three chapters focus on how parents and other caregivers can help promote basic skills that can overcome many of the deficits characteristic of ASDs: communication, socialization, and emotional relationships. Chapters 7 and 8 address the most common behavioral challenges experienced by children with ASDs, and the final chapters focus on a child's daily life as a member of her family, school, and community.

THE AUTISM EPIDEMIC: AUTISM SPECTRUM DISORDER PREVALENCE

Part of parents' fear emanates from the newspaper headlines and articles in magazines they've read and programs they have seen on television that claim that the country is awash in an autism epidemic. It is true that there are many more identified cases of autism than was believed to be the case in the past, but increasing evidence suggests there is no autism epidemic. In the 1980s it was estimated that about 2–3 in every 5,000 children had autism (Ritvo, Freeman, Mason-Brothers, Mo, & Ritvo, 1985). To qualify as having autism, a child had to present symptoms like those we now associate with autistic disorder, the most severe form of the disability. At that time, many pediatricians were never exposed to a child with autism during their training, and in public schools, children with this unusual condition were usually sequestered away in classrooms for students with severe developmental disabilities or emotional disorders. General education teachers had no contact with students with autism. Autism was considered a rare disability. But in the early 1990s epidemiologists, people who study the spread of diseases such as influenza, began reporting that the number of children identified with ASDs in public schools was growing. Over the following years the trend increased, with mounting numbers of children identified by schools as qualifying for services in the category of ASDs. The Centers for Disease Control and Prevention (CDC), the U.S. government agency that tracks trends in diseases, began reporting marked increases in autism prevalence. The CDC's figures were based on the number of children receiving autism services in public schools, using the Department of Education's *Child Count* statistics. That number was growing by leaps and bounds. Alarm spread across the country, especially among parents of young children. Media outlets declared that there was an "autism epidemic." The choice of the word *epidemic* was especially unfortunate and inaccurate because it refers to the occurrence of more cases of a disease than would be expected in a given time period, most often involving a communicable disease such as chicken pox, measles, or meningitis. *Epidemic* usually implies a rapidly spreading outbreak of a contagious disease. If there were an autism outbreak, then many people reasoned that there must be a disease agent causing the condition. Parents whose children had recently been diagnosed with autism began asking what agent could have caused their child's autism on the assumption that there was an autism epidemic. Autism's onset is often recognized between 3 and 4 years of age. Many parents noticed that the onset of their child's autism symptoms appeared around the same age that their child had received childhood vaccinations, a year or so earlier. Speculation grew that the culprit must have something to do with childhood vaccines. Some parents were terrified that their child would "catch" autism from a childhood vaccination, and others who had already been diagnosed were preparing litigation aimed at the pharmaceutical companies that made the vaccine, feeling certain that immunization had caused their child's condition.

The Publication that Ignited a Cultural Wildfire

In 1998 an article appeared in the prestigious English medical journal *The Lancet* proposing a link between the measles–mumps–rubella (MMR) vaccination and autism. Appearance of the article was followed by a rash of letters and responses from researchers and clinicians in British medical journals presenting evidence that there was no such connection (Horton, 2004; Kaye, del Mar Melero-Montes, & Jick, 2001; Taylor et al., 1999). Parents in the autism advocacy community were especially alarmed. An investigation of the chief author of the initial *Lancet* article, Dr. Andrew Wakefield, was launched when most of his co-authors wrote a retraction indicating that they did not believe there was any evidence of a connection between the MMR vaccination and autism. They said Dr. Wakefield added his speculation to the article without their approval. The article was discredited and the journal removed the article from its pages. But the wildfire had been set and took on a life of its own. Internet Listservs were awash with frightening claims and conspiracy theories. Allegations of cover-ups by both the pharmaceutical industry and doctors who immunized children to prevent childhood diseases spread. The claim appearing in a discredited report became a fact in the minds of many people overnight, especially parents (Deer, 2007).

Do Measles–Mumps–Rubella Vaccines and Thimerosal Cause Autism?

The fact that a vaccination can produce an exaggerated immune response and is capable of producing meningitis or encephalitis in a small number of immunized children has been known for many years. There is nothing new about that uncommon event, but it does happen. Occasionally, MMR vaccinations can cause high fever and convulsions. The live Urabe strain of the MMR vaccine can cause mumps in a small percentage of children receiving the immunization (Demichelli, Jefferson, Rivetti, & Price, 2005). But there had been no previous reports that it had caused autism, though the MMR vaccine had been used for many years. Moreover, the risk of meningitis among children who had not been vaccinated and who contract measles or mumps is much higher than that associated with the vaccine.

Over the intervening years there have been 16 studies of the MMR vaccine and the preservative thimerosal. Based on the results of these studies, there is no convincing evidence of a connection between the MMR vaccine and autism. Klein and Diehl (2004) examined studies in the National Institutes of Health MEDLINE database using the terms *measles, mumps, rubella,* and *autism*. They found 10 well-conducted studies that evaluated the relationship between the MMR vaccine and autism. Based on those studies, Klein and Diehl concluded that there is no evidence of a relationship between the MMR vaccination and the development of autism.

Several other studies revealed similar findings. Afzal et al. (2006) used sensitive laboratory tests to determine whether the measles virus was present in white blood cells of children diagnosed with regressive autism as had been suggested. In regressive autism, the child appears to be developing normally for 18 months to 2 years, then begins to lose skills and develops autistic signs. Afzal and colleagues failed to find any evidence of persistence of the measles virus in children with autism with any of the tests they used. Honda, Shimizu, and Rutter (2005) studied the incidence of ASD diagnoses in Yokohama, Japan, before and after the MMR vaccine administration was discontinued. They found ASD incidence increased up to age 7 regardless of whether the MMR vaccination was done. They concluded that the MMR vaccination could not explain the rise over time in the incidence of ASDs. Smeeth et al. (2004) used the United Kingdom General Practice Research Database to study children diagnosed with pervasive developmental disorder-not otherwise specified (PDD-NOS) and controls matched for age and sex. They found no differences in MMR vaccination rates among those who were later diagnosed with autism as compared with controls. Having been vaccinated did not increase the risk of developing autism. Parker, Schwartz, Todd, & Pickering (2004) reviewed all epidemiological studies through 2004. Of particular interest were studies in which thimerosal had been used in a country and was then discontinued. They found 12 publications, 10 of which found no connection between the MMR vaccination and thimerosal. The two epidemiologic studies that supported a possible association were of such poor quality that the results could not be interpreted (e.g., Geir & Geir, 2003, 2004). Parker and colleagues concluded that evidence from available studies did not demonstrate a link between vaccines containing thimerosal and ASD.

In 2004, the Institute of Medicine (IOM) of the National Academy of Sciences conducted the most credible evaluation of available evidence. In the IOM report of the Immunization Safety Review Committee, it was concluded that the body of epidemiological evidence did not support a causal relationship between the MMR vaccine or vaccines containing thimerosal and autism.

What *Is* Responsible for the Increase in Autism Cases?

If the MMR vaccination and thimerosal are not responsible for the reported increase in ASD cases, what *is* responsible? The problem with this question is that it begins with the assumption that there has been a sudden and unexpected increase in the number of new autism cases. But increasing evidence suggests that *the actual number of cases* may not have increased. What increased may have been *the number of identified cases*. It appears that there were *always* more children with ASDs than was apparent from earlier prevalence studies that relied on older diagnostic criteria. Many cases simply weren't recognized using older diagnostic methods. What has contributed to the appearance that there has been an autism epidemic?

Lovaas's 1987 Landmark Study

Prior to the late 1980s, it was generally believed that there were no effective interventions for young children with autism. In 1987, psychologist Ivar Lovaas reported follow-up results for a group of children who had received intensive early intervention, which indicated that half of the children with autism diagnoses greatly profited from intensive early behavior therapy, so much so that they tested in the typical range intellectually and could participate in regular education classrooms. Following Lovaas's (1987) publication, parents began clamoring for better methods of identifying autism among young children and greater access to such early intervention services. But up to that point there had been no generally agreed upon test for autism, which made diagnosis difficult.

A New Test for Autism and More Professionals Trained to Classify and Diagnose Autism Spectrum Disorders

The first widely recognized and accepted test for autism, the Autism Diagnostic Observation Schedule (ADOS), was published in 1989 (Lord, Rutter, DiLavore, & Risi, 1989), the year before the abrupt increase in reported autism cases. A very large number of university-based and community professionals and public school personnel began training to administer the new test. Many medical and educational professionals began recognizing, in children, signs of autism that had been labeled something else in the past. Autism diagnoses began emerging like crocuses in springtime. As the number of people trained to diagnose autism increased, the number of identified cases increased.

Introduction of Autism as a Special Education Service Category

Prior to 1991, children with autism were often included in the category of "emotionally disturbed" or "other health impairments" in special education school programs. Many were also categorized as having either an intellectual disability or learning disability. There was no separate educational category of "autism." In the 1991–1992 school year, the U.S. Department of Education issued a directive indicating that among the special education services categories, a new one be added: autism. In testimony before Congress in 2002, the Autism Society of America announced that over the 9 years from 1991 to 2000, the number of students with autism (ages 6–21) in America's schools increased 1,354%. What the report didn't include was that there was no autism category prior to 2001, so there were no meaningful statistics regarding the number of children with autism in schools. From one year to the next, the number of children receiving autism services in public school programs doubled and tripled according to Child Count statistics, a clear misrepresentation of reality on the ground (Gernsbacher, Dawson, & Goldsmith, 2005). Children with autism had been in our schools all along but had received a different label.

Change in Diagnostic Criteria

In 1994, the American Psychiatric Association released new diagnostic criteria in the fourth edition of the *Diagnostic and Statistical Manual of Mental Disorders (DSM-IV)* that broadened the definition of ASDs. Many children who may have been labeled emotionally disturbed or intellectually or language disabled in the past were now being diagnosed as having mild ASDs using more inclusive, modern criteria. When I began working in the autism field in the late 1960s and early 1970s, only children with severe autistic disorder were diagnosed with autism. These children typically were minimally verbal or altogether nonverbal, engaged in repetitive stereotypical flapping and twirling, and exhibited either aggression or self-injury. Today, children who are diagnosed with milder ASDs, such as Asperger syndrome or PDD-NOS would not have been so diagnosed at that time. It is also likely that children with high-functioning autism would not have been identified unless they exhibited dramatic signs, such as repetitive stereotypical hand flapping and severe tantrums.

Increased Parental Demand for Autism Services

These events made it clear to parents that early diagnosis was very important and that effective intervention was possible for many children with ASDs. As more parents became aware of ASD signs, they began seeking diagnoses from pediatricians and autism services in public schools. Public schools responded by creating more autism services. Once more services were available, schools began identifying more children as qualifying for specialized autism services, and the number of children receiving autism services greatly increased. Presumably, those children had been in school all along, but they had been identified for educational purposes as having another condition.

The National Research Council Report

In 2000, a committee of experts on early intervention convened to review evidence from studies of early interventions for children with ASDs and was commissioned to prepare a report on its findings. Lord and McGee (2001) summarized the committee's findings, which indicated that ASDs could be reliably diagnosed as early as 2 years of age, and they proposed that all preschool-age children with ASDs should receive a minimum of 25 hours per week of structured intensive early intervention. That increased the pressure even more for early identification and enhanced services.

Misidentification by Schools

There is growing evidence that school identification has led to inaccurate prevalence estimates. It appears that children previously identified as having learning disabilities, dyslexia, or mild intellectual disabilities were now being identified in public schools as having autism. As the number of students receiving ASD classification increased (from 0.6 to 3.1 per 1,000 from 1994 to 2004), the percent of students qualifying for learning disabilities and mental retardation services decreased proportionately (Shattuck, 2006). Laidler (2005) studied the U.S. Department of Education statistics for children receiving autism services and found that within a group of children born in a given year, the number identified as having an ASD increased with time. This increase is puzzling because within a group of children of the same age, there is no obvious reason why more should develop ASDs as they grow older. Autism is typically apparent by 3 years of age if it is going to occur. In addition, this progressive increase was substantially reduced when children reached 12 years of age (i.e., entering junior high school). This suggests that administrative factors may have partially determined which children were identified as qualifying for autism services. Because fewer specialized autism services may be available for older children with ASDs, perhaps they were assigned a different classification for educational purposes (e.g., learning or intellectual disability, emotional or behavior problems) rather than ASD services. Consistent with this idea was a study by Palmer, Blanchard, Jean, and Mandell (2005) that examined the relation between school district funding and autism prevalence within school districts. Districts with more financial resources identified a larger proportion of children with autistic disorder. This may mean children with ASDs in less affluent districts went unidentified, whereas students receiving an ASD classification in more affluent districts were more likely to be incorrectly identified as having autism because specialized services were available.

Misdiagnosis by Community Providers

Pediatricians, child psychiatrists, and other community practitioners providing services to children with autism are often not trained to accurately diagnose ASDs. They may be experts in attention-deficit/hyperactivity disorder (ADHD), mood disorder, or other neurodevelopmental disorders but may have had little experience with ASDs. Moreover, they are often unable to provide interdisciplinary team evaluations, which are often important in identifying alternative reasons as to why a child may exhibit some ASD signs but not have an ASD. A study conducted in Queensland, Australia, sheds light on this issue. Queensland is the second largest and third most populous state of Australia. Skellern, McDowell, and Schluter (2005) conducted an anonymous survey of pediatricians and psychiatrists in Queensland who had diagnosed or treated children with ASDs and related developmental disorders. They found that 58% of surveyed psychiatrists and pediatricians reported that when they were unsure of a child's diagnosis, they had erred on the side of providing an ASD diagnosis for educational purposes, and 36% of clinicians had provided an autism diagnosis in order to make it possible for the child and family to receive funding for specialized services *even when they knew the child did not meet the criteria for an autism diagnosis*. Comparable studies have not been conducted in the United States or Canada, though it seems unlikely that these diagnostic problems are limited to Australia.

SUMMARY OF AUTISM PREVALENCE

Though spectacles were used prior to the 1860s, they were primarily used by people who did a lot of close-up work, such as doctors, lawyers, writers, and surveyors. If other people complained of blurred vision when trying to make out objects at a distance, their doctors or pharmacists often recommended they try wearing spectacles. They purchased eyeglasses at a nearby pharmacy or general store, determining the appropriate strength by trial and error. But when the Dutch eye doctor Hermann Snellen published his famous letter chart for visual acuity in 1862, it became possible for any doctor's office to screen for nearsightedness in a matter of minutes. Snellen eye charts were hung on pharmacy walls and in doctors' offices, and optometry practices began springing up in the 1870s and 1880s. Over the next decade, a great many people who hadn't had a formal diagnosis in the past discovered that they suffered from nearsightedness. Had *Time* magazine and *Newsweek* magazines existed at the time, no doubt they would have announced the nation was experiencing a myopia (nearsightedness) epidemic.

Make no mistake, ASDs present huge challenges to families as well as educational, medical, and social service providers. There are far more people with ASDs than was believed in the past; however, many experts in the field now believe that if the same diagnostic criteria and the same tests that exist today for ASDs had been applied to a very large sample of children in 1980 who had been referred because they had signs of developmental disabilities and behavioral challenges, similar ASD prevalence figures may have been obtained. The previous autism prevalence figures of 4–6 out of 10,000 using older diagnostic criteria and evaluation methods grossly underestimated actual ASD prevalence at that time. Many children who could have profited from ASD services failed to receive them because they were not identified. Increasingly, experts are coming to the conclusion that there is no autism epidemic; rather, ASDs have always been more common than was once believed. If there was an epidemic, it was of fear and misinformation spread by word of mouth, through the Internet, and by the mass media. If there is a positive side to the claims of an autism epidemic, it is that it has made professionals and policy makers aware that ASDs have always been far more common than was previously believed, which poses challenges for improved early diagnosis, education, and treatment.

A FAMILY OF DISORDERS

Autism isn't a single disorder like a ruptured appendix. Autism is a *syndrome* that has more in common with epilepsy, which can affect different parts of the brain to differing degrees, than to an acute illness affecting a specific organ. ASDs are developmental disorders due to errors that occur early in brain development. Autism isn't caused by cold mothering, despite what Bruno Bettelheim (1967) said. Parenting can make ASD symptoms better or worse, but parenting doesn't cause autism. ASDs can be mild to severe. For a given child with an ASD, he or she may have minimal effects in one area of functioning, such as language, and moderate effects on another, such as social skills. Or the disability can profoundly interfere with a child's abilities in all areas. Some children with ASDs can have physical features that closely resemble those of other members of their families, and others may look distinctively different, with unusual physical characteristics, called *dysmorphic* features. Some ASDs run in families, others do not. When someone says that a child has autism, that doesn't tell the listener enough to know what the child is really like. A great deal of additional information is required in order to begin to develop a clearer picture about any given individual with an ASD.

Familial and Nonfamilial Autism

It has been known for a long time that some families include several individuals with autistic disorder or a combination of ASDs, whereas others have none. It is more likely that another family member will have an ASD when one child in the family has autism, as compared with a randomly chosen child in the general population having a brother or sister with autism (Folstein & Rutter, 1977; Ritvo et al., 1985). But as you will shortly see, that isn't true of all individuals with autism. Dr. Judith Miles and her colleagues at the University of Missouri in Columbia operate a regional autism center where they receive many referrals of children suspected of having autism. They use a battery of medical and psychological tests to evaluate each child. The more children she evaluated, the more Dr. Miles was convinced she saw an emerging pattern and began to more systematically study those patterns among her young patients. From 1995 to 2001, she and her colleagues studied 260 individuals who met diagnostic criteria for autistic disorder (Miles et al., 2005). Some children had a small head size or other significant unusual physical features. The unexpected physical features included such things as lacking a crease in the palm of the hand, backward whorls of hair in the head, or unusually shaped ears. Unusual physical features and small head size define what she called the "Complex Autism" subgroup, comprising one of five individuals she and her colleagues studied. The remaining children who lacked those features, Dr. Miles said, had "Essential Autism." On average, individuals with Complex Autism have lower intellectual functioning, are more likely to be nonverbal, have more seizures, have more brain-wave abnormalities, and have more brain structural abnormalities as shown by magnetic resonance imaging (MRI). Children with Essential Autism were more likely to have a brother or sister with autism and more of their other relatives had autism (20% compared with 9%). Children with Essential Autism were twice as likely to be male as those with Complex Autism. Dr. Miles's study tells us that when autism runs in families the outcomes tend to be better, and the children are more responsive to early education and behavior therapy programs.

The fact that autism does not recur among family members of children with Complex Autism to the same extent suggests that it is less likely to be inherited. It appears to be due to an early error in development due to a noninherited factor. It is likely that subsequent studies will reveal that within the Essential Autism group, there are subgroups with different inherited developmental errors. Some may have greater effects on parts of the brain related to language and communication, whereas others may have greater impact on social development or ritualistic behavior. Understanding the basis of such errors holds promise for devising more specific treatments.

Broad Autism Phenotype

Because there is evidence that autistic disorder, Asperger syndrome, and PDD-NOS run in the same families, it is suggested that each is not a different type of disability but is a degree of expression of a single family of disabilities (Lauritsen & Ewald, 2001). In addition, there are increased autism-like symptoms in brothers, sisters, parents, and other family members who are not diagnosed with an ASD (Constantino et al., 2006). These characteristics have been called the broad autism phenotype, suggesting that there may be multiple genes that contribute to varying degrees to the features making up an ASD. For example, Constantino et al. (2006) studied autistic characteristics among brothers and sisters of children with pervasive developmental disorders which did not meet the threshold for diagnosis as autism. Social differences were greatest among sisters and brothers of children with autism who had two or more individuals with autism in their family. Toth, Dawson, Meltzoff, Greeson, and Fein (2007) found that siblings of children with ASDs were below average in expressive language, IQ, adaptive behavior, and social communication skills. Brothers and sisters of children with autism used fewer words, fewer gestures, and exhibited fewer social smiles than comparison children, differences their parents had observed as early as 13 months of age. This suggests that the genes responsible for autism symptoms in a child diagnosed with an ASD are influencing characteristics of his or her brothers and sisters to a lesser degree.

CORE DIAGNOSTIC FEATURES

The purpose of this section is to explain the main diagnostic features of autistic disorder, Asperger syndrome, and PDD-NOS. In the next section I discuss diagnostic methods and tests used and the differences between medical diagnosis and school identification for purposes of autism services.

Sometimes people doubt ASDs can be reliably diagnosed, and even it they can, they question whether it makes a real difference. Distinguishing among clinical conditions or other biological entities requires training and experience. If most of us looked at photographs of trees, we would recognize that some are deciduous, such as maple, oak, or elm. We could tell others are coniferous, such as spruce, pine, and junipers. Beyond that, many of us would be hard pressed to reliably make further distinctions. We wouldn't know for what we are looking. But the coniferous cypress trees that thrive in the Okefenokee swamps of Florida are vastly different from the Ponderosa pine of the Sonoran Desert or red pines growing in northern Minnesota near the Canadian border. Each coniferous tree thrives in a very different environment from the other. An experienced forester would be able to provide a list of specific features that distinguish one from another. He or she would be able to explain how those characteristics are essential to their ability to ward off infestations, obtain the necessary moisture and nutrients, and protect them from heat or cold, features that are essential for their survival. Distinctions among them are critical to understanding what makes them tick and being able to help them prosper in their respective environments.

Because both lay people and some professionals find it difficult to distinguish children with ASDs from children with other disabilities, it doesn't mean that those conditions aren't genuine or that they lack practical significance. As much as understanding habitat differences of various kinds of conifers are important, understanding the types of environments in which children with different ASDs learn and thrive are essential. Well-trained and experienced pediatricians, psychiatrists, and clinical and developmental psychologists who have learned the necessary diagnostic skills are able to distinguish specific differences among children with types of disabilities, as well as among children with the three types of ASDs. These differences are real and measurable. There is a high degree of diagnostic agreement among well-trained specialists, although professionals with less experience and training may at times reach different conclusions. That is why parents are encouraged to seek a professional with extensive training and experience in autism diagnosis prior to making an appointment for a diagnostic evaluation.

Steps in Diagnosis

Diagnosis of an ASD involves two steps: 1) Obtain a detailed history and an interview with parents and other caregivers, and 2) perform autism-specific diagnostic testing, including both screening and diagnostic tests.

Obtain a Detailed History and an Interview with Parents and Other Caregivers

The interview follows a standardized, structured interview format designed to determine which of the features of autism specified by the American Psychiatric Association the child exhibits and to what degree, as well as the age at which symptoms first appeared. This interview is often supplemented by a parent intake questionnaire as well as a teacher questionnaire. The information on the intake questionnaires are reviewed and are then used to guide the professional in asking detailed follow-up questions based on information provided by the child's parents and teachers.

Autism-Specific Diagnostic Testing

There are several diagnostic and screening tests. Parents and teachers should know the difference between *screening* and *diagnostic* tests. Screening tests indicate whether a child has a likelihood of having autism when subjected to more detailed diagnostic evaluation. A screening test indicates that the child may have an ASD, not that he or she definitely has an ASD.

Screening Tests

The Checklist for Autism in Toddlers (CHAT; Baron-Cohen, Allen, & Gillberg, 1992) indicates whether it is likely that a child would be diagnosed with autism upon further evaluation. The Childhood Autism Rating Scale (CARS; Schopler, Reichler, & Renner, 1988) is used to help clinicians and educators recognize and classify children with autism. Although it is correlated with other diagnostic scales, many professionals consider it a screening rather than a diagnostic instrument. The national autism screening program FirstSigns employs several instruments but recommends the Modified Checklist for Autism in Toddlers (M-CHAT; Robins, Fein, Barton, & Green, 2001) Online to be administered first followed by the PEDS Online (*FirstSigns,* n.d.). The M-CHAT is a modified American version of the United Kingdom test CHAT. The Parents' Evaluation of Developmental Status (PEDS; Glascoe, 1997) Online is a more comprehensive developmental screening test. The Social Communication Questionnaire (SCQ; Rutter, Bailey, Lord, & Berument, 2003) is a screening instrument designed to evaluate communication skills and social functioning in children who may have autism or ASDs. Questions on the SCQ were developed to identify ASDs accurately and to differentiate them from other developmental disorders. The SCQ provides a measure of ASD symptoms with a cutoff score that can be used to indicate the likelihood that the individual has an ASD. The SCQ may be less useful as a screening instrument for young children and for families who are less familiar with ASDs.

Diagnostic Tests

The Gilliam Autism Rating Scale–2 (GARS-2; Gilliam, 2006) is used to diagnose autism in individuals ages 3–22. The child's parents or caregivers answer 42 items describing the characteristic behaviors of persons with autism. The items are grouped into stereotyped behaviors, communication, and social interaction. It also estimates the severity of the child's disability. Items on the GARS-2 are based on the American Psychiatric Association diagnostic criteria.

Autism Diagnostic Observation Schedule (ADOS; Lord et al., 2000) is considered the "gold standard" autism diagnostic test. It is a standardized observation assessment of behaviors related to autism or ASDs. Previous versions of the ADOS and the Pre-Linguistic Autism Diagnostic Observation Schedule (PL-ADOS; DiLavore, Lord, & Rutter, 1995) have been combined into this single test. The ADOS is a semistructured, standardized assessment of communication, social interaction, and play or imaginative use of materials for individuals who have been referred because of possible autism or an ASD. An examiner and the child are seated at a table in a testing room, and a series of play activities are used to elicit responses from the child and are scored. The ADOS can be used to evaluate individuals at different developmental levels and ages, from toddlers to adults, from individuals with no speech to those who are verbally fluent. Depending on the degree of the child's cooperation, the test can be administered in 30–60 minutes. The test provides cutoff scores for autism and a broader diagnosis of PDD.

Because the ADOS does not include a measure of repetitive, nonfunctional behavior, other tests, such as the Repetitive Behavior Scale–Revised (Bodfish, Symons, & Lewis, 1999; Bodfish, Symons, Parker, & Lewis, 2000), may be used. It includes five autism symptom measures: Ritualistic/Sameness Behavior, Stereotypic Behavior, Self-Injurious Behavior (SIB), Compulsive Behavior, and Restricted Interests. Though it is not as widely used as other tests, it may provide useful information regarding the type and severity of repetitive behavior.

The Autism Diagnostic Interview–Revised (ADI-R; Rutter, LeCouteur, & Lord, 2002) is a diagnostic interview to assess behaviors related to autism or ASDs. Based on the American Psychiatric Association criteria for autism and PDDs, the ADI-R contains questions about a child's early development, communication, social interaction, and patterns of behavior. The ADI-R yields scores for current behaviors and history and results in cutoff scores indicating the presence or absence of autism. A classification of autism is given when scores in all three domains of communication, social interaction, and patterns of behavior meet or exceed the specified cutoffs and onset of the disorder is evident by age 3. The ADI-R typically takes between 90 minutes and 3 hours and is administered by an experienced clinician to the main caregiver of an individual with autism. The examiner's clinical skills and experience with the ADI-R are crucial to administration. Because extensive training is required to correctly administer the ADI-R and because the assessment is very time consuming, it is seldom used in routine clinical diagnostics.

DIAGNOSTIC FEATURES OF AUTISM SPECTRUM DISORDERS

The following features of each diagnostic category must be relatively constant for a given child across various people and situations and be stable across time and emerge before 3 years of age. If these features occur with some people (e.g., teachers) but not others (e.g., parents), in some situations (e.g., school) but not others (e.g., home), and if they occur for a week or two and then stop occurring, they would fail to meet the specified diagnostic criteria. Specific autistic behaviors wax and wane in severity, but they seldom disappear altogether. Often, one ritualistic behavior will replace another, but the tendency to display *some type* of ritualistic behavior is relatively constant across time. I worked with a very bright 11-year-old with high-functioning autism who, for some time, had been preoccupied with weather. He asked his parents repeatedly throughout the day about the weather forecast and whether it was going to rain or snow or whether there would be a tornado. He insisted on watching the Weather Channel on television and frequently checked the thermometer outside the porch door. His interest, however, abruptly changed to the topic of a video game he had played involving bank robbery. He began asking his father if he could rob a bank. His father said he couldn't because it is illegal and the police would arrest him. The boy next asked if he could *pretend* he was robbing a bank, and his father replied that was also illegal and would get him into trouble. Later, the boy insisted that his father drive by a nearby bank on their way to school in the morning, at which point the youngster asked his father if he could throw a rock through the bank's front window. This type of alternation among preoccupations (e.g., weather versus robbing banks) is very common among high-functioning individuals with ASDs; however, perseverative preoccupations persist over time, though the specific focus may change.

Autistic Disorder

Children receiving a diagnosis of autistic disorder must exhibit deficits or abnormalities in social interactions, communication, repetitive behavior, and fixed routines. They must have at least one communication and repetitive behavior problem and two problems in the social behavior domain.

Social Impairments

Children who have autism often have little ability to use eye contact, facial expressions, gestures (e.g., pointing), or body posture to communicate. For example, it is unlikely that a child with autism would notice that a person is bored based on facial expressions, or the fact that the person is rising to a standing position preparing to leave the room. Most children with autistic disorder either have no meaningful peer relations or have inappropriate relationships for their age. They do not appear to be interested in sharing their interests with others and fail to recognize others' achievements. Perhaps most strikingly is their lack of social give-and-take and empathy. They seldom understand taking turns, and it would not occur to them to be spontaneously helpful to others.

Communication Impairments

Children with ASDs often have no spoken language or have minimally useful speech. Some high-functioning individuals have speech, but it lacks changes in intonation and is seldom used to communicate. They are typically unable to use gestures to indicate their needs or wants. Not surprisingly, they are unable to initiate or sustain a conversation. Children with ASDs who exhibit spoken language often display nonfunctional speech, such as repeating

Figure 1.1. Four-year-old boy fascinated by shiny objects, including the shimmering surfaces of the bubbles he has blown.

phrases from television advertisements, which is called *echolalia.* Finally, they seldom play make-believe games with peers or siblings, and they lack spontaneous imaginative play. When given a toy farm to play with, including a barn, tractor, farmer, and cows, the child may fixate on opening and closing the barn door repeatedly and ignore the other farm items.

Restricted and Repetitive Interests and Behavior

Nearly all children with autistic disorder exhibit highly specific interests or activities. They are often interested in such topics as dinosaurs or geography. Lower-functioning children may collect pieces of string or other nonfunctional items. They often become upset when an attempt is made to deflect the topic of conversation away from their preoccupation. They exhibit rigid rituals and routines that are not functionally useful or necessary. If those routines are interrupted, they often have tantrums. Most children with ASDs exhibit repetitive behaviors (see Figure 1.1 for an example of a boy who is fascinated by shiny objects and repeatedly blows bubbles). This behavior is far more intense than in a typical young child (e.g., rocking in the bed), and each episode lasts longer. Finally, when playing with toys or objects, they often focus on a specific part of the object and ignore the intended use (e.g., spinning the wheels of a toy car rather than driving it along the floor).

Asperger Syndrome

Children with Asperger syndrome have most of the features of autistic disorder, but their language emerges at about the same age as their typical peers and they usually have less severe social impairment. They often develop age-appropriate self-help skills, adaptive behavior (other than in social interaction), and curiosity toward the environment. Nonetheless, they have significant and persistent limitations in social behavior and restricted and repetitive interests.

Social Impairments

As with children with autistic disorder, children with Asperger syndrome rarely exhibit eye contact, don't use facial expressions, don't use or understand body postures, and don't use gestures for social purposes. They often prefer to be with adults and fail to develop peer relationships appropriate to their developmental level. They appear disinterested in other's achievements or in sharing their own interests with their parents, teachers, or peers. They lack empathy and social give-and-take, such as taking turns. If a peer is upset and crying, they may simply walk away or tell the child to stop crying.

Restricted Interests and Repetitive Behavior

Children with Asperger syndrome are often preoccupied with highly restricted interests that appear abnormal in their intensity or that have a highly restricted focus. They often have very good verbal skills, but they repeatedly focus their comments about specific topics, such as a preferred television program, specific wild animals, or geographic formations such as mountains or rivers. Attempts to change the topic of conversation makes them upset and may provoke a tantrum. They inflexibly follow specific, nonfunctional routines or rituals. They may insist that their socks be arranged in a specific order in their dresser drawer according to color, or they may insist that they eat their food in a specific order at mealtime. Some exhibit stereotyped and repetitive motor mannerisms such as waving their arms or twirling in a circle when they are excited or upset. It is common for higher functioning children with Asperger syndrome to dismantle or take apart objects so they can see specific parts of them. They don't mean to be destructive; it is just that they are curious as to what is inside an object. They may dismantle a toy or appliance to discover its inner workings.

Though children with Asperger syndrome are often very verbal, their language can be expressed in unusual ways. I met an 8-year-old boy who insisted on knowing the make, model, and year of the automobile I drove. Then he wanted to know the names and ages of my children in chronological order. A month later when I next saw him, he initiated a conversation with me without a greeting or other preamble: "How is your Audi? It's an A6 with all-wheel drive. How is Rebecca…Jennifer…Andrea…Peter?" He remembered my children's ages; however, on this occasion he asked what each of them did (i.e., attend school, work as a musician, and so forth). After I replied to his questions, he thought for a moment then abruptly turned and walked away without further comment. Having obtained the information he wanted, he had no other interest in my company.

A general education teacher who has a student with Asperger syndrome in his or her classroom may find the student very confusing. He or she may seem to have exceptional verbal skills and islands of knowledge in some areas that are striking. During a lesson about dinosaurs, a child with Asperger syndrome may respond to his or her 3rd-grade teacher's question by saying, "Triceratops was an herbivore that lived during the late Cretaceous period." The child's teacher and the other students would most likely look at the student in disbelief, wondering how he or she knew that. When asked a follow-up question, the student with Asperger syndrome may reply, "Triceratops had three horns on his head." The child's remarkable knowledge of dinosaurs is better understood in context when the teacher asks a question such as, "Was Triceratops a reptile?" After a moment the child may reply, "Tyrannosaurus was a meat eater that lived at the end of the Cretaceous period." To probe further, the teacher might ask him or her which was larger: Triceratops or Tyrannosaurus. After a few moments, the child with Asperger syndrome is likely to reply with something such as, "Tyrannosaurus had spines on his back." When children with Asperger syndrome fail to understand or are unable to respond to a question, they often provide the answer to another question they *are* able to answer rather than admitting they don't know or aren't sure. Sometimes they simply change the subject altogether. As a result, conversations with children with Asperger syndrome are often oddly disjointed and lack meaningful transitions from one idea to the next. It is very easy to be misled regarding the depth of knowledge and pragmatic understanding of a child with Asperger syndrome based purely on his or her vocabulary regarding a single topic.

Pervasive Developmental Disorder-Not Otherwise Specified

Children with PDD-NOS either do not fully meet the criteria of symptoms clinicians use to diagnose any of the specific types of ASDs previously mentioned, and/or they do not have the *degree* of impairment described in any of the aforementioned ASD types. For a child to be diagnosed with PDD-NOS, he or she does not need to exhibit repetitive, fixed interests or stereotyped behavior patterns. It is often assumed by nonspecialists that PDD-NOS refers to high-functioning autism with few severely limiting features, but that is usually incorrect. A person with PDD-NOS may exhibit similar, but somewhat less severe language and social impairments than individuals diagnosed with autistic disorder. Their verbal skills will usually not be as advanced as those of a child with Asperger syndrome.

SCHOOL IDENTIFICATION AND MEDICAL DIAGNOSIS

The purpose of school evaluations of children referred for autism services is to determine whether such educational services are appropriate for a given child. School districts vary widely in their assessments by region, state, and individual district. Some districts employ the ADOS, along with language and other testing, and often do an excellent job of evaluating children for services. Others use teacher and parent checklists and screening tests, which are not intended for diagnosis. Though the assessment process may seem similar to a medical diagnosis, depending on exactly how it is carried out, it often yields different outcomes. One of the major differences is the purpose of the assessment. The purpose of a medical diagnosis of an ASD is to determine whether the child meets diagnostic criteria for an ASD and, equally important, to answer the question of whether there could be any other reason the child exhibits symptoms similar to those seen in autism. As in any other medical diagnostic process, it is as important to rule out a diagnosis as it is to rule it in. Could there be other reasons for the presenting signs and symptoms than the hypothesized autism diagnosis? School identification determines whether a child presents a sufficient number and intensity of autism symptoms to benefit from an autism educational placement.

Reasons for Misdiagnosis

There are various reasons a child may exhibit some autism symptoms but not have autism. Believing and accurately interpreting what one has seen are not the same thing.

Seeing and Misinterpreting

Believing one has witnessed something doesn't always make it true. As an adolescent I was fascinated by astronomy, reading books and magazines about the solar system, Milky Way, and beyond. I loved science fiction, voraciously reading H.G. Wells and Ray Bradbury. I pored over instruction manuals for building telescopes and taking photographs of stellar objects. When I was 13, I built a 6-inch reflecting telescope, typical of many amateur astronomers. Standing alone in the nearly pitch-black darkness that still existed at night in the early 1950s, I routinely experienced what seemed to me to be miracles peering through my telescope. The craters of the moon were breathtaking, and the rings around Saturn were an astoundingly beautiful secret between the remote planet and me. And Mars had an orange tint as Lowell had written, and on exceptionally clear nights I could make out darker land masses and lighter polar caps. I felt as though I was witnessing astounding things few people were privileged enough to experience.

In late October of that year, I situated the tripod of my telescope between furrows in a nearby farmer's field and peered with my dark-adapted eyes toward the southern horizon. A bright star in the Aquarius constellation seemed to be behaving oddly. Sometimes it was very bright, but then it would dim and occasionally disappear altogether. I trained my telescope on that star. Small telescopes like mine didn't increase the diameter of stars, but they appeared brighter, so the waxing and waning seemed more pronounced. I had read about novas and rapidly circling double stars, but neither seemed feasible. The timescale was completely off. No, I must be seeing an airplane, I reasoned. I stood up and peered for several minutes with my naked eye, but the object didn't move as an airplane would. It was fixed, but it continued blinking.

As I watched through my telescope's eyepiece, I felt my heart beating more rapidly, overcome with excitement. Perhaps it *really was* the beginning phase of a nova about to explode. I felt as though I may have been witnessing a remarkable astronomical event. When I watched more closely through my telescope, there was something odd. It was almost as though something periodically obscured the star. What could that be? The night sky was crystal clear as happens in late autumn in Minnesota. I stood stark still and studied the star again with my naked eye. The star was only 5–10 degrees above the horizon. A sinking feeling weighed upon my chest. I started walking toward the blinking star, and then broke into a run, stumbling on the furrows as I ran. I fell at one point, bloodying my hands and knees on the frozen ruts, but I got up and continued running. A quarter of a mile across the field I approached a county road along which a series of telephone poles stood with wires hanging between them. As I approached the seldom-traveled road, the wires became visible swinging slowly in the darkness. I felt my cheeks burning with embarrassment in the brisk October air. I felt I had been a fool to have so deceived myself. My nova had been a wire swinging in the breeze, periodically obscuring the star that shone steadily now that the wire was no longer separating the star and my eyes. I had wanted so badly to believe I was witnessing a remarkable stellar event, when in fact I had misinterpreted what I had seen. The phenomenon I had witnessed was real, but the cause was other than what I had believed it to be.

In the field of autism, misinterpreting what one has seen is a very common phenomenon. Teachers, therapists, and parents see some signs of symptoms they believe indicate that a child has autism, but they are often due to something else.

Communication Deficits

A child may have oral-motor speech apraxia, a physical condition that makes it difficult to form speech sounds. Such children have a speech delay well beyond the age when other children are speaking in words or phrases. Because they have difficulty speaking, they often appear to ignore parents or teachers who are talking to them because they are unable to reply intelligibly. A child may have another specific language impairment that limits the ability to distinguish speech sounds and also delays the use of spoken language. Children with selective mutism may rarely, if ever, speak in school. This is a learned behavior pattern that can be very confusing to school personnel who may suspect the child is unable to speak. If a home visit is conducted, school personnel may be surprised to discover that the child speaks freely with siblings when at home. Children adopted from other countries who lived in an orphanage where they experienced very little adult attention are often extremely delayed in the use of language as well as social skills. They often display stereotypical rocking and other autism-like behavior as well. Children living in households where the only other child is deaf or has autism and is nonverbal often exhibit significant speech and social skills problems. If any of these speech-language problems are combined with those mentioned next, it is very possible a child could exhibit some signs suggestive of an ASD but not have an ASD. A child with anxiety problems and borderline intellectual functioning may be particularly prone to appearing autism-like if he or she also has a significant speech-language disorder.

Social Skill Deficits

A child who has parents or siblings diagnosed with social phobia, obsessive-compulsive disorder (OCD), or other serious anxiety problems has an increased risk of having the same problems. The child may appear shy because of social phobia or may appear to insist things be done his or her way because of his or her OCD. Such a child will often have few, if any, friends because his or her peers can be annoyed by his or her rigidity. If an only child grows up in a family with reclusive parents who seldom have adult friends with their children over for meals or to spend leisure time together, the child has few opportunities to learn the basic social skills other children routinely learn incidentally. This may occur among some immigrant families who are not well-integrated into a majority Anglo neighborhood. Parents who are overprotective and don't allow their child to play outdoors with other children or don't have other children to their home to play have no opportunity to learn child-to-child social skills, and will often appear socially diffident. A child who has a chaotic home life (e.g., living with a single parent who works unpredictable hours or who has multiple partners) may appear withdrawn and distrusting of adults. This is especially true if a child has been abused. The child will often avoid adult eye contact, such as social overtures by teachers or classroom aides. He or she may not answer when spoken to and may appear withdrawn and fearful. A child who lives with a parent who is seriously ill (e.g., has AIDS, terminal cancer), and whose other parent is depressed because of the impending loss of his or her partner, may have little interaction with either parent. The child's parents may have limited emotional time or energy to invest in their child. As a result, the child will often appear depressed, unresponsive, and withdrawn.

Repetitive Fixed Routines

Children whose parent(s) suffer from OCD are at risk for OCD themselves, often displaying fixed repetitive routines and emotional outbursts if they are disrupted. Teachers may describe them as "having to have their own way," which can be a sign of OCD rather than autism. Highly anxious children often rock in their seat, appear distracted, have difficulty concentrating, and may appear aloof to other children. They may resist trying new things because of fear of failure. It is normal for typical preschool children to line up cars or other toys as a means of creating structure; however, if those same children display any of the foregoing signs *in addition to* these otherwise typical childhood organizing rituals, teachers may begin to suspect they are seeing signs of autism. Children with ADHD are especially prone to appearing distracted and exhibiting temper outbursts when demands are placed upon them. They follow teacher directions poorly, refuse to take their seat, and may appear agitated. Again, a combination of ADHD and any of the above conditions or circumstances can create the impression that the child may have an ASD.

Situational Autism?

A diagnostic interview or ADOS assessment may suggest that a child has a less severe form of an ASD, such as Asperger syndrome or PDD-NOS. When circumstances such as those described above are explored in depth, however, it may become apparent that the reason the child displays those symptoms is unrelated to autism. The child may be socially avoidant with some adults, but interact freely with others. The child's speech may be delayed, but he or she clearly understands the use of gestures to meet his or her needs and occasionally uses vocalization communicatively. The child may smile and exhibit eye contact with siblings and their parents but not with people outside of the family. The child may appear emotionally withdrawn and exhibit little imaginary play in school but may be highly expressive and may willingly engage in pretend play with his or her siblings at home. By definition, ASDs are pervasive developmental disabilities, meaning that core symptoms are exhibited in nearly all aspects of life across different people and settings. *There is no such thing as situational autism.*

Specialty Clinic versus Routine Community Autism Diagnosis

Some university-based autism specialty clinics report that nearly half of all children are referred because an informant believes they have an ASD, but after a thorough differential diagnostic evaluation it is determined that they do not have an ASD (C.E. Lord, F. Volkmar, P. Szatmari, M. Reiff, & R. Rumsey, personal communication, 2007). A child evaluation may reveal he or she approaches the cutoff scores on the ADOS but often has another developmental problem, such as those previously described, that better account for his or her symptoms. Parents and teachers often initially react with consternation because they are convinced the symptoms they see indicate that the child has autism, but often they do not understand the various other reasons the child may exhibit symptoms similar to those seen in ASDs.

The mother of a 4-year-old child who had been diagnosed with autism by his doctor in a small town in a rural area brought him to a specialty clinic for an autism diagnostic evaluation. Based on his doctor's initial evaluation, the family received funding for a personal care attendant (PCA) 15 hours per week, and the child was receiving preschool special education services from the public school district under the autism category. The boy was very sociable and outgoing, readily established eye contact, engaged in imaginative play, oriented toward the examiner when spoken to, used gestures to communicate, was able to take turns, and asked the examiner several questions about her family. He was exceedingly active, however, crawling under and on top of a table, continually squirming in his chair, banging toys destructively, refusing to be seated when asked to do so, and shouting "no" defiantly when asked to pick up a toy he had thrown on the floor. After a thorough evaluation, including a review of a parent checklist for emotional and behavior disorders, it became apparent the boy had ADHD and oppositional defiant disorder as well as a substantial speech-language disability, not autism. When the child's diagnosis was discussed with his mother, she became very angry and indicated that he would not qualify for PCA services without an autism diagnosis. She questioned the accuracy of our diagnosis and said she would take him to another doctor "who knows what he is doing." The child certainly needed intervention services, but not 30 hours per week of intensive early behavior therapy services designed for children with autism. He was obviously very challenging and undoubtedly frustrating to his parents. He would likely profit from speech therapy and ADHD medication, and his family needed assistance learning parenting strategies for dealing with a child with oppositional defiant disorder.

A more common reaction from parents whose child receives an ASD diagnosis at a specialty clinic after being told by their pediatrician that their child "has the terrible twos" is relief that they are finally told why their child is behaving so oddly. Although they are invariably saddened when they hear the diagnosis, parents are also grateful that someone has taken the time to thoroughly evaluate their child and make detailed recommendations for the most appropriate interventions. Obtaining an accurate diagnosis is a critical step in understanding your child and laying the foundation for a short- and long-term plan for his or her education and treatment.

SUMMARY

Parents often report that at times their child with an ASD is like a little stranger in their midst. The child is like his or her siblings in many ways but in others seems so very unusual. It is so difficult to see the world through his or her eyes, to feel what he or she is feeling, to understand his or her perspective. Learning to understand your child's world requires time, patience, and understanding, which is the topic of the remainder of this book.

ASDs, in all likelihood, have always been far more common than was indicated by older prevalence studies. Though diagnosed or identified cases of ASDs have dramatically increased since the early 1990s, that trend appears to be due largely to increased awareness, greater case identification, and availability of services. There is no compelling evidence of a growing "autism epidemic."

Properly trained and experienced clinicians can reliably differentially diagnose ASDs in young children beginning at 2 years of age. Moreover, it is possible for them to distinguish among ASD subtypes: autistic disorder, Asperger syndrome, and PDD-NOS. Although agreement among trained diagnosticians in distinguishing high-functioning autism from PDD-NOS is somewhat lower than other diagnostic categories; nonetheless, agreement is generally high. Valid ASD diagnoses accompanied by intellectual, communicational, psychopathological, and psychoeducational assessments are essential steps in developing an overall intervention plan for a child with an ASD.

Misidentification and misdiagnosis of ASDs is common. This problem occurs partially because many practitioners and educators aren't adequately trained to differentially diagnose ASDs. Medical schools and universities must do a better job of training community practitioners and school personnel to differentially diagnose, identify, treat, and educate children with ASDs. In addition, there is growing evidence that administrative factors play a role. It appears that some children are misdiagnosed or identified as having an

ASD in order for them to qualify for specialized services or in order to obtain funding for other services. Misdiagnosing children prevents them from obtaining the service they really need, which may not be intensive autism therapy or specialized school programs for children with ASDs. Because openings in community treatment programs for children with ASDs are generally limited, every child misdiagnosed as having an ASD limits access to those necessary services for other children.

Elliott: A Parent's Story

Kammy Norman Kramer

Elliott was our firstborn, and he was a bright-eyed, happy baby. I stayed home with him for 3 months and then returned to work. Several co-workers also had babies around the same time, and each day over lunch we would all share stories of what our little people were up to. They all had funny tales of how their babies were starting to use words and as Elliott approached 1 year and still had none, I remember having this tiny little uncomfortable feeling in the pit of my stomach. Elliott had started in a child care center at 3 months of age, had almost constant ear infections, and was on every antibiotic imaginable. He finally had ear tubes inserted at 7 months of age, and when I first mentioned to our pediatrician that I was concerned that he was not talking, she told me he would likely be delayed because he had not been hearing sounds due to all of the infections. We sort of expected the delay and moved on eagerly awaiting his first words.

They didn't come. Now Elliott was 18 months old, and I knew something was not as it should be. It was just a feeling I had, and as much as I tried to reassure myself it nagged at me. He didn't seem at all interested in the other children at playgroups. I visited our pediatrician, who was getting irritated by my repeated appointments and questions about language development. Other parents tried to reassure me that boys commonly develop later and not to stress out.

Finally, I called our school district, which sent a speech-language specialist to our home to evaluate Elliott. One day near the end of her visit, I could tell something seemed to be bothering her. She asked me if Elliott had ever pretended that a toy was a telephone (no), and if he pointed (yes). She then spoke slowly, choosing her words very carefully, and said that we might be dealing with something more than just a speech delay—something called a pervasive developmental disorder, or PDD. I had never heard those words before and asked for clarification, at which point she said the word *autism*.

I thought she was crazy. Though she had warned me not to do so, I spent the entire night on the Internet, searching for every reference to PDD I could find. It was frightening and depressing, and each site had various lists of what types of things to look for, and he had only a few of the "signs." I resigned myself to the notion that she was just wrong and found myself defending some of his "quirky" behavior to her and ultimately to myself.

Then the aggression started, and our world changed overnight. Elliott was 21 months old when his brother, Henry, was born. One day at a McDonald's Play Land, Elliott saw a little girl hit her mom and about 5 minutes later he hit me. I will never forget that moment because it was the beginning of a very dark period for our family. He began hitting, biting, kicking, and pushing us constantly. Then he started attacking baby Henry. He reached behind him in the double stroller and scratched his nails against the baby's head until Henry was bleeding, chased him with a knife that he got from breaking the child guard on our dishwasher, and pushed him down a flight of stairs after removing the gate when I was in the bathroom. I was falling apart at the seams. Tom, my husband, was having difficulty at work because I was calling every day in tears asking him to come home and help me because I was afraid that Elliott would kill the baby.

In addition, we could not leave our home because he had started attacking people in public. One day at a playground he began running, and before Tom could catch him he pushed over an elderly woman. Many parents either gave us the look (i.e., your child is out of control and you're not good parents), or they would yell at us because Elliott had hurt their child. Our marriage was falling apart, I was on the verge of a nervous breakdown, and we had no friends and limited family support.

A day arrived when Elliott seemed ill and I could not get an appointment at our clinic, so I called a new one in town and got right in. It was a practice of nurse practitioners, and their post card that we received in the mail suggested that they would not hustle patients in and out but take whatever time was needed. When the door closed and she asked what was wrong, I just fell apart. I told her everything, and she let me talk and cry until I was done. It was like letting a complete stranger in on our darkest secrets that we could not even share with our families, and it felt so freeing to be able to honestly talk with someone who was not going to judge but find our family some help. She referred me to a pediatric neurologist she had worked with and also referred us to a clinic that provided speech therapy for children. It took all of about 5 minutes for the pediatric neurologist to tell us she indeed believed Elliott had a form of autism called PDD-NOS but that she could not make that diagnosis and referred us to a specialty center that dealt only with autism. The bad news was that the autism clinic had a waiting list of 2 years. I broke down again, and Tom's voice was shaking as we described Elliott's aggression and our fear for what might happen to Henry. Six days later, we were sitting in the waiting room of the autism clinic where we would receive an official diagnosis of PDD-NOS.

Though I had initially tried everything to fight a diagnosis on the autism spectrum, even making myself believe that poor school district speech-language specialist was just crazy, when Elliott was actually diagnosed, we were relieved. Tom and I agreed that the psychologists could call it whatever they wanted as long as we could begin helping Elliott overcome aggression and hopefully learn to talk.

Slowly, we started to come up for air. Elliott began attending day treatment two mornings a week at the autism clinic and a special education preschool class the other three. Just having that break was so helpful because although Elliott was still having the aggression problems, having him occupied in an activity that was helping him gave us space at home to catch our breath and give Henry some much needed attention.

Then one day I started chatting with another mom who had twin boys on the autism spectrum. She told me about a home-based early intervention therapy program their family had started called applied behavioral analysis (ABA). They were thrilled with how much their son had learned in a short time and how much he enjoyed it. I looked it up on the Internet and found some frightening articles. There was mention of turning children into robots, using corporal punishment, and basically having children sit in their basements at a table doing drills for hours at a time. This was nothing like what my friend had described, so I asked some educators about it in our local school district. They, for the most part, had unfavorable comments about ABA not that different than the Internet.

Tom and I decided to get on waiting lists and see what ABA was all about. A short time later we got a phone call that indicated a local service provider of intensive early behavioral therapy (what I had mistakenly been referring to as simply ABA) services had an opening and wanted to meet us. A program director and supervisor came to our home to talk with us and begin doing assessments. They were very kind and helped answer many of the questions we had about why they needed to work with Elliott so many hours per week (around 30), and how they would begin very slowly as not to overwhelm him and gradually increase hours and allow him to continue his naps.

Elliott was thrilled to have new people in our home from the moment the doorbell rang. They were so fun, physically tossing him in the air and flipping him over, dragging him on blankets, all of the kinds of activities he craved. In between, they conducted assessments trying to pinpoint where he was developmentally so that we could have a baseline. Then we needed to have approval from the supervising psychologist prior to beginning our program. When our director told me that he was a very talented well-known psychologist in the field, I Googled his name and got really nervous about having this person visit our home. My fear was unwarranted because he was warm, friendly, and absolutely brilliant, and Elliott and Henry adored him.

That meeting changed the course of Elliott's future and has saved our family. He listened to all of our questions and fears, and helped us understand the science of behavioral therapy. Most of all, he was the first person who gave us hope. Although careful not to make any promises, he believed that progress was very possible based on the assessments and on the treatment plan. It was the greatest news in the world that Elliott had a fighting chance and that there was a way for us to help him and to be a part of it. Three months later, he returned to our house. For us, a miracle had happened. Elliott had gone from more than 100 aggressive acts per day to maybe one or two per week and even those were fairly typical for his age. He was also tested as being on the edge of age-appropriate in language development conducted by an independent clinic. We were enjoying activities together as a family and learning from the therapy team how to help him in the natural environment.

Since then, Elliott has continued to make amazing gains. He is now 6 years old, in a typical classroom with some aid, and is learning to navigate the social circles of kindergarten with increasing success. He continues to have difficulty with pragmatic language and loves elevators way too much, but he has an amazing relationship with his brother and is gentle with and interested in his new baby sister. Sitting in that autism clinic 3 years ago we could never have imagined our life today. Elliott is a happy, outgoing, adorable little boy who continues to amaze us, teach us, and renew our faith in possibility.

2

Need for Control

Moment-to-moment events of daily life seem utterly out of control to many children with ASDs. Their life appears to them to be chaotic and unpredictable. In his astute description of autism, Leo Kanner wrote,

> The child's behavior is governed by an anxiously obsessive desire for sameness that nobody but the child himself may disrupt on rare occasions. Changes in routine, of furniture arrangement, of a pattern, or the order in which everyday acts are carried out, can drive him to despair. (1943, p. 245)

Kanner continued,

> Objects that do not change their appearance and position, that retain their sameness...are readily accepted by the autistic child. He has a good relation to objects...When with them, he has an undisputed sense of power and control. (1943, p. 246)

NEED FOR CONTROL

With these insightful words, the man who provided the first detailed clinical account of autism captured one of the most important features of ASDs: need for control. Parents often see a child who is obstinate and displays tantrums, teachers see a child who is being oppositional and refuses to follow directions, and friends and relatives see a spoiled child who must have his or her own way. When I see a child with an ASD displaying such frustrating, challenging behavior, I try to remind myself of Kanner's words: "Changes...can drive him to despair" (Kanner, 1943, p. 245). It is difficult for anyone to be truly effective at parenting, teaching, or providing therapy services to a child with autism without fully grasping the depth of distress a child with an ASD experiences when he or she feels that he or she has no control over a world that seems in unpredictable disarray.

Children's Early Learning About Gaining Control

Young children, including those with ASDs, experiment from a very early age with strategies for controlling things and people around them. Carmen, who has an ASD, is seated in her highchair. She holds her spoon out and releases it. It goes downward and makes a noise as it hits the floor. That is really quite interesting. She does it again, and the spoon always falls downward and makes a clanging noise. She soon discovers that she can also make her parents do things the same way. When she drops her spoon on the floor and it makes a noise, her mother, Maria, bends down and picks it up. She tries that a few times and it always works: Her mother or father always bends down and picks up the spoon and returns it to her. Next she discovers that if she drops her spoon so it falls under the dinner table she can make her father, Silvio, get down and crawl around on his hands and knees. That's even more interesting. When her father retrieves the spoon and hands it to the girl, he opens his mouth and sounds come out (e.g., "Now don't do that again!"), which the child doesn't understand, but it's very interesting, nonetheless. She rather likes the sounds when he opens his mouth, but she is confused by his facial expression, which seems to be different from usual.

Children discover that if they put a block in a particular place on the floor, crawl across the floor, and then return to the block, it is still in the same place. That is reassuring to a child with an ASD. A child with an ASD learns very quickly that things like blocks and stuffed bears are predictable. Once the child does something with them they stay put, but people are different. After the fourth or fifth time Carmen drops her spoon on the floor, instead of her father retrieving it, he stands up and takes her out of her highchair and places her on the floor and says, "All done," which she doesn't understand, but she realizes there is no more food. Carmen begins crying and screaming. It wasn't supposed to work that way. It is very annoying to a child with an ASD when adults keep changing the rules.

Children with ASDs learn very early that if they want to reliably cause their parents to do things, their own actions have to be dramatic. It isn't as easy to make adults do things as it is to make a clown pop out of a box when you push the button. If a boy with an ASD screams and cries, he discovers that it causes his mother to pick him up and hold him. If he continues to cry more loudly, his mother rocks him and bounces him on her knee and sounds come out of his mother's mouth (e.g., "It's going to be okay."). He doesn't understand what his mother is saying but at least she's holding him. Children with ASDs learn that in order to make parents behave in more predictable ways, they have to do things that are louder and involve screaming, crying, or throwing things. Children with ASDs quickly learn that their parents stop responding to less dramatic overtures. Adults are annoyingly unpredictable. Because children with ASDs don't have the skills to ask their parents for things or to be held or tossed up in the air and caught or to be sung to, they have to devise other ways to control their parents' behavior. That usually involves crying and throwing themselves on the floor and screaming, which reliably causes their parents to do things, sometimes in the way the child had wanted in the first place. Children learn that their parents always do *something* when they have an outburst. That makes parents more predictable. Children with ASDs usually learn that lesson between 18 months and 2 years of age.

Relation of Need for Control of Obsessive-Compulsive Disorder

Adults seldom realize that the smallest change, one they think is inconsequential, may be perceived as intolerable to a child with an ASD. The Thanksgiving dishes had been cleared from the dining room table and it was time for dessert. Pumpkin and apple pie were placed on the table along with ice cream for those who chose to indulge themselves. Grandma had made 6-year-old Tony's favorite dessert just for him, chocolate cake with thick, rich, creamy chocolate frosting. She placed his cake in front of him as others began savoring their pie à la mode on matching dessert plates. Tony sat motionless with an expression midway between horror and torment on his face. His sister Amelia said, "What's wrong, Tony? It's chocolate cake. You love chocolate cake!" Tony's lower lip began to quiver and a tear ran down his cheek. He sniffed and wiped the tear away with the back of his hand. He pushed the dish with the chocolate cake away as though to distance himself from it. The more his family encouraged him to try the cake, the more upset he became, eventually sobbing quietly as though he were in pain. At the opposite end of the dining room table, Tony's grandmother, a retired special education teacher, stood watching him intently. "Would you like your blue plate, Tony?" she asked. His head shot up and he nodded vigorously while sniffling and wiping away his tears on his shirtsleeve. She picked up his untouched dessert, took it into the kitchen, and returned with the same piece of chocolate cake on his blue plastic plate, the one in the shape of a puppy's head with the tongue hanging out in the corner for a spoon rest. It was the plate Tony had used for all of his meals at Grandma and Grandpa's house ever since he could remember. It was *his* plate. When Grandma placed his blue plate in front of him with the cake on it, he beamed with joy. Tony dug in and asked for seconds before others had finished their first piece of pie.

On a drive to the family farm up the interstate, the father of another child with autistic disorder decided to take a different exit because the side road they usually used was under construction. As their car passed their usual exit, his 5-year-old son who was seated in the back seat began screaming and hitting his father over the head, and though he seldom spoke, he shouted, "No, no, no!" In anguish, he pointed toward the "missed" exit.

Such compulsive need for sameness and control is a critical feature of ASDs. There is evidence that there are overlaps in symptoms of typically developing people with OCD and people with high-functioning ASDs. Russell, Mataix-Cols, Anson, and Murphy (2005) studied a group of adults with high-functioning ASDs and a matched group of adults with a primary diagnosis of OCD. They used standard psychiatric scales designed to measure OCD symptoms. They found that the two groups had similar frequencies of OCD symptoms with only bodily obsessions and repeating rituals being more common in the typically developing OCD group. Zandt, Prior, and Kyrios (2006) studied obsessions and compulsions in typical children diagnosed with OCD and high-functioning children with ASDs matched for age. The types of compulsions and obsessions tended to be less sophisticated in children with ASDs than those with OCD but were similar in other ways. Several studies indicate that parents with OCD or OCD symptoms are at an increased risk of having a child with autism suggesting a possible shared genetic mechanism (Abramson et al., 2005; Bolton, Pickles, Murphy, & Rutter, 1998; Hollander, King, Delaney, Smith, & Silverman, 2003). There is also evidence from brain imaging studies of possible brain similarities between OCD and autism. Hollander et al. (2005) found increased volume of a structure deep inside the brain (basal ganglia) of individuals with high-functioning ASDs similar to those observed in OCD patients (as compared with matched typical controls).

OBSESSIVE-COMPULSIVE EXPRESSION IN CHILDREN WITH AUTISM SPECTRUM DISORDERS

Children and adolescents with ASDs engage in several types of rituals that are similar to those seen in typical psychiatric patients with OCD as well as individuals with Tourette syndrome, which share common brain chemical differences.

Obsessions

Obsessions are persistent, disturbing preoccupations often involving an unreasonable idea or feeling. According to the American Psychiatric Association, obsessions are recurrent and persistent thoughts, impulses, or images that cause marked anxiety or distress (1994). The thoughts, impulses, or images are not simply excessive worries about real-life problems. In a typically developing adult, the affected person is aware that the thoughts and feelings are irrational, but he or she can do nothing to stop them despite their efforts to do so. But in young children and individuals with developmental disabilities such as ASDs, they are generally not aware that their obsessions are irrational and that they arise from their own thoughts rather than from something provoking fear outside of themselves. Among the more common obsessions exhibited by people with ASDs are

- Emergency vehicles (e.g., fire trucks, police cars, ambulances)
- Frightening animals (e.g., snakes, spiders, vicious dogs)
- Television cartoon characters (e.g., villains, heroes)
- Video games (and associated characters)

- Water (e.g., bath tubs, showers, rain, swimming pools, lakes, rivers)
- Weather (e.g., tornadoes, hurricanes, lightening, thunder)

Although many typical children engage in fantasy play involving police cars and television cartoon characters, they can usually be easily redirected from these activities or interests. These activities usually occupy only a small portion of a typical day. For children with ASDs, however, it may be nearly impossible to change the topic when discussing terrifying weather or fire engines and fires. Moreover, they typically spend a substantial part of some days persistently talking about an obsession if permitted to do so. I was involved in evaluating a 6-year-old with PDD-NOS who was obsessed by the letter *A*. He thought about it constantly, printed the letter, cut out the letter from magazines, and stored the pieces of paper containing the letter *A* neatly in labeled boxes. During diagnostic testing, he took a special interest in the ADOS when he noticed on the manual that it started with the letter *A*. He complained that thoughts about the letter *A* kept intruding when he was trying to do something else, such as math problems. The letter *A* was a true obsession for this little boy.

I evaluated a 21-year-old young man with a high-functioning ASD some years ago who was obsessed with hymns. He knew each hymn in his church's hymnal by number and name and insisted on talking about hymns with anyone who would listen. Because few people were interested in talking about hymns, his parents had attempted to redirect his interest to other topics, but he became very agitated and at times aggressive if they refused to discuss hymns. While interviewing him I tried to shift the topic of conversation by asking if he watched television. He replied that he did, and then in the next sentence he explained that his favorite program on television was the 700 Club, a religious program that featured numerous hymns. That is typical of the obsession of a person with a high-functioning ASD.

Compulsions

Whereas obsessions are ideas or preoccupations usually manifested by persistently talking about specific topics, compulsions are intensely repetitive behaviors (e.g., hand washing, ordering, checking) or mental acts (e.g., counting, repeating letters or words silently) that the person feels driven to perform. In response to an obsession, a child feels compelled to follow specific rules in carrying out ritual compulsive behavior. In typical individuals these behavioral rituals seem designed to reduce distress or prevent some dreaded event or situation. But these obsessions and compulsive rituals are not connected in a realistic way with what they are designed to neutralize or prevent. They are clearly excessive and unrelated to any real threat or problem. Among the most common compulsions in typical adult psychiatric patients are those revolving around cleanliness and order, such as repeatedly washing hands, fastidiously checking clothing for spots or wrinkles, lining up objects, making certain all of the curtains in a room are exactly the same length, or repeatedly locking windows and doors to be absolutely certain they are locked. The person with a compulsion to do these things realizes that he or she is excessive and irrational and may even describe him- or herself as being "crazy," but the urge is so intense that he or she can't stop doing them.

Figure 2.1. Five-year-old boy with autism engaging in repetitive hand flapping in his kindergarten classroom. Such nonfunctional compulsive rituals are common, especially among children with little language and more severe autism.

Compulsions among individuals with ASDs vary with intellectual and verbal ability. Some compulsive rituals are similar to those of typical OCD psychiatric patients, such as insisting that the individual always eat off of the same plate and use the same cup and that the bottoms of the spoon and fork are precisely aligned on the dining room table. The child who was obsessed by the letter *A* had a bout of crying and extreme distress when his shirt got a spot of paint on it in school during an art activity. He had to change his shirt immediately; it seemed imperative for him to do so. Younger children and individuals with mild to moderate cognitive limitations are more likely to exhibit rituals that involve specific physical movements similar to those in Tourette syndrome. They may repeatedly flip light switches on and off or open and close closet doors. The movements are usually simple and repetitive and take almost precisely the same form on each occasion (see Figure 2.1). With higher-functioning children, compulsions usually involve more complex activities, such as running a toy popcorn popper across the floor for an hour at a time, or riding a tricycle in circles for hours. When a child is engaged in these activities, it does not appear that he or she is experiencing pleasure. To the contrary, he or she often displays an agitated glassy-eyed appearance. It is easy to see why parents and teachers use the expression "something has gotten into him" to describe these episodes.

Children with autism often visually fixate on shiny objects and use them for compulsive self-stimulation. Many children with ASDs are attracted to long thin objects, such as pencils or long-handled spoons, which they hold to one side of their face, waving to and fro, and peer at them out of the corner of their eye. No one understands the basis for this unique form of visual self-stimulation. Among children with poor language and more cognitive limitations, compulsions tend to involve nonfunctional materials or body parts, such as repeatedly twirling pieces of string, crumpling and throwing bits of paper, retaining saliva in the mouth and then spitting, or rocking backward and forward and flapping hands. Children with ASDs who have severe intellectual disabilities, with little or no language, are prone to the most disturbing compulsive rituals, such as twirling in circles for hours or banging their head with their fists or against hard surfaces, such as the floor, wall, or table. Self-injury will be discussed in detail in Chapter 10.

Various strategies have been used to reduce obsessive and compulsive rituals and behavior in children with ASDs. Behavioral intervention techniques can be helpful, but at times, especially in the most severe forms of destructively compulsive behavior, psychotropic medications are used as well. In the following section, I will discuss several behavioral techniques used to reduce the perceived unpredictability of the child's world and to provide a feeling that the child has more control of what is happening around him or her.

Dealing with Obsessions

In dealing with obsessions and compulsions, the first questions parents, teachers, and therapists must ask themselves are, "How pervasive is it? To what degree is it actually interfering with his or her (and our) daily life?" Occasionally, caregivers will decide that although a specific ritual is very annoying and causes some interference in the child's and their own daily lives, they decide to leave the obsession (or compulsion) alone and hope that it will diminish with time. These rituals are often transformed into another obsession or compulsion. Obsessions and compulsions often spontaneously remit with time. But an obsession is often truly maddening to caregivers and others around the child and may seriously interfere with daily life. Telling the child with an ASD that he or she may never talk about the topic of the obsession is rarely effective, because the child will throw a tantrum and may become aggressive, which make it impossible to follow through on the admonition not to talk about the obsession; however, there are several specific things you can do.

Limit Time Devoted to Obsession

Tell the youngster that he or she may talk about his or her obsession at a specific time each day. Set aside 5 minutes once in the morning and once in the afternoon during which he or she can talk about fire engines, tornadoes, or another topic of his or her obsession. While he or she is talking about his or her obsession, it is best to show little interest in his or her obsessive talk, but do not try to interfere with it during this time period. Don't answer his or her questions, such as, "Is there going to be a tornado?" And don't try to be reassuring by saying, "Don't worry, there isn't going to be a tornado." That will generally make matters worse. Discussing his or her obsession usually perpetuates it. At all other times, if the child begins talking about his or her obsession say, "We can talk about it at 2 o'clock" and show him or her the hands on the clock indicating the time that the child can talk about the topic. It is best to walk away and involve yourself with an activity that makes it appear as though you are busy and not paying attention to the child. The child may follow his or her teacher or parent to another location if the adult leaves the area. The child may insist on talking about his or her obsession. It is best that caregivers not respond to persistent obsessive talk. The first few times that teachers or parents employ this procedure the child may scream, throw him- or herself on the floor, flail his or her arms and feet, and otherwise appear upset. If caregivers are able to walk away and ride out the tantrum, the child's tantrums usually stop after the second or third episode. While ignoring the outbursts it is worthwhile to try to determine whether there is anything else making the child anxious because OCD behavior is often associated with increased anxiety.

Limit Places Obsessive Talk Can Occur

Tell the child that if he or she wants to talk about an obsession, he or she must do it in a designated room. It is best if the selected room is not the child's own bedroom. If there is a family room or spare bedroom that is seldom used during much of the day, tell the child that he or she may go in that room to talk about that topic by him- or herself or with a parent seated nearby who is busying him- or herself with another activity. Make certain that there are no other family members, other caregivers, siblings, TVs, or video games in those rooms. That ensures that no one will talk with the child about his or her obsession, which usually makes matters worse.

In most cases, obsessions change with time. One obsession will disappear, and several months later the youngster will focus on another topic. Occasionally, a child who is experiencing a particularly anxiety-producing period, such as starting a new school, may exhibit marked worsening of obsessions. As children become more comfortable in their new setting, the obsessions often subside and disappear. If a child's persistent obsessions are associated with nightmares (e.g., being chased by monsters), or are accompanied by self-injury, the child should be seen by a developmental pediatrician or child psychiatrist. That usually suggests that something else is going on in the child's life that is contributing to his or her high degree of anxiety. In many instances, a combination of modified sleep, updated hygiene practices, and prescribed medication can be useful in enabling the child to sleep through the night without terrifying dreams, which reduces daytime obsessions.

Dealing with Compulsions

Compulsions are usually anxiety-driven and are much worse in situations that are disturbing to the child or when he or she is surrounded by uncertainty. The birth of a younger sibling, family discord, or a change of schools or teachers often aggravate compulsions. Anything parents or teachers can do that will give the child the feeling that he or she has more appropriate control of his or her circumstances will generally reduce compulsiveness. It is not appropriate, however, for the child to coercively control his or her parents' or teachers' behavior by threatening to throw a tantrum if he or she is unable to engage in a compulsive ritual. A kindergarten teacher had a 5-year-old nonverbal student with autistic disorder who exhibited significant self-injury. The teacher's strategy for dealing with his self-injury was to hold him on her lap (or the educational assistant's lap) all day and restrain his arms. If his teacher tried to put him down, he screamed and hit his head. If the assistant was holding him and she had to attend to another child, he immediately engaged in self-injury. A child shouldn't have to control his teachers' or parents' behavior that way. A child with an ASD can achieve some measure of appropriate control over how daily activities occur and thereby has less need for inappropriate compulsive behavior. We taught this child to use a combination of icons and gestures to communicate and increased his independence in doing routine classroom activities. We helped his teacher identify several of his positive activities and encouraged her to selectively attend to him when he was constructively engaged. He was allowed to sit on his teacher's lap when he completed a classroom activity but not when he threatened to self-injure. His self-injury stopped after several weeks and he seemed far more relaxed and at ease in school.

Making Choices

Children with ASDs should have opportunities to make choices throughout their day and as often as possible. A child might choose whether to have apples or grapes with lunch, whether to work on the shape-matching or sequencing activity first, and whether to go to the supermarket first or to the hardware store with a parent. Those are the types of choices that help the child feel as if he or she has some control over what is going on in his or her life. Children may not choose whether they attend school, go to a doctor's appointment, or go to bed at 9 p.m. Remember, children with ASDs thrive on structure and are made far more anxious by erratic, unstructured daily routines. A child who has the opportunity to make legitimate choices within a predictable structure has less reason to be anxious about what will happen next because he or she helped determine the next activity.

Reducing Compulsive Rituals

When children exhibit compulsive rituals, such as turning light switches on and off repeatedly, it occurs partially because they have an urge to engage in that behavior (i.e., a compulsion), but it is made worse by the attention they receive for doing so. Parents or siblings tell them to stop or may physically remove them from the light switch. Inevitably, the child's compulsive urge becomes intertwined with the attention he or she receives for engaging in compulsive behavior. Some compulsive rituals are not as disruptive or disturbing to others as repeatedly opening and slamming a door shut. A child who flaps his or her hands or twirls in a circle is engaging in behavior that is stigmatizing but minimally affects others. As previously described, paying little attention to a child who is discussing an obsession works well with many children with compulsions because it eliminates any possible attention he or she might receive for engaging in behavior that is disturbing or annoying to others.

Habit Reversal and Compulsive Behavior

Higher-functioning verbal children with ASDs can occasionally be taught to stop exhibiting specific rituals through a technique called Habit Reversal (Woods, Miltenberger, & Lumley, 1996). This begins with helping children realize when they are engaging in problem behavior. Children with ASDs are often unaware of when they are flapping, twirling, or repeatedly flipping a switch. The behavior just happens spontaneously. It becomes an automatic bad habit. Once children are made aware of when they are engaging in the compulsive behavior, they are taught to do something else that is incompatible with the ritual. In one case, a high-functioning elementary school–age child with Asperger syndrome who twirled in circles and flapped his hands when he was excited was videotaped. One of his classmates was also videotaped when he was excited (e.g., laughing with excitement, clapping his hands together, giving his friends high fives). We played the videotapes back to the boy with Asperger syndrome and asked him which he thought looked better. He was embarrassed by how he looked when he twirled in circles. He said the other boy looked better when he was excited. We said that when he was excited and felt like twirling in circles we needed to think of something else he could do instead, such as clapping his hands once or twice or saying, "That was great!" We practiced the new alternative skill, and a classroom assistant agreed that she would signal him by calling his name and holding up one finger when we saw him starting to become excited. This way he could become aware of when he was about to engage in the compulsive behavior. As soon as the classroom assistant held up her finger, he practiced one of the other responses, such as clapping his hands or enthusiastically saying, "That's great!" Although this procedure was effective most of the time, he periodically lapsed into flapping and twirling when he was excited. Other students laughed at him and his classroom teacher said, "Stop flapping." We discussed this residual problem with him and agreed that if he simply couldn't control his urge to twirl, he would go into an adjacent room near his classroom (an unused occupational therapy room) and twirl or flap his hands. The compulsive behaviors stopped within a week, which suggested that part of the reason the flapping and twirling persisted was due to the attention it generated, even though the attention appeared to be negative in most respects.

Functional Assessment of Compulsive Behavior

At times, particularly with less capable students who have limited communication skills, compulsive behavior is multiply determined. There appears to be an OCD component that is very difficult to control, but there is also a social component. The compulsive ritual often occurs more in some situations and rarely in others. By keeping track of episodes over a 1-week period and recording what the child was doing immediately before face slapping, repeatedly screaming, and so forth and what happened shortly thereafter, a pattern often emerges. For example, we worked with a 14-year-old nonverbal boy with severe autism who would self-bite and head-hit, which his special education teacher said had occurred randomly over the course of the school day. We discovered that when we kept careful records of each episode, self-injury often occurred when his classroom teacher or aide shifted their attention from him to another child. So the trigger event was taking attention away from him and giving it to another child. Shortly after he began self-biting and hitting his head, his aide or teacher approached him on each occasion, restrained his arm or head, and said, "Stop, no biting (or hitting)!" Part of the solution involved teaching the youngster to use an appropriate gesture to request teacher attention and teaching staff to ignore minor self-injury that presented no risk of physical harm (Symons, Fox, & Thompson, 1998). That procedure, along with others described in Chapter 10, eliminated his self-injury.

Medications and Compulsive Behavior

Though psychotropic medications are beyond the scope of this book, appropriate use of specific medications can be extremely helpful in reducing some obsessive-compulsive behavior. The same medications as those used to treat OCD in typical psychiatric patients (Anafranil, selective serotonin reuptake inhibitors [SSRIs], antidepressants, and some atypical antipsychotics) can be very effective with older individuals with ASDs in reducing severe compulsive behavior including self-injury (Thompson, 2007). Although some physicians prescribe atypical antipsychotic medications to younger children as well, many doctors encourage parents to explore other options first.

ACTIVITY SCHEDULES TO REDUCE OBSESSIONS AND COMPULSIONS

When Juan arrived at school in the morning, he asked his teacher if he could feed the fish in the aquarium, though he usually fed them just before lunch. Even before he hung up his coat, he seemed very frustrated that he was unable to feed the fish. Helen is anxious about what is going to happen when she finishes with occupational therapy. She keeps asking, "Now what? Now what?" Cory has a meltdown because he thought he was going to have cookies and juice next but instead was asked to join the other children for circle time.

Executive Function Deficits in Autism Spectrum Disorders

Children with ASDs have great difficulty understanding and coping with sequences of events. These problems are believed to be due to dysfunction with their frontal brain area called the prefrontal cortex, which regulates planning sequences of actions and organizing ideas. Youngsters with ASDs have special difficulty organizing and planning a sequence of activities and even greater problems grasping times at which events occur (i.e., according to the clock). They often repeatedly ask their mother or teacher when a specific event will happen. These are called *executive functions* because they are required to organize other activities involving functions of other brain areas. A task as simple as putting on socks and shoes requires planning. If a child slips his or her feet into shoes before putting on socks, he or she is unable to dress properly. Deciding what to do next requires understanding sequences (i.e., what things must be done in a specific order). A child's learning to ask his or her mother to get juice out of the refrigerator requires understanding the sequence of events that will gain him or her access to juice rather than just pounding on the refrigerator door. Children with executive function deficits often have difficulty learning from past mistakes and make the same mistake repeatedly.

Schedules and Task Lists

Teachers and parents often assume children with ASDs have organizing abilities that they really don't have. It is common for an adult to prepare a meal, write a grocery list, and talk on the phone to plan the agenda for the next PTA meeting all at the same time. That is what is commonly called *multitasking*. One activity may be interrupted and then resumed later where it was left off without missing a beat. That attests to the tremendous computing power of a normal adult brain—abilities that a typical child with ASD does not have. Helping children with ASDs make their world more predictable is critical in working with youngsters on the autism spectrum. That is where schedules and task lists come in. A *schedule* is a temporally organized plan for activities, or, alternatively, an ordered list of times at which things are planned to occur. A *task list* is list of tasks to be completed (i.e., a "to do" list) but without reference to a specific order or designated time. A schedule often implies tasks to be completed at specific times and in a specified order. Children with ASDs thrive on schedules and task lists. They transform a chaotic world into one that is predictable and understandable.

Sometimes parents and teachers are concerned that imposing schedules and lists on their students or children with ASDs will be too regimented and will aggravate the child's preexisting rigidity.

One mother told me that sticking to her child's activity schedule made her feel as though she were in the Marines. Although activity schedules may initially rankle some teachers and parents, effective use of these tools usually reduces anxiety and improves children's abilities to make sense of their daily lives. This can lead to greater independence over time. Activity schedules help a child anticipate what is forthcoming. An effective activity schedule compensates in part for a child's executive function deficits. Adult caregivers usually find that within a week or so of implementing an activity schedule or task list, their life with a child or student with an ASD has become much easier than in the past.

The secret of using activity schedules involves choosing the most effective cues for a given child to prompt them and creating a schedule that is inherently flexible and easily changed to meet changing needs.

Activity Schedules for Young and/or Nonverbal Children

Brandon is $4\frac{1}{2}$ years old and uses some words and short phrases as a result of speech therapy and intensive home-based behavior therapy combined with his parents' diligent practice with him on the evenings and weekends. He eats with his fingers at mealtime and uses the toilet to urinate but is not bowel trained. Brandon has learned to pull up his own pants and push his feet into his shoes after his mother has helped put on his socks. He attends early childhood special education on Monday, Wednesday, and Friday mornings and has speech therapy on Tuesday and Thursday mornings for an hour each. After lunch each day, behavior therapists work with him at home for 4 hours. During the afternoon, he and his therapists work on skills leading to 4–5 goals in his individual treatment plan as well as other activities used as rewards that also strengthen his leisure and social skills.

Brandon's complicated schedule differs somewhat each day and involves different people, places, and activities. He often becomes confused about what he going to be doing on a given day and has tantrums when an activity he is expecting is planned for a different day. His lead behavior therapist suggested making him an activity schedule that would help him anticipate what he would be doing throughout each day. Two excellent resources to help teachers and parents understand and use activity schedules are McClannahan and Krantz's (1999) book *Activity Schedules for Children with Autism: Teaching Independent Behavior* and Hodgdon's (1995) *Visual Strategies for Improving Communication: Practical Supports for School and Home.*

Preliminary Assessment

Before beginning to construct an activity schedule, several preliminary steps are necessary. We first need to determine whether a clip art picture or a photograph represents the same thing as an actual object does to the child. We print a clip art drawing of a child's potty chair from the Internet and take a photo of Brandon's own potty. We also print out clip art drawings of a boy eating with a spoon and a photo of Brandon eating with a spoon. Brandon had already learned to point to actual familiar small objects, such as a spoon, a crayon, and a grape, so he grasped the idea of pointing to something to identify it. We place the clip art potty chair and the photo of Brandon's own potty chair, and say, "Brandon, point to potty." If Brandon is like most children his age and ability, he would point to the photo of his own potty chair, but he may not point to the clip art version, which is more abstract. We then place a clip art image of a child eating with a spoon next to a clip art image of a potty chair. This time we want to see if he can recognize clip art drawings of actual things and we say, "Brandon, point to eat." Often, children like Brandon will randomly select one or the other. The clip art drawings are too abstract for him to use as symbols on his visual schedule without being trained to recognize them first.

How to Present the Activity Schedule

Next we begin planning how to best present the schedule. Rather than beginning with a complete schedule for each day of each week, preliminary training would be recommended to include only activities beginning with lunch and ending at 5 p.m. when his therapist leaves in the afternoon. For a young child Brandon's age, photographic picture schedules are often most effective. For older children who have already been taught to name people, objects, and activities from pictures in books or magazines, it is possible to create activity schedules using such pictures or clip art. Each afternoon for the next week the therapists working with Brandon will take digital photographs of each activity in which he engages beginning with eating lunch and ending with waving "bye-bye" to his therapist as she walks out of the front door of his house. Brandon's parents and the lead therapist look through the photographs and decide which ones they will use and arrange them in a sequence for the entire afternoon. They may decide that they have missed an activity or that a photograph for a specific activity isn't sufficiently clear and decide to shoot additional pictures. Once the entire sequence is arranged, it is broken down into smaller groups of activities, typically 3–5 per group.

What Activities to Include

How does one know which activities to photograph? Every time one activity is going to end and another begin, a photograph of the new activity will be needed. Each photograph is designed to provide a tangible cue that 1) there is going to be a change in activity and 2) indicates the specific activity that is going to occur next. It is important to intersperse photographs of enjoyable, reinforcing activities that will be used as rewards for completing especially challenging tasks. If brushing teeth after lunch is often a struggle, the photograph following brushing teeth should be a highly preferred reinforcing activity, such as playing a tickle game or going on a horseback ride. For younger children and those with more cognitive limitations, no more than 3–5 activities should appear per page of a spiral notebook corresponding to each day's activities. The entire schedule for a given child's afternoon might include four pages with 3–5 activities per page. The last activity on a given page should always be an enjoyable and rewarding activity. For Brandon, the first page of his activity book would resemble the example shown in Figure 2.2, a morning schedule. It would begin with Brandon eating breakfast, brushing his teeth, and then playing a tickle game. The next page would begin with a "Do this..." imitation activity, followed by a matching activity, then a sequencing activity, and ending the page with snack time (see Figure 2.3 for an example of an after-school schedule). It isn't always possible to end an activity schedule with a preferred activity, such as when the child goes to bed at night (see Figure 2.4).

This schedule should be followed for a week or until Brandon has adjusted to the activity schedule. The following week, 2–3 minor changes should be made in the specific order of activities or the rewards that will be available. For example, after toothbrushing a photo of Brandon having a horseback ride might be substituted for a tickle game. The matching and sequencing activities might be reversed. The purpose of these changes is to reduce Brandon's rigidity while making the sequence of events very clear to him so he will readily tolerate changes.

Activity Schedule Formats

Another common format for a visual schedule involves printing the photos or clip art images onto heavy card stock and stick Velcro on the back of each. On a vertical piece of cardboard or foam core attach a matching strip of the opposite side of the Velcro material. The vertical foam core or cardboard strip should be large enough to accommodate up to five photos or images arranged one above the other. Each morning, arrange the sequence of activities for the morning and give it to the child to place on his or her desk in school or the area at home where he or she spends most of his or her time. Repeat the same procedure for the afternoon with a new set of images. As the child completes each activity, he or she can pull off the corresponding image and place it in a heavy envelope that is attached to the bottom of the cardboard or foam core strip.

Morning

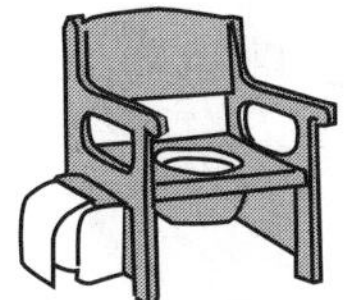

Figure 2.2. Example of a morning schedule.

If Brandon's teacher had decided to use clip art instead of photographs, she could identify appropriate drawings and print them on card stock, one for each activity in his schedule. Because Brandon recognizes photos of actual familiar things, she could use a matching procedure to teach him which clip art drawings are the same as actual objects. A clip art image of a school bathroom and another of children playing with a ball are placed side by side. Above them is a photograph of

After School

Figure 2.3. Example of an after-school schedule.

Brandon sitting on the potty. The teacher points to the two clip art images and says, "Point to potty, like this" pointing to the photo of Brandon on the potty. This may be too difficult at first. If it is, back up a step and begin with a clip art of a school bathroom as the correct choice and a large red square as the alternative incorrect choice. Repeat the instruction, "Point to potty, like this." Most children point correctly to the clip art image. Over a period of steps, the incorrect choice is transitioned to look increasingly like an alternative clip art image (e.g., a balloon, a tractor, an airplane, an image of a boy eating). In most cases, the child will point to the correct image. During this process, it is important to randomly place the correct image on one side or the other to avoid simply choosing the image on one side. This series of steps needs to be repeated until the child selects the correct images that will be used on his or her visual schedule for a given week or two.

For individuals with ASDs with more severe cognitive limitations and attention problems, an alternative activity schedule format can be used (Thompson & Carey, 1980). The plastic holder for a single page-per-day desk calendar with pages that can be flipped over each day can be used effectively. The calendar pages are removed and pages are cut from heavy stock paper the same size as the calendar pages. Photographs of one activity per page are printed or pasted on the pages that fit the desk calendar. The photo on the left side of the calendar will be the activity to be completed by the child, and the corresponding reinforcer will be shown on the right side. The pages can be laminated in plastic with holes punched for the metal calendar page hoops. The day's schedule is inserted into the holder with all of the pages on the right side except the first activity of the day, which will appear on the left side. Instead of a calendar holder, some teachers or parents use a bragging book that can be purchased at most photography supply stores. They are composed of plastic pages into which photographs can be inserted by proud parents to show pictures of their children as they grow up. No more than one or two plastic sleeves are on a page. Once the child has learned to use the activity schedule, 2–3 tasks can be inserted sequentially followed by a reinforcing activity rather than one reinforcing activity per task completed. It is helpful to vary the number of tasks before each reinforcing activity to promote persistence without the child's expecting a reward. This type of activity schedule is especially helpful for children and adolescents who are especially distractible or have difficulty focusing on one aspect of a complex stimulus array. Bopp, Brown, and Mirenda (2004) provided a tutorial regarding the use of functional communication training and augmentative and alternative communication interventions employing visual schedules for students with more severe communication limitations, including the roles that speech-language pathologists can play in assessment, intervention design, and implementation in school and home settings.

After Dinner

Figure 2.4. Example of an after-dinner schedule.

Whichever schedule format is selected, flexibility is important because it should be easy to change or substitute activities in order to help a child tolerate changes as long as they are signaled. It is usually a mistake to use the same activity schedule week after week. That will create greater rigidity and intolerance for changes in daily routines. Higher-functioning and older children can often be taught to use a computer-based visual schedule. Rehfeldt, Kinney, Root, and Stromer (2004) described a computerized PowerPoint activity schedule that includes photographs, text, and sound that would be extremely flexible and easily used once the basic program has been created.

Older Children Who Can Read

Once children begin to read, visual schedules can be transitioned and replaced by a printed text schedule. This usually begins by including both text and pictures alongside one another (e.g., "do this" is printed alongside a photo of an imitation activity). One at a time, the photographs are removed and only the text remains, beginning with text information that the child is able to read most reliably. Usually within several weeks the photographs have been faded out entirely and only a text schedule is used. If a child has difficulty switching from pictures to printed words, a computer program that fades the ink density can be used over several weeks (i.e., 90%, 80%, and so forth until 10% is reached, at which point the pictures can be eliminated). When a new activity is added that a child has yet to be able to read reliably, a photograph is paired with the activity until he or she is reliably reading the text, then the photo is removed. Text schedules are often more portable and provide practice reading. Moreover, it is easier to produce each schedule and make changes. A text schedule also generalizes more easily between and among settings, such as school and home and speech therapy and school.

Activity Schedules and Choices

After a child has mastered either a visual or text schedule, teachers and parents can begin each day's activities by inserting activities first in the day's schedule that must be completed at specific times (e.g., lunch, bathroom, getting on the school bus), and then lay out all of the remaining pictures or textual cues corresponding to other activities to be completed on a table in front of the child. The child is encouraged to arrange them in order. This is often very difficult for younger children and those with more severe cognitive limitations. Practice choosing only one activity at a time (e.g., what will be done first after going to the bathroom), which gives the child some control in the situation but doesn't overwhelm him or her with too many choices.

Many children with ASDs who are higher functioning enjoy creating their own daily schedules by writing down the order in which they will complete activities. To ensure that some activities aren't omitted, parents or teachers usually provide a list of all activities from which the child chooses their order. Once a child has mastered creating his or her own daily schedule, he or she may elect to add a preferred activity of his or her own choosing from time to time. Watanabe and Sturmey (2003) studied the effectiveness of a choice procedure in connection with an activity schedule with young adults with ASDs. Under the baseline condition, staff assigned the order of the tasks. In the "choice" condition, the participants chose the order of tasks that supervisors assigned to them. They made their own activity schedules by writing down the order of their tasks for that morning. Praise was provided contingent on the participant's task completion. The same tasks were used in baseline, intervention, and maintenance phases. Client engagement was substantially higher when they could choose their own activity schedule and subsequently their behavior was well maintained without praise following task completion.

TASK LISTS

Task lists are a type of "to do" list but will appear similar to an activity schedule to a youth who has had experience with them. Task lists are often used with adolescents and young adults to help them organize their daily lives, especially as they are transitioning to more independent settings and activities. If a youngster has had experience with activity schedules, it is usually easiest to say that his or her task list is an activity schedule that can be done in any order. It is very common for youngsters to insist on completing the items on the list in the order they were written, at least in the beginning. After a week or so, teachers or parents can suggest to the child that he or she might want to do some things first even it they aren't first on the list. By selecting a "to do" activity that you think the child will strongly prefer, he or she is often willing to try doing items on the list in a different order. For example, a teacher could say, "What would you like to do first? How about helping me put the books back in the bookshelf?" Once the youngster has made it over that initial hurdle, he or she is usually willing to ignore the order of the items on the list and select items according to his or her preference.

Task lists are useful at home, not only to help a youngster remember household chores, but to help in planning ahead. For example, a teenager may want to invite a friend to watch a video Saturday evening but he "forgets" to call the person. People with

ASDs are shy and often find it difficult to initiate such a telephone call. If calling a friend to invite over on Saturday is an item on his task list, it is less likely the child will "forget" because he or she is more likely to see it as only another thing to do, such as taking out the trash. Task lists also teach skills useful in school, like planning the steps in writing a report for biology class. Adolescents who are not as high functioning can also make use of visual task lists. Photographs of a youth doing various household tasks, such as sorting laundry, can be prepared and reviewed each morning. "What should we do first?" his father might ask, pointing at the four photographs of "to do" items. Minimally verbal children can learn to point at the activity they are willing to do, and then they can be prompted through the steps of completing the task.

SUMMARY

The world of many children with ASDs appears confusing, disorderly, and even chaotic. The more understandable and predictable a child's life can be made, the less anxious he or she will be and the smaller the need to gain control of his or her world through unusual compulsive rituals will be. Through using visual schedules, lists, and regular routines, most children's compulsive rituals and obsessions can be managed. Promoting choice making provides a child with a legitimate way to have some control over his or her daily life. Most children, adolescents, and adults diagnosed with ASDs continue to exhibit some compulsive tendencies even after having completed successful therapy or specialized educational services as children. They may insist on talking about a narrow range of topics regardless of the listener's obvious disinterest. They may be excessively fastidious and become annoyed with roommates who violate their rituals by leaving the cap off the toothpaste or by disrupting their belongings. Nonetheless, many children with ASDs can grow into young adulthood with an array of coping skills that permit them to navigate their way through a less than predictable world.

3

Time Is Your Enemy

You glance at your watch and realize you should have gotten your son into the car and headed for school 10 minutes ago. In an urgent tone of voice you say, "Jacob, hurry up. Put on your shoes. We're late!" Jacob continues playing with his Legos as though he hasn't heard you. You nearly shout, "Jacob, I told you to put on your shoes. You're going to be late for school!" As you begin closing the cereal box before putting it in the cupboard, Jacob suddenly looks up when he hears the paper crackling, then he resumes playing with his Legos. You feel like screaming. "Jacob, get a move on!" you shout. After another few seconds, he looks up at you with a puzzled expression, and he begins to cry. You are at your wits' end. You pick him up and forcefully begin shoving his feet into his shoes as he resists, stiffens, and sobs. The artist Ben Hecht (1957) remarked, "Time is a circus, always packing up and moving away." The same is true when living with or teaching a child with an ASD. Time is forever escaping.

PROCESSING DEFICITS IN AUTISM

Children with ASDs have deficits in processing speech, have limitations in pragmatic use of language, and have difficulties in changing strategies or activities due to compulsiveness that interferes with their ability to respond to spoken instructions or questions in a timely fashion.

Delayed Processing of Speech Sounds

Children with ASDs perceive most nonspeech sounds normally, such as musical notes or the crackling sound of a paper wrapper across the room, but they have difficulty recognizing sequences of speech sounds (Oram Cardy, Flagg, Roberts, Brian, & Roberts, 2005). The length of time from the onset of speech sounds until their brain begins to react to those sounds is delayed. When sounds come in rapid succession, their brain detects the first sound but may show no response to subsequent sounds that occur in rapid succession. When people with ASDs are presented with speech and their brain responses are measured using brain-imaging methods, they show significantly less activation in the left brain speech-related areas. In another study, the ability of the brains of children with high-functioning ASDs to detect speech sounds was measured by presenting acoustically matched simple tones, complex tones, and vowels. The task was to detect one "odd" sound among a sequence of identical sounds. The children's brain responses were normal when unexpected simple or complex tones were presented but were entirely absent when an odd vowel change occurred amidst a sequence of other identical vowels. In short, children with ASDs specifically have problems processing speech, especially speech sounds in rapid succession (Boddaert et al., 2004). The net result is that they may appear not to hear what is said to them. It is likely that they perceive portions of what is said, especially if it is stated slowly, but will miss portions of what their parents or teachers say if it is rushed. It would be like trying to pour water through a funnel that drains very slowly. If you empty more water into the funnel than it can handle, it overflows. That is one of the main reasons that time is your enemy. It takes children with ASDs far longer to process and fully understand what you have said to them.

Pragmatic Language Limitations

A second related problem is that children with Asperger syndrome or high-functioning autism may have substantial spoken vocabularies, but their understanding of the full meaning of those words may be more limited than you realize, especially in combination. A teacher says, "Maya, let's put our toys in the cupboard, then we can take them out again after we come back from music." What sounds like a simple statement is far too complex for many children with ASDs to negotiate, even bright children with good speech skills. If we parse the statement, we begin to see why Maya is having problems:

"Let's put our toys in the cupboard" is one thought that Maya will likely understand.

"Then we can take them out again" is a second thought. But this is part of an "if–then" statement ending with *again*, which makes comprehension much more difficult.

"After we come back from music" is the third and final thought that Maya must integrate with the first two distinct thoughts, which is a tall order for most youngsters with ASDs.

It shouldn't come as a surprise if Maya sits motionless with a puzzled expression on her face. She isn't being noncompliant, she is trying to figure out what in the world the teacher said.

Compulsiveness and Difficulty with Strategy Shifts

Compulsiveness is a third problem underlying the time crunch facing teachers and parents in working with their student or child with an ASD. Although many children do not meet all of the diagnostic criteria for OCD, most exhibit several traits characteristic of OCD. As noted in Chapter 2, compulsions are repetitive behaviors (e.g., repeatedly opening and closing doors, lining up objects, arranging and rearranging toys or other items repeatedly) or mental acts (e.g., counting, repeating words silently, or in the case of children with ASDs, repeating the words aloud) that the person feels driven to according to "rules" that must be applied rigidly. Among children with ASDs, it is often difficult to verbalize the rules, but if given the opportunity, they will demonstrate them through their actions. Among typically developing children and adults with OCD, the behaviors or mental acts are aimed at preventing some dreaded event or situation, but they are not connected in a realistic way with what they are designed to prevent or they are clearly excessive. But individuals with ASDs are not able to explain what will happen if they are unable to engage in the compulsive ritual, but they exhibit great distress if they are prevented from doing so. In a study comparing OCD symptoms among typical children diagnosed with OCD and a comparison group with ASDs, it was found that children with OCD reported more compulsions and obsessions than children with ASDs

(Russell, Mataix-Cols, Anson, & Murphy, 2005). Both groups, however, reported more compulsions and obsessions than a typically developing comparison group. Types of compulsions and obsessions tended to be less sophisticated in children with ASD than those with OCD.

Typical people with OCD have difficulty with decision making and tasks that involve changing strategy. For example, a child with OCD is given a stack of cards with colored pictures or animals on the cards and told to sort all of the red animals in one pile and the green animals in a second pile. After sorting half of the stack according to this rule, the child is told to stack the rest of the cards according to whether the animals have two legs versus four legs. Individuals with OCD as well as those with ASDs have great difficulty making this shift in strategy (Yerys, Hepburn, Pennington, & Rogers, 2007). This type of strategy shift task requires intact functioning of executive function circuits in the frontal part of the brain (frontal cortex). Individuals with damage to these areas often find it difficult or nearly impossible to complete certain tasks involving more complex executive function demands. There is considerable brain-imaging evidence that children with ASDs often have frontal cortical dysfunction (Just, Cherkassky, Keller, Kana, & Minshew, 2006).

When a parent gives a child an instruction such as, "It's time for dinner," that implies that the child is to stop what he or she is doing (Task 1) and shift to another activity (Task 2). The more complex the demand, or if the situation involves divided attention (e.g., distracting sounds, visual signals), the child will have far more difficulty processing and responding to the instruction. While the parent is setting the table for dinner, the television is on in the next room, and the phone has just been ringing. When the parent says to Matthew, "It's time for dinner," no wonder he doesn't respond. He has no idea to what he should be paying attention. Many errors by children with ASDs in educational settings are often related to compulsiveness and language problems rather than the inability to perform the requested task. If one spelling rule has been taught, and then a second added, the child tends to persist in following the first rule even with repeated urging by the teacher to incorporate the second rule as well. A longer period of time is required to process and adjust to changes in task demands than with a typically developing child of the same age.

STRATEGIES FOR COPING WITH TIME PROBLEMS

Assisting your child coping with time difficulties involves a combination of planning, allowing more time, and alerting your child to upcoming changes in activities. In addition, speaking more slowly and calmly and avoiding overestimating how much speech your child can understand can head off problems before they happen.

Plan Ahead

Anticipating upcoming events can make a world of difference in helping a child with an ASD deal with time. Adults who procrastinate and tend to do things at the last moment when a deadline looms are destined to have problems with their child or student with an ASD. The adult feels rushed and finds it necessary to improvise in order to get there on time or complete a task before a deadline. Children with ASDs cannot be rushed, and have little tolerance for improvisation. The secret in helping them avoid crises is to plan ahead well in advance of activities. Many parents of children with ASDs create a daily schedule, much as classroom teachers write the day's activities on a chalkboard each morning before the students arrive. That helps keep everyone on track and reminds them of upcoming events. If a visual schedule is used, as discussed in Chapter 2, it will also help the child anticipate forthcoming events.

Allow More Time

If you think it should take 10 minutes for an activity, allow 20 minutes. It is better for a child to complete an activity ahead of schedule than to be hurried to complete it. Any activity that involves multiple steps, such as brushing teeth, will take longer because the child is called upon to repeatedly stop one activity and begin the next. The child first must wet the toothbrush under the running water, then squeeze the toothpaste on the toothbrush, then close the toothpaste tube, then brush his or her teeth, then rinse out his or her mouth and spit in the sink, rinse off the toothbrush and hang it up, and finally wipe his or her face on a towel and hang up the towel. This sequence may seem simple to an adult or typical child but is precisely the kind of activity that creates problems for a child with an ASD. It takes longer because making switches between activities takes longer.

Alert the Child to Upcoming Changes

Changing from one strategy or activity to another is challenging for youngsters with ASDs. Adults can facilitate transitions by providing an alert several seconds before a change will occur, which gives a child's brain time to process the forthcoming change. It is a mistake to provide a warning too far in advance because a child may either forget the alert or begin to ruminate about the upcoming change, especially if the upcoming activity is one he or she prefers less. Five minutes before going to physical education, a teacher may say, "Bronco, we're going to gym in a few minutes." Bronco remembers being knocked down by another child during physical education and is afraid of falling from the monkey bars. As the minutes elapse, he becomes increasingly fearful and begins to cry. It usually is more effective to provide the alert between 30 seconds and 1 minute before the change, and within a few seconds after the initial signal, engage the child in a transition activity that occupies him or her, preventing him or her from thinking about what he or she dislikes about the upcoming activity. A statement such as, "Bronco, it's almost time for gym (pause and silently count to 5). Let's begin putting away our crayons" provides Bronco with a concrete transition activity (putting away the crayons) that will prevent him from thinking about and resisting the change. Another strategy involves handing a child a transition item that he or she can give to the adult in the next task situation who will reward him or her for doing so. "Isabel, it's time for Music. Give this (hand her a card with a picture of a piano) to Mrs. Jones and she will give you a treat."

Use Fewer Words and Speak Slowly

Areas of the brain involved in interpreting speech are not well coordinated for many children with ASDs, so it takes them longer to process spoken instructions or respond to questions. By definition, speech sounds usually come in rapid succession. If there are too many words and the words are spoken rapidly, it is very likely that the child will not understand what has been said. For many children with ASDs, speaking and interpreting speech is like dealing with a tongue twister: "Peter Piper picked a peck of pickled peppers." We can all say the words slowly but we have difficulty when we try to say the words rapidly. For children with ASDs, that also applies to interpreting the spoken words of others. A parent may say, "Would you like some butter on your potatoes?" That seems simple enough, but for a young child with autistic disorder who is just learning to speak it would be more effective to say, "Emily, butter on potatoes." This accomplishes two things: It indicates that you are talking to Emily, and it eliminates unnecessary words. Such telegraphic speech that omits articles and pronouns is often effective early in communication intervention. As a child begins to understand and use speech, it is appropriate to begin adding articles and pronouns.

If one listens carefully to typical spoken exchanges, it becomes apparent that a speaker expects a verbal response from the listener within a few seconds. If the listener fails to respond, the speaker assumes something is wrong. Perhaps the person wasn't paying attention, or he or she may be upset by what was said and is deciding how to respond. If a father reads the story *The Three Little Pigs* to his 5-year-old son, Shou, who has Asperger syndrome, and asks why the third pig made his house out of bricks, it is likely he may receive either no reply or one he doesn't expect, such as, "So he can live in it." When we attempt to correct such a miscommunication, linguists refer to that as a *repair*. Shou's father may try to give a hint (a repair) by asking what happened to the other little pigs' houses. At this point, Shou's father has spoken 18 words in about 15 seconds. If he is like many of us, Shou's father's second question might be stated more loudly to make certain the child has heard the question. Such lengthy utterances are very difficult for children with ASDs to understand, especially if they are spoken rapidly. If Shou's father wanted to ask a question about the story, it would better to ask "what happened" questions rather than "why" questions that require an understanding of a character's motives. It might be more effective to ask what the wolf did to the straw house. Spoken instructions or questions should be enunciated clearly and slowly. For example, to a child with an ASD, hearing "going to" may not mean the same as the informal contraction "gonna." If a caregiver asks, "D'ya wanna M&M?" to a child with an ASD, it is likely all the child may hear is "M&M." If a child appears not to understand, try to restate the instruction or question as clearly as possible with fewer words, avoid contractions, and speak more slowly.

Don't Overestimate What a Child Understands

It is common for children with Asperger syndrome to exhibit spoken vocabularies and reading abilities at or above grade level. The depth of their understanding of the words they use or read, however, may be more limited. This is particularly true of abstract concepts and language that pertains to the reasons for people's actions. An elementary school child with Asperger syndrome may know all of the *Star Wars* characters but is unlikely to understand what "May the force be with you" means. I have known children with Asperger syndrome who knew the names of all of the states in the United States and their capitals but wouldn't be able to explain why people seldom drive from New York to California but often drive from Maryland to Virginia. It is very easy for adults to mistake a child's "knowing that" for "understanding that." A child with an ASD may know many facts but not understand their relationships with one another. Pragmatic language may be more limited than syntactically correct speech. Speaking to a child with high-functioning autism or Asperger syndrome on the assumption that he or she thinks like typical children his or her age and can perform comparable inferential reasoning can create problems. Such a child still requires more time to process the meaning of speech than typical peers.

Keep Calm and Don't Raise Your Voice

When a teacher has a classroom full of children to attend, or a parent is in the midst of daily family responsibilities, it can be very frustrating to speak to a child on the autism spectrum and receive no response or an echolalic response, such as repeating an advertisement from television. If an adult raises his or her voice, speaks harshly (e.g., "What's wrong with you? Aren't you listening?"), or, worse yet, yells at a child, the youngster will hear nothing that is said subsequently. Children with autism tend to be overly fearful, and a harsh tone of voice sets off alarms in their brain that interferes with their ability to think and listen. Responding harshly or loudly teaches a child that interactions with adults are unpleasant and frightening.

It is best to take a deep breath, stay calm, and repeat the instruction or question more slowly in an even tone of voice. If the child refuses to stop what he or she is doing (e.g., a preferred activity) in order to move on to a necessary new activity, try to look at the situation from his or her vantage point. Think of your job as being like that of a customer service representative dealing with frustrating customers. They usually have a reason for being upset, though their response is often exaggerated. Raising your voice, being more forceful, or physically forcing a child to do as you say will only make matters worse. By remaining calm, you will have an easier time soliciting the child's cooperation next time. Say the child's name, wait until he or she orients toward you, and then make your request.

Dangerous Situations: An Exception to the Rule

The one exception to this general rule is when a child with an ASD is about to do something that is potentially dangerous to him- or herself or others. If Ariel is about to insert a paper clip into an electrical outlet or Ashley appears to be poised to poke another child in the face with a pencil, it is appropriate to call them by name and firmly and loudly say, "stop" (e.g., "Ariel, stop!"). The child should be frightened by the situation in which he or she finds him- or herself (about to do something dangerous), which startles him or her long enough to keep from harming him- or herself or others and is reasonable and responsible.

SUMMARY

Nearly everything you do with a child with an ASD requires more time than with a typical sibling or student peer. Parents who prefer to go with the flow have far more difficulty communicating with and enlisting the cooperation of their child with an ASD. Classroom teachers who are frequently harried, rushed, and a bit muddled will find themselves having repeated problems with their student with an ASD, even a high-functioning student. A combination of planning, using alerts before changes in activities, slowing down spoken communication, and avoiding complex language can prevent problems.

4

Once Upon a Time

Discovering the Mystery of Words

Words are mysterious things. They create pictures in our mind's eye of things both past and in the future, real and imagined. When I was in third grade, and not a very good reader, I received three volumes of Lone Ranger books for Christmas. They were festooned with wonderful color prints of artists' renderings of the masked man on his horse, Silver, accompanied by his companion, Tonto. At first, my reading was plodding, but as I delved further into the first book, my reading speed accelerated, and I became entranced by the stories. Before New Year's Day, I had read all three books and my mind was filled with the smell of campfires, images of tumbling sagebrush and reddish sunsets over the painted desert, and, of course, shoot-outs with the bad guys. Needless to say, because I was growing up in Minnesota those were all images in my imagination and were not based on actual experience. Words do indeed have magical powers.

Words are the means by which people we love tell us about important events in their lives. Steve, the father of a child with an ASD, arrives home a half hour late from work and says in an exasperated voice, "Sorry I'm late. I got stuck in traffic." His wife, Helen, asks, "What happened? Was there an accident?" Steve replies, "Yeah, there was a pileup north of downtown. A tractor-trailer jackknifed. It was a real mess!" Try to imagine what a child with autistic disorder makes of this exchange. He tries to think about what it means to get *stuck*. Was there an *accident*, like spilling your milk? What is a *pileup*? What does *jackknifed* mean? The child might wonder whether the *real mess* was like his bedroom when his mom told him to pick up his toys and socks off the floor because it *was a mess*.

TYPICAL CONVERSATION IS INCOMPREHENSIBLE TO MANY CHILDREN WITH AUTISM SPECTRUM DISORDERS

Normal conversation swirling around children with ASDs is often incomprehensible to them, replete with figures of speech. Words come in rapid succession as the child is still trying to decipher the first part of the sentence while more words pile on top of the previous, which often creates a jumble of confusion.

Figures of Speech Are a Barrier to Communication

Common forms of expression are very confusing to most children and youth with ASDs. We say, "It's been raining all day!" A child will wonder what has been raining all day; to what does *it* refer? Worse yet, if we say, "It's been raining cats and dogs" a youngster may look outdoors to see if there are animals on the lawn. Or consider the situation in which a sibling comes home from school and says, "Boy, I've had a lousy day." A youth with autism will think of this as simply a statement of fact and may say, "Oh?" and turn around and walk away. A child with an ASD doesn't realize that his or her sibling's comment is an overture, to which he or she is expected to respond by asking what went wrong. A child's father says, "I wonder where I put my keys?" If the child knows that the keys are on the kitchen table, he or she may not know to tell his or her father. The child just thinks his or her father is wondering something and not specifically asking for help locating the keys. If a parent says to his or her daughter, "It's time for dinner," meaning please sit down for dinner, the daughter may simply take that as a statement of fact and not as a request. Her failure to take her seat may be interpreted by the parent as noncompliance rather than not understanding the intention of the statement. Our daily language is stuffed with puzzling expressions, such as "I'm fed up," "tickled pink," or "sick and tired." When a child with an ASD hears one of his or her peers say their teacher's tie is *cheesy*, this will befuddle the child. It doesn't look like cheese to him or her. Language pertaining to feelings is even more elusive. If a child's mother says, "You hurt your sister's feelings," that will mean little to a child with an ASD. He or she understands what it means to hurt someone by hitting them, but how do you hurt someone's feelings, and where are they located?

Limited Ability to Use Context to Interpret Speech

It is no wonder that children with ASDs are often at a loss to understand what is going on around them, and as a result they tune out adult conversations. Typical children also have difficulty deciphering such exchanges, but they learn a great deal from the context (e.g., getting stuck in traffic is like getting stuck in your booster seat). They learn from the second adult's replies (e.g., getting stuck in traffic has something to do with having an accident), which enables them to learn the ins and outs of vernacular communication. Youngsters with autism have greater difficulty using context to provide cues in interpreting speech and they don't understand figures of speech, such as *getting stuck.*

GRASPING THE PURPOSE OF COMMUNICATION

Communication problems are one of the three primary deficits of children with autistic disorder and PDD-NOS. Children with Asperger syndrome have less difficulty with speech, though they also have problems with the practical use of speech, called *pragmatics*. The first problem many children with autistic disorder and PDD-NOS face is understanding that communication has a purpose, one of which is that it is a tool for solving problems.

Promoting Communication

Ethan, who is 12 years old and has been diagnosed with PDD-NOS, wonders what people have to talk about all of the time. He hears people talk and talk, but they seldom say anything interesting, such as discussing the length of the Mississippi River or how many places they can remember the value of pi or which presidential stamps are in their collection. Adults are always talking about who said what to whom: he said, she said. Ethan overhears his mother saying to his father that she thinks they are having problems with their relationship. Ethan tries to conjure up an image of a relationship but draws a blank. People, like Ethan, who have ASDs watch television, but they find the talking between people on sitcoms and soap operas incomprehensible. Men and women stand around on those shows saying such things as, "You know that's not what I meant" and "I didn't want to hurt you" that don't seem to have practical meaning to youngsters like Ethan. He wonders why people would they say things like that. People with ASDs watch the news and weather shows and the Discovery Channel. People on those shows talk about avalanches and describe isotherms traveling across maps, and wildlife biologists discuss how goats are adapted to climbing up the side of mountains. Those things make sense. Most talking doesn't seem to serve any purpose as far as he can tell. Therein lies one of the most basic reasons that communication is so difficult for most people with ASDs.

A great deal of day-to-day communication establishes and strengthens relationships among people. We share experiences with others because we assume they will be as interested in the details of our lives as we are interested in theirs. We discuss our trials and tribulations and receive encouragement, support, commiseration, and helpful suggestions from our family members and friends. Little of our conversation is actually about things. Conversations are mostly about what happened to us, our friends, and our loved ones and our (and their) feelings about those events. This aspect of communication is intangible to most people with ASDs. They have limited understanding of how others think and feel and have no sense that their own experiences will be interesting to others. They find that talking among people is puzzling and are unsure of its function. For people with ASDs to be interested in communicating with others it must serve a practical purpose.

The Role of the Speech-Language Pathologist

While parents and teachers can accomplish a great deal to promote a child's communication on their own, their effectiveness can be multiplied by working closely with a SLP experienced in working with children with ASDs. Public school programs for youngsters with ASDs, as well as community preschools and diagnostic centers specializing in ASDs, usually have SLPs available on staff to aid in this process. Throughout this chapter it is assumed that parents and teachers will be consulting with an experienced SLP regularly concerning the most appropriate communication strategies for a given child.

Teaching the Purpose of Communication

It does not occur to a young boy with autistic disorder that if he wants juice from the refrigerator he can use words to ask his mother to get him juice. Instead, he tugs at her sleeve and cries hoping she will figure out what he wants. If that doesn't work, he has a tantrum as his mother frantically tries to discover the problem.

Sometimes, even children with good verbal skills who have ASDs fail to use language to solve practical problems. They just don't seem to think about using their language to overcome obstacles. The mother of a 9-year-old girl with high-functioning autism told me that her daughter, who had been toilet-trained since entering kindergarten, suddenly began wetting her pants in school. The child's pediatrician ruled out any physical cause for the problem. She was otherwise doing well in school and seemed to enjoy school. A team meeting was called at school and the behavior analyst presented a plan for a token system for the girl, in which she would receive tangible rewards and access to preferred activities the longer she went without wetting her pants and for correctly urinating in the toilet. As the meeting was drawing to a close, the child was asked to explain the token system, which she was able to do, and whether it was okay with her. She replied that the token program was fine, but she said her teacher could also take the spider out of her preferred stall in the bathroom. It turned out the little girl, who was highly compulsive, would only use one toilet stall in which to urinate and that a large spider had made a web in one corner of the stall, and she was terrified of the spider. So rather than use the stall, she wet in her pants. When her mother asked her why she hadn't said anything previously about the spider, she seemed puzzled and said she didn't know. She said she didn't think about saying anything. It apparently hadn't occurred to her to use her words to ask for help.

It is important that parents and teachers teach children with ASDs at a very young age to use spoken or augmentative communication, such as Picture Exchange Communication Systems (PECs; Bondy & Frost, 2001), to solve problems such as asking for things, asking for help, and asking to delay doing certain things that they strongly dislike. The first step in learning communication skills is to use gestures, which are taught through imitation.

Overcoming Unorthodox Speech

Many 2-year-olds with ASDs do not speak at all or they use words because they like their sounds. They may repeatedly say short phrases from television commercials, song lyrics, or nursery rhymes. They do not use these utterances to communicate; they are a form of self-stimulation called *echolalia.* Grace walks around her house repeatedly saying, "Dickory Dock, Dickory Dock," which she learned from her parents who read nursery rhymes to her before bedtime. Jonathon repeats, "Apply directly where it hurts" from a television commercial. He has no functional speech, but he occasionally repeats the phrase when asked a question by his parents. Echolalia can be misleading because it suggests the child is able to use words, but it is important to realize that it is often a form of self-stimulation, not communication. In some cases, echolalic responses to questions are attempts to respond (because the child realizes he or she has been asked a question), but in the absence of knowing what to say or how to say it, the child employs a rote echolalic phrase.

The secret to overcoming unorthodox speech lies in focusing on what a child is trying to communicate, not the words he or she said. By providing practice saying what is actually meant in context, (e.g., question: "What do you want?" reply: "Juice," instead of "Dickory Dock") the child will gradually engage in less unorthodox speech and substitute more appropriate intentional communication. Scolding or making disparaging comments, such as, "That doesn't make sense," will only make matters worse because it doesn't teach alternative skills and it punishes communicative attempts.

IMITATION AND GESTURE

Children almost always first communicate by pointing or holding up their hands to be picked up or held. Gestures are usually learned through imitation. Knowing where to begin with intervention can be aided by a preliminary assessment. In her book *Do-Watch-Listen-Say* (2000), Kathleen Ann Quill provided excellent functional assessment tools that can be used to evaluate the beginning skills a child brings to the communication situation. The inventory is beyond the scope of this book but is highly recommended, especially to teachers and therapists working with children with ASDs. Parents are encouraged to consult with a SLP when planning to conduct such assessments and develop communication plans.

Motor Imitation and Gesture

Typically developing children begin to imitate sounds and facial expressions and struggle to reach objects that are out of reach with outstretched hands between 6 and 7 months of age. They return their parents' smiles and engage in eye contact. By 12 months, they imitate gestures, such as clapping, orient to their name when it is called, enjoy playing peek-a-boo, and extend their arms as if to reach for things they want, as a requesting gesture. They are beginning to imitate some words by 1 year. By 15 months, most children are combining two words to create phrases (e.g., "more milk"), and by 2 years children point to objects or pictures when they are named (or body parts, such as nose or ears).

Gestures, posture, and body language provide important visual information for most of us. A drooping posture suggests a person is tired, feels discouraged, or perhaps doesn't feel well. Animated movements and gesticulations indicate a person is in good spirits. An averted glance suggests a person is uncomfortable. We detect these signals in a few seconds or less. Although most young children learn to produce and interpret gestures through imitation learning very early in life, that isn't true of many children with ASDs. The best predictor of rapid learning among children with ASDs is how well they engage in motor and/or verbal imitation between 2 and 3 years of age (Sallows & Graupner, 2005). About half of young children diagnosed with an ASD between 2 and 3 years of age do not spontaneously imitate their parents' gestures, such as clapping hands. They must be taught to do so.

Simple Motor Imitation

Motor imitation is a first step in communication. The following gross motor imitation procedure can be repeated 3–4 times over the course of a typical day. Choose times the child is in a good mood and is not engaged in a repetitive self-stimulatory activity, such as hand flapping, rocking, or other preferred compulsive behavior. It is best to fit the activity into a naturally occurring activity in your daily routine; for example, when the child is splashing in the bathtub or engaging in a tickle-and-chase game, a parent can clap his or her hands and say, "Yay! That was fun."

Hand and Arm Imitation

Seat the child in a child-sized chair, booster seat, or on the floor facing you. Call the child's name and wait until he or she orients toward you. Hold your hands up in front of you and say, "Do this" and clap your hands. Some children with ASDs will attempt to imitate clapping, but many will not. If the child does not attempt to imitate, hold the child's hands in your hands and bring them together in a clapping motion. As soon as the child's hands meet in a clap, smile and praise the child. For example, say "Wow, that was great!" With children who are resistant, sips of juice, small bits of fruit, or other treats can be used to reward imitation attempts.

Wait for about 5 seconds and then repeat the above step. Make certain the child is looking toward you before giving the instruction, "Do this." As soon as he or she is looking at you, clap your hands again and say, "Do this." Use a lot of praise and encouragement with phrases such as "This is fun!" "What a smart girl!" or "You're such a good boy!" In working with 2- to 3-year-olds, this procedure can be repeated every 5–10 seconds for approximately 5 minutes, followed by a rest or free play period. Always stop on a positive note, so make certain you conclude the session before the child has become fussy or is crying. At the end of the imitation period, sit with the child and provide him or her with a preferred treat or activity, such as milk and a cookie, and comment on how well he or she has done.

In many cases, within a week, as soon as you say, "Do this," and hold up your hands, the child will immediately clap his or her hands. Then you are ready for the next step, imitating patting the top of your head. Use exactly the same procedure. Begin with five repetitions of the familiar clapping hands exercise, then shift to patting the top of your head. Pat your head and say, "Do this." At first, the child is likely to clap his or her hands. Say the child's name (wait for the child to look at you), and then say, "Do this," and pat the top of your head again. Make certain the child is looking at you before you model patting your head. If the child claps his or her hands or otherwise doesn't imitate patting the top of his or her head, guide his or her hands to the top of his or her head and praise him or her for doing so. If the child resists, don't force him or her. Wait for several seconds and try again. Alternate five trials of clapping your hands with five trials of patting the top of your head. By repeating this over the course of several days, the child should eventually perform both motor imitation responses correctly when you present a model.

The foregoing procedures are repeated by next adding rubbing your tummy while alternating with trials of clapping hands and patting your head. Finally, add a fourth gross motor imitative response, patting both thighs with your hands with the palms turned downward. Once your child has mastered all four gross motor body imitations you are ready to work on object imitations. Your child has begun to develop a skill called *generalized motor imitation*. Once a child develops this skill, he or she will usually attempt to imitate any other movement you perform when you say, "Do this." Additional enjoyable activities, such as doing actions along with songs (e.g.,"Itsy Bitsy Spider," "Head, Shoulders, Knees, and Toes"), are more captivating and maintain their interest while practicing generalized motor imitation.

Object Imitation

Your child understands that "Do this" is a cue that means he or she is to repeat the movement you make. The child has learned that this is an enjoyable activity and it is always followed by a treat, so in most cases resistance has stopped or is minimal. Beginning object imitation is often more effective if you use responsive toys, such as maracas, bells, or xylophones. These toys have the advantage that the child can immediately tell that his or her movement has produced a concrete effect and therefore teaches cause–effect relationships. The procedure is identical to those that involve imitation of body part movements, but instead you shake a toy or strike the xylophone with a small mallet. Select two of the previous body part imitation activities and insert five trials of shaking the maracas. For example, you clap hands, rub your tummy, shake maracas, and repeat this sequence. In most instances, children catch on to toy imitation activities more quickly than they initially mastered body part imitation. Once the child has learned to imitate one toy movement, add a new toy imitation activity (e.g., hit the xylophone) and substitute one of the previously learned body part imitation tasks (e.g., pat head, clap hands, hit xylophone).

A next step involves learning gross motor toy imitation activities that produce minimal auditory feedback (unlike the maracas or bells that make a distinctive sound). A good activity is to drop colored blocks in a box. Give the child a block, pick up a block yourself, and say, "Do this," and drop the block in the box. If you give the child a pile of blocks, he or she is likely to drop all of them in the box or may throw them, so it is better to hand him or her the blocks one at a time. Interpolate five trials of the block activity among one gross motor body imitation activity and one reactive toy imitation activity. Continue to give the child practice with previously learned skills that makes certain he or she doesn't forget them. Another similar toy imitation activity involves stacking rings. Once the child is successfully imitating 2–3 gross motor toy imitation activities, you can begin teaching him or her to imitate use of other common toys or playthings, such as rocking a baby or pushing a car across the floor or the top of a table. This prepares the child to engage in spontaneous play that is similar to that of his or her peers. The same methods are used as with teaching previous skills.

Video Modeling

Some children find it difficult to imitate toy play from watching a live model. They are distracted by the teacher's checkered shirt, the child talking next to them in school, or the sound of the fire truck driving by outdoors. For highly distractible youngsters, substitute a video of an adult or older sibling modeling the toy play movement to eliminate distractions. Charlop-Christy, Loc, and Freeman (2000) and LeBlanc et al. (2003) have effectively demonstrated the use of video modeling and reinforcement to teach toy play and perspective-taking skills to children with autism. The basic materials are available to many families, and the procedures can be easily learned. Many families have digital video cameras that can be used to make short videos showing a parent or older sibling repeatedly driving a car back and forth across the floor, stacking blocks, or rocking a baby doll. When the recording is made, the adult or sibling model says, "Do this," and drives a toy car back and forth across the floor. Segments should be no more than about 5 seconds long. It is wise to make several slightly different versions of the same toy play model so the child doesn't expect the actual adult model to be identical on each occasion. The video models are played back on a television monitor, and the child is encouraged to watch the video and then imitate what he or she sees. Once the child is imitating a video model, it is usually easy to shift to a live model engaging in the same movement. Now the child is less likely to be distracted and will focus on the toy movement.

Once a child has reached this stage of imitation learning, he or she will attempt to reproduce any gross movement you make. This is called *generalized motor imitation*. This serves two important purposes. It makes it easier to teach any new skill simply by demonstrating it to the child. Once the child has learned "Do this," you can demonstrate how to set the table, hold a crayon, or brush his or her teeth by demonstrating and saying, "Do this." The second and more important reason is that teaching the child "Do this" is a stepping stone to learning to speak or communicate augmentatively. Augmentative communication involves using an object or symbol to represent another thing when communicating, such as a three-dimensional object, a picture, or a graphic symbol.

Children who are making no speech sounds or who are only saying vowels or consonants repetitively should be evaluated by a licensed SLP to determine the most appropriate communication approach. Califiero (2005) provides a good discussion of augmentative and alternative communication strategies for children with ASDs who are minimally or not communicating with speech. The focus is on spontaneous functional communication using naturally aided language, signs, picture communication symbols, and communication boards as well as voice output devices.

Imitating Mouth Movements and Speech Sounds

Children are more likely to begin developing speech sounds after they have started babbling or saying "word-like" sounds, called *jargon*. Children who have difficulty chewing, swallowing, or making lip or tongue movements should be evaluated by a SLP to determine whether they are capable of making speech sounds.

Teaching spoken language begins by teaching a child to imitate mouth movements. Mouth movements involving the lips and tongue at the front of the mouth are usually more easily learned because a child is able to see the adult model more readily. As a result, one usually begins with forming lips in a fashion that will help a child with "mmm," "bbb," and "ppp" sounds.

Evan has been responding to 9 out of 10 trials correctly on gross motor and toy play imitation. His teacher decides to introduce prelanguage imitation. Evan vocalizes making "eee-eee" and similar vowel sounds, but doesn't produce words or many consonants. Mrs. Glazer sits down across from him at a small table and holds her finger up to her mouth and says, "Evan, do this," and she closes her lips in an exaggerated way so her mouth makes an "mmm" sound. Evan watches her closely and claps his hands. Mrs. Glazer lowers her hand so Evan won't think her hand is part of the "Do this" request and repeats, "Do this," closing her lips and saying "mmm." After the third repetition, Evan closes his lips but doesn't make an "mmm" sound. Mrs. Glazer says, "Super! That's right!" She repeats five more "mmm" trials and then switches to five trials of "Do this" pushing the car across the table. Evan imitates correctly. Now she returns to mouth movement imitation. She repeats, "Do this," closing her lips and saying "mmm." This time Evan imitates correctly, including making an "mmm" sound. "Great job, Evan. You're a good talker," she says. She repeats the mouth movement imitation once more in the morning and again in the afternoon. After completing the session, she sits with him as he has some apple slices and juice, and repeats, "Evan, you're such a good talker." Mrs. Glazer is trying to instill in Evan the idea that he uses his mouth to talk even though he isn't saying any words yet.

The following Monday, Mrs. Glazer introduces a second mouth movement: sticking out her tongue. Moving the tongue toward the front of the mouth will be useful for demonstrating how to make the "T" sound. When she says, "Do this" and sticks out her tongue, Evan laughs. She says, "That's funny, isn't it? But it's okay. Do this." She sticks out her tongue again. Evan immediately imitates her tongue thrust movement. She continues intermixing toy imitation trials with mouth movement trials adding putting wooden shaped pieces in a four-piece shape matching board as a motor toy imitation activity. He needs some manual guidance at first to insert some pieces in the puzzle board.

By Thursday, Evan is doing so well that Mrs. Glazer decides to teach him to say "more." She gives him a jellybean. After he has eaten it, she says, "Evan, want mmmore?" Even watches her mouth intently. Mrs. Glazer says, "Do this. Say 'mmore'" closing her mouth with an exaggerated "mmm" sound. Evan closes his lips and says, "mmmr." She says, "Super, Evan. Here are more jellybeans" and gives him two jellybeans. By Friday afternoon, Evan is reliably saying "more" when he wants more jellybeans.

TEACHING REQUESTS: MAKING COMMUNICATION USEFUL

Linda Hodgdon (1995) provides an excellent discussion of the use of visual supports to promote communication by children with ASDs. One of the best ways to teach children with ASDs to use speech or augmentative communication systems is to gain access to things and activities they want (i.e., by making requests).

Facilitate Making Requests

In order for children with autistic disorder and PDD-NOS to be interested in speaking, talking must serve a useful purpose for them. Evan's mother has been repeating the same mouth imitation movement exercises at home that Mrs. Glazer has been using at school. She decides to see if he will generalize saying "more" at home. This is a first step in teaching him to make requests. Saturday morning as Evan is finishing breakfast, his mother notices he has drunk all of his orange juice. She points at his empty glass and says, "Want more? Do this, say 'mmore'" as she points to her lips. Evan looks from his juice glass to his mother's mouth and says, "mmore," and she says, "Terrific talking, Evan!" and immediately pours a small amount of juice in his glass. He promptly drinks the juice and looks at the glass again and then at his mother. She asks, "Want more?" and waits a few seconds. Evan quickly says, "More." His mother says, "Great job, Evan," and pours some more juice into his glass. Evan is enjoying this game. He points to his glass (gestural communication) and his mother says, "Want more, Evan?" This time when he imitates his version of "more," it is a closer approximation to correct pronunciation. The "more" request taught at school transferred almost immediately to home, which bodes well in the future for transfer across settings.

Evan has a peanut butter sandwich with milk and an apple for lunch. His mother pours his glass half full of milk, which he uses to wash down the sticky peanut butter. He looks at his glass and says, "More." She gives him additional milk. The next time he asks, she says, "Say 'more milk'". Evan tries to imitate the word *milk*, but omits the *l* in *milk*. He has learned the concept but will need to work on articulation. Over the next 2 weeks, Evan gradually learns the names of common food items he wanted: *juice*, *milk*, and *cookie*. He also learned to add "more" in order to request additional preferred activities, such as "more tickle" and "more TV." This is a big step that means Evan has learned an important function of language: to make things happen that he wants to have happen.

Using Card Readers and Button-Activated Recorders

Some children learn to speak quickly using card readers and scripts (McClannahan & Krantz, 2005). Card readers are devices that play back short segments of speech (up to 8 seconds) that a parent or teacher has recorded. The cards are heavy card stock with an audio-tape magnetic strip along the bottom. An adult caregiver records a word or phrase that is saved on the magnetic strip. The child can later play back the recording by placing the card in a card reader. This strategy is most effective when used in conjunction with a visual activity schedule and when the child is taught to use scripts. The cards are inserted into the activity schedule alongside the photo of the activity. When the specified activity is to occur the child pulls out the corresponding card and places it in the card reader. Once a given script has been learned, the prompts are gradually faded and the child learns to simply say the phrase. After the child has learned to use the card reader, other readily portable recording devices can be attached to locations in which specific words or phrases are likely to be needed, such as on the refrigerator door, by the door leading outdoors or on a toy storage closet. Mini-Me and Voice Over are button-pressing devices that serve the same purpose as card readers. If a child wants to make a request, such as, "Juice, please," he or she pushes the button on the refrigerator door located next to a photograph of a glass of juice, and his or her mother's voice says, "Juice, please." The child is asked to repeat the phrase and then is given juice. In school, a button device might be placed on the cabinet where the toys are kept, and when the child presses the button, the teacher's voice might say, "Toys, please," and the child is asked to repeat the phrase. Over time, the button-pressing devices are faded out and the photograph remains. Eventually, the photos are faded out and the child is expected to say the word or phrase without additional prompts when he or she wants juice or access to toys or to go outdoors and play. Specific details in using these devices and script fading can be found in McClannahan and Krantz's *Teaching Conversation to Children with Autism: Scripts and Script Fading* (2005).

Requesting Things that Are Not Present

The first step usually begins by teaching children to request items that they can see but not reach, or have recently seen, such as milk in a glass. As children gain more communicative competence, they are taught to request things that they want but cannot see.

Faduma has learned to request food that is present or request an activity that is associated with a particular person who *is* present, such as being tossed in the air and caught when she sees her father. Before breakfast, Faduma's mother notices that her daughter seems to be looking for something. Yogurt, toast, fresh berries, and jelly are on the table but no cereal. Her mother says, "What do you want, Faduma?" Faduma appears to be thinking for a moment and walks into the kitchen and looks up at the cupboard and then looks at her mother expectantly. Her mother repeats, "What do you want, Faduma?" After a few seconds Faduma says, "Lups" and her mother thinks for a moment and then realizes she wants Fruit Loops cereal that is inside the cupboard, which was closed. She reaches for the cereal box and places it on the table next to Faduma's bowl and places the carton of milk next to it. Faduma no longer needs to see the actual desired stimulus to remember the name of what she wants. Over the next few weeks, Faduma began spontaneously saying, "Daddy come?" shortly before he came home from work and "Go park" when she wanted to go to the park that was several blocks away.

NAMING, DESCRIBING, AND ELABORATING

In order for children with ASDs to be able to carry on conversations, they must know the names of people, things, places, and actions.

Developing Receptive Vocabulary

The next step begins by teaching a child to point to concrete objects, such as a ball, a dog, and a baby doll when they are named, which is called *receptive vocabulary*. A ball and a dog are placed on the table in front of a child. A teacher says, "Point to ball." If the child doesn't respond, the teacher says, "Do this. Point to ball," and points to the ball. Because the child has already learned "Do this," most children begin pointing at the object very quickly. The child is rewarded with praise and intermittently given a tangible treat following correct answers. A baby doll is placed on the table next to the ball, and the teacher says, "Point to ball." The child does so correctly. To make certain the child is learning the object and not its position (by selecting the object on the left side), the ball is moved from the left to the right and back again. Next, a toy block and a baby doll are placed next to one another on the table, and the teacher says, "Point to baby." Once the child is correctly identifying three-dimensional objects receptively, the next step involves substituting two-dimensional photos for three-dimensional objects. The teacher has taken photos of the ball, the baby doll, and the blocks and repeats the same training procedure using the photos in place of the actual objects. Most children readily transfer from actual three-dimensional objects to photos of those same objects.

A photo of the child's mother and a comparison photo very unlike her mother are selected, such as a dog or cat, and are placed on the table alongside one another. The teacher says, "Point to Mommy." Nearly all children will respond correctly by this point because Mommy is especially important to them. The incorrect choice is periodically changed (e.g., policeman or farmer are substituted for the dog or cat) and the sides are alternated between left and right. After 8–10 trials have been correct in a row, a photo of a younger brother or sister is placed alongside the picture of the child's mother. The teacher says, "Point to Mommy," which the child usually does. On the next trial the teachers says, "Point to Andrew" (the child's younger brother). Often a child with an ASD will continue pointing to his or her mother. The teacher says, "Do this. Point to Andrew," and models pointing to the photo of Andrew. Many children will begin to respond correctly after three or four repetitions alternating between "Point to Andrew" and

"Point to Mommy." Once the child is responding correctly, the "Do this" prefix is eliminated. One by one, photos of all family members, grandparents, and the family pets are added in various combinations until the child is correctly pointing to all members of his or her family, indicating that their names are now part of his or her receptive vocabulary. This ensures that the child can correctly identify all members of his or her family, which is a prerequisite to naming them.

Naming People

The names of immediate family members are usually easily taught because the child is familiar with how they sound, though some children with ASDs have articulation problems and may have difficulty pronouncing some names. This is true of typically developing children as well. When a young mother became engaged to a man who had two daughters, Allison and Madison, their names created a communication problem for the young woman's 2-year-old daughter, Emily. She had difficulty pronouncing the initial "Al" sound in Allison, so she called both of the older girls "Madson," though she knew their names receptively. Emily had been told the older girls were coming for dinner. She said, "Madson and Madson coming." If Emily were asked to give a toy to one (Allison) or the other (Madison), she did so correctly. Young children with ASDs often have similar articulation problems that are usually overcome with practice. It is often useful to consult with a SLP who can make suggestions for improving articulation.

Two pictures of family members are placed in front of the child with an ASD, one adult and one child. The child's teacher says, "Point to Mommy. Say 'Mommy'" (the photo on the left). The child will point to the picture but often not repeat the name. "Say 'Mommy,'" the teacher repeats. Any approximation of "Mommy" should be immediately rewarded. The two pictures are removed and the photo of the child's mother is placed on the opposite side (e.g., right) and a new incorrect photo is placed alongside of it (a photo of his or her sibling on the left side). "Who is this? Say 'Mommy'" (pointing to the photo). Again, any approximation of "Mommy" should be reinforced. This procedure is repeated with a photo of the child's father ("Who is this? Say 'Daddy.'") and another incorrect photo as the comparison (e.g., Grandma). As the

Figure 4.1. Therapist assisting child in naming family members.

number and percent of correct responses increases, the instruction becomes "Who is this? Daddy?" The word *say* is faded out. Eventually, many verbal children will develop the skill to name most family members, though, as noted above, there often are articulation problems, so Andrew might sound like "Drew" and Grandpa may come sounding like "Papa" (see Figure 4.1).

Names of Objects

The same procedure is used to teach the names of common objects a child encounters in everyday life, such as a cup, spoon, shirt, soap, toothbrush, and so forth. Although one could teach these receptive names using actual objects, it is usually a good idea to continue using photographs because all subsequent vocabulary will be taught using photos. After such familiar items from everyday life are taught, things a child might encounter outdoors are taught, such as a tree, street, lawn, sky, cloud, rain, or car.

After familiar indoor and outdoor "thing" names have been learned, the names of places, such as rooms in the child's house ("kitchen"), the school building ("school"), grandma's house ("Gramma"), and McDonald's ("Donal"), are taught. Having mastered things and places, the child is next taught which things belong in which places. For example, Ben's mother may ask, "Where is the soap?" and the child may have photos of several rooms on the table as reminders. Ben looks over the pictures and replies "bathroom." "Good job," Ben's mother says. Once the child can match objects with places (e.g., "Where is the toothbrush?") using visual prompts, the photos are removed and the same questions are asked, and answers are repeated without visual prompts. When the child is able to say where things belong without a visual prompt, these questions should be incorporated into normal daily routines incidentally. When a parent is folding laundry, he or she may say to a daughter with an ASD, "Becky, take this to the bathroom," handing her a washcloth. Now the child can say people's names, names of familiar objects inside and outside her house, and where objects belong in her house.

Recalling and naming items from memory that have specific properties may not be achieved until much later. Recalling things that belong together or that are used for a specific activity is practically very useful. This skill is useful for later activities involving planning. For example, if a child is going to paint a picture, the teacher might ask, "What do we need to paint a picture?" The child will have to recall that he or she needs paper, a cup of water, paintbrushes, paint, and a smock to cover clothing. Although it is good practice to employ visual prompts (e.g., a list of supplies needed), there are many situations in daily life in which a child will be called upon to anticipate what will be needed for a future activity and no visual prompts may be available.

Naming Actions

Learning the names of actions is often difficult for children with autism, many of whom appear to have a dysfunction in their mirror neuron system that is used to detect gestures. For most of us, if we watch other people perform a movement (e.g., reaching for a coffee cup) the neurons in our own brain that would be active if we ourselves were reaching for a coffee cup become active. These are called *mirror neurons.* Mirror neuron responsiveness to seeing a model appears to be one of the mechanisms by which we understand the meanings of other people's gestures and movements. This process appears to be faulty among some children and adults with ASDs. That makes it particularly difficult for them to respond appropriately when watching others' movements.

A good starting point involves teaching children with ASDs to name familiar actions and movements with which they have had a good deal of experience, such as swinging, jumping, and running. The same technique as previously described is used (i.e., presenting children with pictures of the target child or siblings swinging on a swing, jumping up and down, or running, and teaching them to name them). "What is Billy doing? Say 'running.'" After several repetitions, "say 'running'" is faded out. The same techniques can be used to teach recreational activities, such as riding bicycles, swimming, throwing a ball, and so forth. Again, it is a good idea to incidentally insert practicing this skill into daily activities. When walking in the park, Mom asks, "What is she doing?" while pointing to a child on a swing. The child with an ASD answers, "Swinging," to which Mom replies, "That's right. She's swinging." In school Mrs. Johnson may say to Chay, who has PDD-NOS, "What is that boy doing on the sidewalk?" while pointing to a boy on a bicycle. Chay replies, "Riding bicycle," to which his teacher replies, "You're right. He's riding his bicycle."

As instruction or therapy transitions to more subtle and complex actions, movements, and gestures, the task becomes more difficult, especially when it involves interactions among people. Studies have shown that when high-functioning people with ASDs view movies or videos of interactions between people, they tend not to focus on people's eyes. Instead they look at the mouths of the people talking, their hair, or other aspects that provide little information about the social meaning of the interaction (e.g., arguing, expressing affection). Aspects of social interactions, such as hugging, are usually taught either using still photographs or videos combined with practicing the actions themselves, such as "Give Mommy a hug."

DESCRIBING AND ELABORATING

Conversational skills require being able to describe objects, events, and actions, which eventually lead to the ability to elaborate. As noted earlier, McClannahan and Krantz's (2005) book, *Teaching Conversation to Children with Autism: Scripts and Script Fading* has helpful strategies based on scripts and script fading. Other detailed methods have been developed as part of The Assessment of Basic Language and Learning Skills–Revised and its associated curriculum (Partington, 2006). The Spontaneous Vocalization Scale (L) is divided into 19 subskills that assist in teaching some of the following.

Teaching Describing

Children with more severe autism have difficulty developing skills in using adjectives and adverbs, which are useful to describe their world. Adjectives are words that describe or modify another person or thing in the sentence, such as the *blue* cap. Words that modify verbs, such as descriptors of actions, are adverbs (e.g., *fast*). Teaching usually begins with properties of things, such as size, shape, texture, or color. Sorting into categories is often a good way to begin teaching properties. Some properties are categorical (e.g., *red* versus *green*), whereas others are relative (e.g., *bigger* versus *smaller*) and more difficult to learn. A red and a blue block are placed in front of a child, and he or she is asked to say the color of the blocks. By the time children with ASDs are 3–4 years old, many have already learned basic color names. If they haven't, they are taught the same ways as recognizing things (e.g., "Point to red"). The next step involves teaching them to distinguish a single property of objects that differ in other ways, such as a red circle, red triangle, and red square (as distinguished from blue shapes). Then a child is given a pile of objects differing in shapes and asked to sort the red objects in one box and the blue objects in another. At home, a parent may give a child a pile of colored socks from the clothes dryer, and say, "Sort the socks. Put blue socks here (pointing), red socks here, and green socks here." The purpose of this activity is to make certain the child can reliably distinguish one property (color) and not confuse that property with other properties such as shape, size, and texture.

Once this strategy has been extended to several properties, the child is asked to say a short sentence involving the property. Point to an object (e.g., a ball) and say, "What is this?" The child will likely say, "Ball." Say, "Right. What color is the ball?" The child will likely answer, "Red." Respond by saying, "Right. It's a red ball." You then show the child a blue ball and say, "What is this?" while pointing to the ball. With several repetitions, the child will begin to understand that he or she is being asked to name the object and its color and will appropriately name the object and its color. The same strategy is used to teach other properties, such as size and texture. Point to a picture of a small boy alongside a larger boy and ask, "What is this?" The child will answer by saying, "Small boy." It is useful to integrate this skill into daily activities, such as asking the child to take the red ball to Mrs. Johnson and show Daddy the big dog. Place a colored object inside a larger box alongside a smaller box, and while the child is watching ask, "Where is the car?" The child should answer by saying, "In the big box." Then ask the child to find his or her green shirt. The child goes into his or her room and returns with the green shirt. Ask the child what he or she is wearing today. The child should answer appropriately. This is a sequential process of layering the child's combined verbalizations on top of previously taught information about the properties of everyday things he or she encounters.

Teaching Elaborating

As children approach kindergarten and first grade, they are taught to tell parents about things they have recently experienced.

Parent: What was in the park?

Child: Boy on a bike.

Parent: What did you see in the sky?

Child: Clouds and birds.

Parent: What did you do at the library?

Child: Get a book.

Teaching children with ASDs to accurately report actions is often a challenge. For a child's safety, the child needs to be able to report things that happen to him or her. Preschool teachers can send home a note to parents indicating what was done at school, such as singing a song or playing with bubbles or that a clown came to class. Before leaving school, the child's teacher provides a form with pictures of the day's activities that prompts the child to recall what he or she did over the course of the day. When a child with an ASD comes home from school, parents often ask what he or she did at school (e.g., "What did you do at school?"). If the child can't remember or seems unable to report what happened, parents should prompt the child based on the teacher's note: "Did you see someone special today?" or "What did you play with today?" Once the child recalls what happened, parents can ask leading questions, such as, "Tell me about the clown's hair," "How big were the bubbles?" "What song did you sing?"

Much as a child was taught to add "more" to desired objects or activities (e.g., milk, tickles), we teach children to add descriptors or qualifiers (adverbs) to action words.

Parent: How is she jumping?

Child: She is jumping high.

Parent: How is he running?

Child: He is running fast.

Words such as *very* and *a little* can be taught the same way.

Parent: How fast is he running?

Child: Very fast.

Parent: How much juice does he have?

Child: A little.

The teaching process is similar to naming people, things, and places.

TEACHING CONVERSATION SKILLS

Children with ASDs have poor conversational skills because they have limited interest in others and because they can't see a purpose in having a conversation. A conversation involves asking another person about his or her daily life or commenting upon it and responding to what he or she tells you.

Parent: What did you do at school today?

Child: Played with the gerbil.

Parent: What color is the gerbil?

Child: Brown and white.

Parent: What does the gerbil eat?

Child: Gerbil eats lettuce.

Parent: Anything else?

Child: Carrots and celery.

Although it isn't a scintillating discussion, it's a good start.

Create Reasons for Conversation

Children with ASDs are generally not interested in what happens to other people or what others are doing, so they seldom initiate this type of conversation. One must create a reason for the child to want to initiate a conversation. The child has to be motivated to communicate. One of my favorite vehicles for promoting conversations between children with ASDs and adults involves the shared activity of cooking, such as frosting cookies and decorating them with colorful sprinkles. A parent seeks his or her child's help rolling out cookie dough and then bakes a batch of cookies. When the cookies are cooled, they are placed on aluminum foil or waxed paper sheets on a table. Frosting that can be squeezed out of tubes is easiest for children to use, but canned frosting that can be spread on with a knife can be used as well. Several bottles of sprinkles—chocolate, red, and green—are placed on a table in front of the child. Some children prefer multicolored sprinkles, so it's a good idea to encourage them to choose. The parent invites the child into the kitchen to help decorate the cookies.

A typical exchange goes as follows:

Parent: Cecilia, come help decorate the cookies.

Child: Decorate cookies.

Parent: What should we do first?

Child: Decorate cookies.

Parent: What should we put on first?

Child: Put frosting on cookies.

Parent: Okay, here's the frosting. Do it like this. (The parent demonstrates how to squeeze the tube so it deposits frosting on a cookie.) You do it. (The parent hands the child the frosting tube and point to the next cookie. As the child squeezes the tube, the parent gives manual guidance as needed.)

Parent: That's great. Putting frosting on the cookie.

Child: More frosting. (The parent points to the next cookie, and this continues until several cookies have been frosted.)

Parent: What should we do next? (The parent points to the bottles of sprinkles.)

Child: Sprinkles.

Parent: What should we do with the sprinkles?

Child: Put sprinkles on cookies.

Parent: Which sprinkles should we put on first?

Child: Chocolate sprinkles.

Parent: That's great. Let's put on chocolate sprinkles. (The parent opens the top and hands the child the sprinkles and shows the child how to shake out the sprinkles on the first cookie.)

Parent: You do it. (The parent hands the child the bottle.)

For many children, it would be helpful to prepare a visual schedule of the activities involved in making cookies, which can be used as prompts. This activity has a naturally built-in reinforcer that will maintain the child's interest. Other similar activities are making popcorn, mixing Kool-Aid, making toast, and spreading peanut butter on toast. Activities that actively engage a child, in which he or she has choices, can provide the grist for a verbal exchange and have a naturally built-in reward (something to eat) and are especially effective. A similar type of activity can be organized around any of a child's special interests rather than edibles, such as painting, or pasting pictures cut out of magazines to construction paper, or collecting leaves and pasting them on construction paper with a glue stick. The activity provides a context within which natural conversations can be nested.

Promoting Informal Conversation

Dinnertime conversations can also be helpful, especially if there are other siblings to serve as models. When everyone in the family is seated at the table and has begun to eat, Mom and Dad engage older siblings in conversation:

Mom: Hannah, what did you do at school today?

Hannah: We talked about food and stuff.

Mom: What kind of food did you talk about?

Hannah: You know, fruit and healthy food, things like that.

Mom: That must have been interesting.

Dad: Did you go to Scouts today, Avi?

Avi: Yeah, we tied knots.

Dad: Why did you tie knots?

Avi: It's for going camping. You tie knots when you go camping.

By now, Michael, who has high-functioning autistic disorder, has observed conversational exchanges between two of his siblings and his parents. He also has had experience answering questions at school and at home, so he uses building blocks for conversation. He is beginning to grasp the structure of conversations. An adult asks a question or makes a comment, the child says something in response, and the adult makes a comment. This basic three-part exchange is the beginning of having a conversation. When his mother says, "Michael, what did you do at school today?" he realizes he's expected to say something. It is very common for the reply to be short and often not very informative. Michael replies, "Ate lunch." His sister Hannah laughs because she realizes her mother was referring to schoolwork. "That's interesting, Michael," his mother says, ignoring Hannah's laughter, and continues, "Who did you sit with?" Michael thinks for a while and replies, "Alice." "What did Alice have for lunch?" his mother asks. Michael replies, "An orange." This series of exchanges is an important part of the process by which children with ASDs learn about family life and about the process of conversing. Over time, Michael's parents ask him to expand on what he has said. For example, his mother might ask, "Did Alice have anything else for lunch?" or "What did you do after lunch?" Occasionally, children are unable to think of what to say when asked such a question, and they relapse into delayed echolalia or scripted speech from cartoons or television advertisements:

Mom: What did you do in school today?

Michael: SpongeBob Krabby Patties.

It is usually best to ignore the echolalia or scripted speech and ask the question again with additional prompts.

Mom: What did you have for lunch at school?

Michael: Macaroni and cheese.

Mom: That sounds good!

Siblings of children with ASDs often understand speech attempts by their brother or sister with a disability more readily than adults because they spend more time with them. They often learn from ancillary cues (e.g., facial expression, posture, context) to interpret speech. During dinner on our deck, I was having difficulty understanding what my grandson Michael, who has an ASD, was requesting. He has moderate to high-functioning autism. He was 4 years old at the time, and his articulation was difficult to understand. He attempted twice to ask for something, at which point his older sister Emma said, "Michael wants more potatoes." I asked Emma how she knew what Michael wanted and she replied, "I speak autistic," at which point I struggled to suppress a chuckle.

Family dinner table conversations can be a good way to teach a child with an ASD about humor.

Mom: When I was a little girl, I loved to have peaches and cream when I came home from school.

Dad: When I was a little puppy, I loved to chew on a bone after school.

Hannah: (makes a silly face) Oh, Daddy!

Avi: (laughs) That's silly.

Michael: (listens intently, and then speaks seriously) Daddy wasn't a puppy when he was little. He was a boy. (Everyone laughs, helping Michael understand that his dad made a joke, so he joins in the laughter, too.)

Children with high-functioning ASDs often find such verbal incongruities funny, which can be a good way to teach them humor and make family conversations enjoyable. Conversations that involve "yes" and "no" replies are less effective than those that elicit a more extended response, such as, "I wonder what we should do next?" or "Who would like to watch a movie?" It takes practice learning to ask leading questions that generate a series of exchanges. "Whose turn is it to feed Fido?" leads to a series of comments such as, "I did it yesterday" and, "It's Hannah's turn," to which Michael might reply, "I'll feed him."

VOCABULARY VERSUS COMPREHENSION

Many higher-functioning children with Asperger syndrome or PDD-NOS may have a substantial spoken and reading vocabulary. They may be *hyperlexic*, but that doesn't mean they fully understand the words they are speaking. As noted in Chapter 1, such children's exceptional vocabulary can be misleading in conversation. After returning from a school field trip to the zoo, the teacher asks her students, "Who would like to tell us about the animals they saw?" Olivia, who has Asperger syndrome, raises her hand. When Mrs. Harlee calls on Olivia, the 6-year-old girl says, "Kangaroos are marsupials. They have pouches." "That's right," replies Mrs. Harlee in amazement. The teacher continues, "Where do kangaroos live?" Olivia replies, "In the zoo," and the other children laugh. "I meant what part of the world do kangaroos come from?" Mrs. Harlee adds. "I saw a kangaroo at the zoo in San Diego," replies Olivia. Her answer was not wrong, but it was unresponsive to the meaning behind Mrs. Harlee's question, which the other typically developing children understood. The correct response was Australia. This type of exchange is typical of higher-functioning children with ASDs. They often possess isolated pockets of information, sometimes well beyond what would be expected for their age, but it is often not well integrated with other information in a way the leads to functional conversation

This deficit is most striking in the realm of interpersonal relationships and motives. Whether the story is *Pinocchio* or *Chicken Little,* children with ASDs have great difficulty engaging in cogent conversation about the reason why Pinocchio's nose grew longer or about the reason why one shouldn't claim the something terrible is about to happen when it isn't. A bright child with Asperger syndrome could recite *Pinocchio* in detail, including correctly recalling the names of the characters (e.g., Gepetto), but may not grasp the intended lesson behind the allegory, which most typical children the same age would readily understand.

Juan, a fifth grader with PDD-NOS, comes home from school distraught. His mother asks him what is wrong. Juan says someone put a thumbtack on his seat in school. He says he sat on it and jumped up and yelled when it hurt. Juan said the other kids laughed when he jumped up but, "It wasn't funny. I don't know why they laughed." His mother puts her arm around Juan and says, "Whoever did that to you is mean. They weren't nice." Juan keeps repeating that "it wasn't funny" and that he doesn't know why the children laughed when he jumped up. His mother tries to explain what playing a trick on another person means, and that sometimes it is cruel, but Juan doesn't understand. "It wasn't funny," he says over and over again, then goes in his room and shuts the door. Juan had no understanding of the motive of the child who placed the thumbtack on his chair. It is very difficult for Juan's mother to explain to him why the other child put a tack on his chair and what Juan can do about it.

The father of a 6-year-old told me about his son, Joseph, who wanted badly to play with other children his age. Joseph has high-functioning autism and a large vocabulary for his age. He is very skilled at building things with Lincoln Logs or Legos but has poor social skills. Joseph's dad loves sports and hopes Joseph will enjoy sports as well. Joseph's father signed him up to play tee-ball in a neighborhood park. The first time Joseph came up to bat, he hit the ball solidly between first and second base, where it bounced into the outfield, but when he ran, instead of running to first base, he ran to third base and was thrown out. Joseph's father was distraught, asking him why he had run to third base instead of first base. Joseph smiled and said, "It was fun! I hit the ball really hard and ran fast!" His father replied, "But Joseph, you can't win unless you run to the right base." Joseph thought about what his father said, and said, "Tony kept yelling 'Run, run,' so I ran fast and stood next to him." Tony was the third baseman. Joseph's father looked up with a wistful expression on his face and said, "Joseph doesn't care about winning. He just wants to be with the other kids." It is very difficult for Joseph and his father to have a conversation about sports because the youngster doesn't understand why someone would want to win, and his father doesn't understand why he isn't interested in winning.

Extending Conversations

Children with ASDs are usually not effective at sustaining a multipart conversation. Situations that are inherently important to them can provide the context for longer exchanges. Billy, who has high-functioning ASD, is in fourth grade. When he comes home from school, he talks to his mother:

Billy: There was a fight today on playground.

Mom: My goodness, what happened?

Billy: Karl called Mickey a bad name and Mickey hit him.

His mother waits a second to see if he will say more, but when it's apparent he isn't going to elaborate, she continues:

Mom: What happened next?

Billy: Karl grabbed Mickey around the neck and threw him on the ground. Then he punched Mickey and made his nose bleed. Mr. Jacobson grabbed Karl and pulled him off Mickey.

Mom: That sounds terrible! What did Mr. Jacobson do?

Billy: He took Karl and Mickey to the office. He looked real mad.

Mom: You must have been scared.

Billy: I don't like Karl. He's mean.

Billy was emotionally upset by the incident and was highly motivated to talk about what had happened. Promoting more extended conversations during less dramatic daily events requires finding ways to create motivation to communicate. Children with ASDs are often intensely interested in specific topics or activities, such as watching favorite television cartoons, building things out of blocks, or talking about scientific topics. Asking your child about what he or she has seen on SpongeBob or Pokémon cartoons is more likely to generate a series of exchanges than asking him or her about school. Sometimes family outings to the zoo, science museum, or aquarium can provide the grist for more extended subsequent conversations. The more practice a child with an ASD has engaging in longer exchanges on one topic, the more likely he or she is to do so when other subjects arise.

SUMMARY

Language serves different purposes at various points in time and in relationships. A hallmark of the process of falling in love includes prolonged conversations with the other person about his or her likes and dislikes, interests, and values. Language is a vehicle for plumbing the depth of our compatibility. Later we tell another friend that we are amazed at how much we have in common with our new-found love. Much of the time in our daily lives, language serves more immediate practical purposes. It enables us to convey and acquire needed information. For children with ASDs, language seldom serves the former function but can come to serve the latter purpose by using specific teaching or therapy methods. Although most language is acquired incidentally by typically developing children, youngsters with ASDs use a methodical process of teaching imitation, making requests, naming, and describing that can ultimately lead to the ability to engage in more sustained social interactions with family members, teachers, and friends. For individuals with ASDs, language and communication can serve very important practical functions that prevent the development of challenging behavior that arises because of the inability to manage their environment and form bonds with other people. Among higher-functioning individuals with ASDs, language makes it possible to represent ideas, things, and events emanating from the creative processes as well.

5

Relationships and Feelings

Children with ASDs have great difficulty knowing who they are in relation to other people. They form relationships with great difficulty. Though they may be surrounded by members of their family who love them, they aren't sure how they fit in. In this chapter, prerequisites to developing relationships and strategies for promoting strong bonds between children with autism and members of their families are examined.

ESTABLISHING RELATIONSHIPS

Not surprisingly, the quality of a child's relationship with people outside of their family depends on their relationship with their parents.

Secure Relationships

Child–adult relationships are often described in terms of the quality of the child's attachment: secure, avoidant, ambivalent, and disorganized (Bowlby, 1988). A *secure* child feels that he or she can depend on his or her parent or caregiver. He or she knows that person will be there when he or she needs support. He or she knows what to expect. *Avoidant* children have learned they cannot depend on parents to provide security, so they attempt to take care of themselves. Children with *ambivalent* attachment have learned that sometimes their needs are met, and sometimes they are not. They may engage in infantile or other inappropriate behavior because it leads to their parents' attention. They are always looking for that feeling of security that they sometimes get, but unpredictably so. Children with *disorganized* attachment don't know what to expect from their parents and are often at the greatest risk for developmental problems.

Sandra Scarr (1984), the distinguished developmental psychologist, wrote, "Most parents can promote a secure relationship with a calm, pleasant, patient baby. Only particularly sensitive and patient parents can promote a secure attachment to a difficult baby" (pp. 95–96). Few infants and toddlers are more challenging for parents than those with an ASD. Parents of a child with an ASD often find it difficult to produce a secure relationship with his or her child because he or she doesn't react to warmth and cuddling like other children. The child appears to ignore his or her mother's hugs or may turn or push away when held. The child stiffens and cries when his or her father tries to comfort him or her. A great deal of establishing a secure, positive relationship with a child with an ASD depends on endless patience and working consistently at developing trust.

Trust: The Foundation of Relationships

To trust another person means to have confidence in, rely on, or depend on that person. Trust involves more than having affectionate feelings toward another person. We trust others to do what they say they are going to do, that they are dependable. We also trust others when, from experience, we have learned they won't do anything to cause us undue anguish or harm. We can depend on them to help us when we need assistance. In the most extreme form of lack of trust, a typical young child who has been abused often loves the abusing parent but doesn't trust him or her. Indeed, the child is very fearful much of the time.

Trust has a cognitive and behavioral component as well as an emotional aspect. It has been said, "To be trusted is a greater compliment than to be loved" (MacDonald, 1877). Some parents behave in loving and comforting ways toward their child much of the time assuming that behavior will establish a trusting relationship. But at other times they may yell at their son with an ASD when he's having tantrums, spank him when he behaves badly, and storm out of the room shouting to their spouse, "You deal with him!" They may give their child hugs and kisses, hold him or her on their laps and say positive things to him or her when all is going well, which are wonderful and appropriate things to do, but these things are not the same as helping the child learn that his or her parent can be trusted. Being trustworthy implies being dependable and preventing your child from exposure to undue emotional distress and uncertainty.

Children with ASDs have problems with trust because they are especially prone to fearfulness and because their world often seems unpredictable, if not chaotic, to them. They are often unable to interpret the meaning of others' actions, which means that they have little way of knowing which things a parent or other adult is doing may lead to a dreaded situation for them. A child sees his or her parent doing something different from usual and wonders, "What is going to happen next?" A child's intolerance for change revolves around the limited ability to understand sequences of events. Small changes in behavior of an adult caregiver may appear to be a new and potentially threatening situation to a child with an ASD. Children with ASDs must depend on parents and other adult caregivers to structure their world so it is safe and predictable.

Structure and Trust

Reinforcement procedures can be very helpful to children with ASDs in establishing trust because it provides easily understood cues that help structure their world. When a parent immediately praises a child with an ASD for using his or her spoon instead of his or her fingers, an explicit structure has been created that the child understands. Providing ambiguous, difficult to grasp, and inconsistent signals does the opposite. It creates uncertainty and anxiety. Children with ASDs strive on structure. Structure means predictable daily routines involving people, places, and activities. Structure tells the child when and where things will happen, and which of his or her actions are appropriate and which are not. A safe, structured environment does not mean one entirely devoid of risks or protection from failure. Indeed, gradually exposing children to situations they fear and may initially resist and confirming for them that nothing bad happens is an important part of promoting competence and trust. When a child is stretching to learn a new skill, it is likely he or she may not succeed some of time. Helping him or her learn that not succeeding every time is just fine. It is part of establishing trust. He or she is praised, hugged, and rewarded for his or her efforts, which is an essential part of growing up to be a more persistent and independent young adult.

Trust and Tolerance for Change

The more a child with an ASD trusts his or her parents or other caregivers, the greater his or her tolerance for changes and new situations. The child eventually learns that his or her mother and father will do nothing to harm him or her. If a parent announces that a change in an expected routine will occur, it must be okay. Nothing bad will happen. If he or she needs help with something, a child depends on his or her parents to help him or her. For adult caregivers of children with ASDs, trust must be earned through a patient process of repeatedly affirming two commitments: 1) Within the limits of my ability, I will do nothing to cause my child undue distress, and 2) I will be there to help my child when his or her world becomes confusing and unmanageable and he or she needs assistance negotiating his or her way.

Trust and Doing What You Say You Are Going to Do

If you promise your child with an ASD that he or she can have chocolate ice cream for dessert, you'd better be able to deliver on your promise. Make certain you have chocolate ice cream in the freezer before making such a promise. Children with ASDs do not understand extenuating circumstances. They are unimpressed by explanations or excuses. The fact that, without your knowledge, your son consumed the last scoop of ice cream the previous evening doesn't help your daughter with an ASD accept the fact that you aren't doing what you promised.

If you tell your son before school in the morning you're going to stop by Grandma's house on the way home in the afternoon, your child will assume you meant what you said. If you are running late so you won't be stopping at Grandma's after all, that doesn't matter to your child with an ASD. He expects you to do what you promised.

The Trust Meter

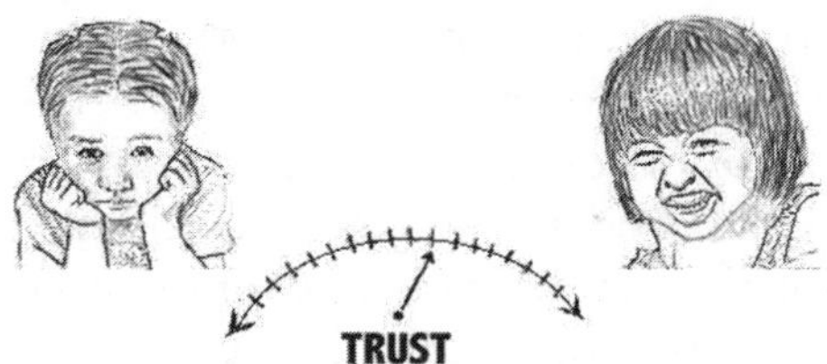

Figure 5.1. Trust that a child with autism has for adults is like a meter that varies with how consistently parents honor commitments to their child. A child's anxiety level and display of behavior challenges is inversely related to his or her level of trust. The greater his or her trust, the less the child engages in repetitive dysfunctional behavior and display meltdowns.

Your relationship with your child is like a meter that counts up and down (see Figure 5.1). Each time you honor a commitment you have made or your child experiences success and you heap praise upon him or her, the meter counts up a point. If you appear to abandon your child because of his or her bad behavior or expose your child to an exceptionally negative experience, such as losing your temper and shouting at him or her, the meter counts down a point or two. The degree of trust your child has for you depends on the meter's balance. If your child's life with you is filled with shared positive experiences, reassuring praise for his or her attempts, and honored commitments, your child will trust you implicitly. Children with ASDs tolerate occasional inconsistencies or harsh words from their parents if they have learned through experience that you are to be trusted most of the time. Everyone loses their temper once in a while, but if it is a regular occurrence your child will be afraid of you. If your home life is unpredictable or chaotic, if you are inconsistent, if you shout at him or her when he or she has a meltdown, or if you frequently scold him or her for failing to do as he or she is told, the needle on the trust meter will likely drift into the negative territory (i.e., lack of trust). Lack of trust translates into increased anxiety, crying, and behavioral outbursts, including aggression. Children who can't trust adults around them engage in more rocking, finger flicking, hand flapping, placing their hands over ears, twirling, and other repetitive nonfunctional behavior.

Trust Is Interactive

Establishing trust is a two-way process. Sometimes creating trust is viewed as similar to sprinkling water on a plant and watching it grow. But trust emerges from shared daily activities that have positive consequences for your child. Your child may become alarmed because of the cacophony of sounds in supermarket aisles crowded with people and shopping carts bumping into one another. He or she frantically demands, "Go now!" If you ignore his or her request, he or she will trust you less. Relationships are established in the course of doing things, not by the child being the passive recipient of expressions of affection. Your child wants to be certain of what you will do when the chips are down, when it really matters.

BUILDING RELATIONSHIPS

Just as tying shoes and catching a ball are skills that must be learned, behaving in ways that promote and maintain positive relationships require learning skills as well. Young children with autism must be explicitly taught many things that typical youngsters learn incidentally, or with minimal effort, in the course of daily interactions with family members. Chapter 6 is devoted to examining strategies that are useful in developing social skills. Here I focus on how those skills pertain to developing relationships.

Relationship Skills

We know someone is listening to us because when we speak, they orient toward us and establish eye contact. If they don't do so, we assume they aren't paying attention to us. Few children with autism look at other people's faces when they are spoken to, or if so, only fleetingly. They have no reason to do so because it appears that the parts of their brain involved in understanding faces (the amygdala and fusiform gyrus) are dysfunctional. They obtain little useful information from looking at faces. But they can be taught to look at their parents, siblings, and others when they are spoken to and can eventually learn what those facial expressions mean.

Children with autism often fail to react at all when spoken to. It isn't that they dislike people or are disinterested in other people, they simply don't know how to respond appropriately. They may appear not to have heard what was said to them. If a neighbor child says, "Let's play ball," while showing your child with an ASD a ball, and if your child either shows no reaction or walks away, it is unlikely the neighbor child will make the same overture again. Teaching a child to respond appropriately to social overtures from others is an essential step in developing skills necessary to establish and maintain relationships.

Teaching Relationship Skills

In the following example, each skill step is taught individually and then combined to create a reciprocal interaction sequence. It is best to begin with one specific situation, like being asked to play ball. Start by having the child look at an adult speaker such as their mother or father when spoken to. Begin by saying, for example, "Emily, let's play ball." Wait until Emily is looking at you before saying or doing anything. As soon as she orients toward you say, "Great! What did I say?" Wait for Emily to say, "Play ball," and reply by praising her and rolling or tossing her the ball. After Emily is responding appropriately to a single adult when spoken to, such as her mother, Dad should repeat the same procedure followed by a sibling. At this point, many children will respond appropriately to any other familiar child when the same sequence of events occurs. Once they have learned a small reciprocal exchange, a second activity, such as playing with action figures or another preferred activity, can be substituted. By the third new response sequence, most children will generalize to nearly any new overture by an adult or a familiar child.

Step 1. Child's goal: Look at the face of the person who is speaking to you.

Step 2. Child's goal: Listen carefully to what they say.

Step 3. Child's goal: Answer them according to what they say. Did they ask you a question or make a suggestion?

This simple exchange enables your child to indicate to others that he or she is listening and understands what they have said. It also indicates that the child with an ASD is an enjoyable person with whom to interact. When children with ASDs first begin learning reciprocal interactions such as these, their behavior seems scripted and lacks spontaneity. The more they practice these skills in their daily lives, however, the more they are exposed to spontaneous comments from caregivers and peers, such as, "Wow, that's great!"

or "Cool!" They begin to spontaneously incorporate such emotional language into their own exchanges. Gradually, the emotions behind these remarks become more authentically incorporated into their interactions with family members and peers. Instead of sounding scripted, their exchanges take on genuineness.

UNDERSTANDING EMOTIONS

Differences in functioning in several brain areas (e.g., amygdala, fusiform gyrus, frontal cortex) make it difficult for children with ASDs to recognize others' emotions and to appropriately express emotions. Many children with ASDs can acquire some of these skills, though they often continue to have limitations in their grasp of more subtle emotions. In this section, strategies for teaching children these skills are examined.

Recognizing Others' Emotions

The striking inability of most children with ASDs to understand feelings and to empathize with others is more difficult to overcome. Children with ASDs often fail to respond to being comforted as do typical children (see Figure 5.2).

Most children with ASDs perceive strong emotions expressed by parents or siblings, such as angry remarks made with a raised voice or crying; however, they often find them disturbing rather than as a source of empathetic feelings. Rather than empathizing with their sister who is crying, they may hit her or otherwise try to make her stop crying. Children with ASDs appear to have differences in the mirror neuron brain system that is used to interpret movements and gestures of other people, such as upraised shoulders combined with outstretched, upraised hands to indicate that they don't know something. Body language, which plays a major role in expressing feelings, is elusive to children with ASDs.

Steps in Responding to Others' Emotions

Understanding emotions and responding appropriately to others' feelings involves identifying what another person feels, what caused them to feel that way, and what one can do in response to

Figure 5.2. This girl with autism is being comforted by her teacher, but she does not appear to respond to being comforted as do typical children. Many children with autism turn their heads away from the adult, push or pull away, and hit or head butt in order to escape the embrace of a consoling adult. Many youngsters with autism come to accept being physically comforted, because they learn their parent or teacher is loving and helpful, but they may not get pleasure from being comforted.

that feeling. That process involves several steps, which when combined, lead to more appropriate responses to people's feelings.

Teaching How to Recognize Emotions on Faces

The following statements include goals of recognition when teaching children with ASDs how to recognize emotions on faces.

1. Discriminate emotional expression on faces: happy, angry, and sad.

2. Determine what events make the person feel that way (e.g., the person wins a prize, a sibling has knocked over the person's blocks, the person's pet runs away).

3. Select an action that corresponds to the other person's feelings (e.g., saying "That was great!" or "That makes me mad," giving the person who feels sad a hug).

Photographs of people displaying happy, angry, and sad facial expressions are a good tool for teaching discrimination of facial expressions. Photos are more effective than line drawings, which are often too abstract for many children with ASDs. If a child is verbal, show a photo of a happy child and ask, "How does she feel?" If a child has little spoken language, place two photos of a child exhibiting different emotions on large pieces of paper in front of the child and say, "Point to happy." Reward correct answers, and prompt correct answers if the child's response is incorrect. Next, place three photos on the table in front of the child: one at the top of the paper (like the point of a triangle) and two at the bottom of the paper, making up the corners of a triangle. The photo at the top of the triangle is of a child with an angry expression. That is called the *sample*. Across the bottom in one corner of the triangle is a picture of a different child who also has an angry expression. At the third corner of the triangle is a child with a happy facial expression. Ask the child to select the photo at the bottom of the triangle that shows the same emotion as the sample at the top of the triangle. This is called *conceptual matching to sample*, in which the child must display the ability to understand the concept of "angry" in order to match the two that are the same, though they are exhibited by different people.

By varying the photos in combinations of happy, angry, and sad facial expressions, many children with ASDs will eventually come to recognize the three basic emotions. Photos can be supplemented with video clips of children displaying various emotions. The Autism Research Centre at the University of Cambridge produced a DVD entitled *Mind Reading–An Interactive Guide to Human Emotions* (Baron-Cohen, 2002), which includes interactive teaching modules for a wide variety of emotions. Six video clips are provided for each emotion and show close-up performances by a wide range of people (i.e., old, young, men, women, boys, girls, and so forth).

Teaching What Events Cause Emotions

The next step is to teach a child the type of events that lead to certain emotions. Again, using photos of children in situations that would lead to happiness, anger, or sadness can be used as follows: Present a photo of a child receiving a wrapped gift. Ask the child with an ASD, "How does she feel?" If the child names the incorrect emotion (e.g., sad), prompt the correct answer and wait for him or her to answer correctly. By repeatedly showing various situations that are likely to lead to specific emotions, the child will eventually be able to anticipate how another person feels when experiencing a specific type of event. This is important in learning to understand why other people feel as they do. Hand puppets can also be used, which are especially effective for higher-functioning children. Have the puppet hold an ice cream cone, and then say, "Oops, the ice cream fell on the ground. How does Bobby (the puppet) feel?" Some children enjoy playing the role of the puppet, which provides additional opportunity to practice situations leading to specific emotions.

Teaching How to Recognize Emotions Using Simulations

The next step involves transferring the learned skills to simulated situations involving family members or friends. Have a sibling or neighbor child play the role of the other person to whom positive or negative things happen. The sibling or neighbor child is coached in how to show an appropriate facial expression when something good or bad happens. In the beginning, it is helpful to display an exaggerated facial expression to make it easier for the child with an ASD to discriminate the emotion. Here are a few examples:

Receiving a Present: Happy

A neighbor child hands a wrapped present to the sibling of the child with an ASD. The sibling smiles and says, "Thanks." Ask the child with an ASD how his or her sibling feels.

Dropped Food Item: Sad

The sibling is eating a piece of orange and it "accidentally" falls on the floor. The sibling says, "Oh, my orange fell on the floor," and shows a sad expression. Ask the child with an ASD how his or her sibling feels.

Knocking Down Blocks: Angry

A sibling and neighbor child are playing with blocks. The sibling has stacked five or six blocks, and suddenly the neighbor child knocks them down. The sibling says, "Hey, you shouldn't do that!" and shows an angry expression. Ask the child with ASD how his or her sibling feels.

Parents can devise numerous other variations on these scenarios to provide additional practice anticipating and judging emotional reactions to real-life situations.

Teaching How to React to Others' Emotions

Finally, the task is to teach the child how to react to others' emotions. These skills can be practiced in simulations as well as in real-life situations. By using the previous scenarios, a parent can model how to respond to the sibling's emotion by making a variety of comments:

- *What to say or do when a person is happy:* "That's wonderful" in a cheerful tone of voice and clapping your hands.
- *What to say or do when a person is sad:* Put your arm around the child and say, "You must feel sad. Let's get another piece of orange" in a comforting tone of voice.
- *What to say or do when a person is angry:* "You must feel angry. I'll help you with the blocks" in a concerned, comforting tone of voice.

Recognizing Emotions in Daily Life

Once a parent has modeled one of the above reactions, each of the foregoing scenarios can be repeated by asking the child with an ASD to do the same thing as his or her mother or father. In most cases, as your child goes about his or her daily life, he or she often sees situations similar to simulated scenarios he or she has practiced. For example, he or she may come upon a child crying in the park as his balloon escapes into the sky. That is a good time to stop and ask, "How does he feel?" and "Why is he sad?" You might encounter boys engaging in horseplay on a playground and one steals another's cap and runs away with it. The boy whose cap was stolen has an angry expression on his face and shouts, "Hey, bring

Figure 5.3. Scott, who has autism, has been taught to give his typical sister Zoey a reassuring hug after she has become upset. While such interactions often have a scripted appearance early in intervention, the more these interactions are practiced, the more natural these actions become and play a significant role in the relation between a child with ASD and his or her family members or friends.

it back!" Stop and ask your child, "How does he feel?" and "Why is he angry?" Once parents begin to think about the common situations they routinely encounter in their daily lives, they realize there are many teachable moments for their child to learn about emotions and why people feel as they do.

The more your child with an ASD practices giving a sibling or a sad friend an encouraging hug and saying, "That's okay," when something bad has happened, the more natural and spontaneous his or her expressions of empathy will become (see Figure 5.3). Parents often ask me whether a child with an ASD feels the same kind of empathy as other children of the same age. There is no way to know for certain. What we can say from talking with highly verbal adults with ASDs is that they readily grasp other people's stronger feelings (e.g., anger, happiness) but often have difficulty interpreting subtle or mixed emotions, such as feeling affection and anger at the same time. Psychotherapists spend a great deal of time with their typical clients helping them learn to interpret and respond to their complex, mixed feelings toward loved ones, supervisors, and friends, so it should come as no surprise that these are very difficult emotional situations for individuals with ASDs to sort out.

ACCEPTING YOUR CHILD'S NEED TO BE ALONE

Parents want their children with ASDs to be integrated into their family and to spend more time playing with friends. They assume that if they often prefer solitary activities to socializing with their family or friends, there must be something wrong.

Being Alone Is Not Being Lonely

Many parents express concern that their child with an ASD seems to spend an inordinate amount of time alone in his or her room building models, making paintings, or building towers out of Legos or Lincoln Logs. They suspect their child must feel lonely or unhappy. It is helpful if parents can accept the idea that just as one of their children is a social butterfly, spending much of their time with friends or family and enjoying being the life of the party, their child with autism is the opposite. That is perfectly fine. Everyone doesn't need to be alike.

Being Alone Can Be Rejuvenating

People with ASDs typically are very comfortable spending a great deal of time alone. For them, being alone is not a source of unhappiness or loneliness. Too much togetherness is not a good thing for most individuals with autism. People with autism are quintessential introverts. They keep thoughts to themselves, watch first and act later, pause before answering questions, prefer isolate or small-group activities, tend to start conversations from their own point of view, and, perhaps most importantly, use time alone to collect their thoughts and feel reenergized. If you ask many highly verbal adolescents or young adults with autism why they spend so much time alone, they will tell you that is when they feel most relaxed and are able to think with greatest clarity without constant bombardment by social demands. They use those quiet periods of reflection to make sense of the previous day's events and get their intellectual juices flowing. As long as a child's family—including grandparents, cousins, and friends—frequently involve their child with an ASD in family events, while providing latitude for the youngster to socially insulate him- or herself as he or she feels the need, most children with ASDs can develop very strong, loving attachments to their family and friends. It is okay to be different.

RELATIONSHIPS, DATING, AND MARRIAGE

At one point or another, most parents ask professionals whether their daughter or son will eventually have dates and get married. Statistically, the answer is that some will date, but it is less likely that they will marry. In any given instance it is impossible to know for sure, but it is safe to predict that only higher-functioning youth are likely to be able to sustain dating and marital relationships.

Desire for Intimate Relationships

Some high-functioning adolescents and young adults meet people to whom they are attracted and develop close relationships. The parents of a teenager with high-functioning autism were asked by their son why he couldn't hug and kiss girls like the other boys in his high school did in the parking lot outside his school. He wanted to know if it was because he had autism, a heartbreaking question indeed. His parents were attempting to protect him from exploitation by typical peers and from getting into trouble because he didn't have a good grasp on the limits of appropriate boy–girl behavior. It was a very difficult time for his parents as they tried to help him negotiate the limits of appropriate intimacy.

Intimate Relationships Skills

Beyond the initial sexual attraction and relationship, the skills required to understand others' feelings and to negotiate differences in what matters to partners in any relationship are extremely difficult for most people with ASDs. Understanding others' motivations is challenging for most people with ASDs, even very high-functioning individuals. Understanding why it is important to compliment the person you are dating on his or her appearance or the meal he or she prepared is elusive to many people with an ASD. Grasping why a young woman's boyfriend is so upset when she comes home several hours later than anticipated from a company party may be confusing to a person with an ASD. This young woman with ASD doesn't understand jealousy and her boyfriend's fear of loss of love that may be implied by her tardiness. Conflicting feelings of love and jealousy and the importance of symbolic acts that are part of any relationship elude most people with ASDs. As a result, though some people with less severe forms of ASDs date, those relationships infrequently lead to successful marriage.

SUMMARY

The family therapist and author Stephanie Martson (1990) wrote, "Children's self-esteem develops in proportion to the depth of trust that is reached in the parent/child relationship." Being reliable, predictable, loving parents is a giant step toward establishing the trust that is the foundation of rearing a strong, emotionally healthy child with an ASD. Children with ASDs can learn skills necessary to develop new relationships and maintain established relationships. Whether those acquired skills are identical to those of their typical peers is less important than that they are effective in creating relationships that build a better life for your child. By accepting and loving your introverted child, you discover new ways of understanding how to bring out the best in him or her as well as discovering the best in yourselves. What future relationships your child may develop no one knows. But if a solid foundation is laid, it is likely that your child will build enduring positive bonds that form the basis for a good life.

6

Letting the Genie Out of the Bottle

Promoting Socialization

Aristotle (trans. 1914) said that man is by nature a social animal, and indeed most of us are very social beings. Our relationships with our families, friends, and co-workers comprise our *raison d'etre.* We know people who are social butterflies and refer to others as exhibiting social graces, skills that make them especially appropriate in polite company. For many, their greatest fear is being seen as a social misfit or outcast. In some societies, banishment or isolation from contact with others is considered among the most severe punishment. It is therefore deeply discomfiting that our own child or a student with an ASD in our classroom appears utterly unconcerned about socializing with others. What others seem to fear most appears to be accepted if not welcomed by many children with ASDs. It seems incomprehensible.

Prefence for Social Proximity but Not Interaction

We hear people say, "What is wrong with that boy? He shows no interest in other children." It would be more apt to say that he has no understanding of other children's behavior, what they are thinking or feeling, or what is involved in being a social partner. It is one thing to lack an understanding of others and to be unskilled at interacting with them and another to lack social interest. Most children with ASDs prefer to be in the same room as their primary caregiver. If their mother (or father) walks into another room, they usually follow within a few seconds. If their brother or sister is seated on the floor playing with toys, children with ASDs may seat themselves several feet away and similarly occupy themselves but may appear to be disinterested in what their sibling is doing. If their brother or sister laughs or makes an unusual sound, the child may look up to see what is happening but often resumes his or her isolate play. The problem is that the child with an ASD is oblivious to social cues and lack skills required for establishing and sustaining social interactions. Our task as caring adults is to capitalize upon his or her interests and teach him or her the necessary skills so he or she can meaningfully interact with and develop relationships with family members and peers, which is the subject of this chapter.

T.S. Eliot wrote in his play *The Cocktail Party*, "To approach the stranger is to invite the unexpected, release a new force, let the genie out of the bottle. It is to start a new train of events that is beyond your control" (1950). Indeed, that is the dilemma of individuals with autism: how to establish relationships with other people without unleashing an intolerable sequence of events they fail to understand and feel is beyond their control.

Social Skills Resources

Weiss and Harris (2001) in *Reaching Out, Joining in: Teaching Social Skills to Young Children with Autism* provide an excellent overview of principles involved in promoting socialization among children with ASDs without causing undue alarm or confusion. It contains an especially helpful appendix of commercially available resources for promoting social understanding and interactions. Jed Baker's (2003) *The Social Skills Picture Book Teaching Play, Emotion, and Communication to Children with Autism* is especially useful. It breaks component play skills down into teachable skills, including understanding social distance, avoiding interruption, greeting playmates, sharing and maintaining a conversation, and ending a conversation. More advanced skills include asking to play and joining in, as well as sharing, compromising, and taking turns. As children progress in developing social skills, they learn to accept "no" for an answer and try something new, which is often especially challenging. In the following sections, ideas drawn from these resources as well as Galmmeltoft and Nordenhof's (2007) game-based approach have been incorporated into strategies that I have found especially effective through experience in developing social skills among children with ASDs.

Observing Others

To children with ASDs, observing another child at play is a bit like trying to understand the behavior of a creature from another planet. Children with ASDs are often fascinated by a peer's activities but have no idea what to make of them. Nearly all children engage in parallel play until around 3 years of age. They sit on the floor building with blocks or playing with baby dolls or action figures and pay minimal attention to the child next to them. They often talk to themselves, describing their own actions or speaking the part of a character with which they are playing, such as a mother doll. Between 3 and 4 years of age, young children often begin showing interest in what other children are doing and attempt to engage another child. That is seldom true of children with ASDs. Many preschoolers with an ASD continue to show limited interest in interactive play, and when they do attempt to interact, their approaches are often inappropriate and rebuffed by their peers.

Inappropriate Social Overtures

Four-year-old Brandon spends three afternoons per week in a preschool with typical children. He has high-functioning autism and has had 2 years of intensive early behavior therapy at home. He has a substantial spoken vocabulary, functions well in most daily living skill domains, and seldom has tantrums. But he lacks social understanding. He stands intently watching two other children playing. He seems to want to join them but doesn't know how to do so. He approaches Gina, a 3-year-old in his class, and places a toy car he has been holding on top of her head. She moves away from him and says, "No!" The car falls to the floor with a loud bang, and Brandon walks away with a confused expression on his face and begins to cry. His inappropriate social overture will make it less likely that Gina will play with him in the future, and his lack of success will discourage him from trying next time.

Joint Attention, Imitation, and Showing

Learning to observe what others are doing and imitating them is an early stage of the socialization process for preschoolers. Learning to look at them and focus on their eyes indicates the child is paying attention to them (see Figure 6.1). Other children are more likely to accept a child with an ASD into their play activities if the child with an ASD engages in the same or similar activity as the intended playmate. Observing others is part of taking an interest in them. Joint attention refers to focusing attention on the same stimulus as another person: a bird flying by outdoors, the ball bouncing across the room, or the activity another child is doing. If Brandon indicates to other children that he is interested in them, they will be more likely to play with him. His teacher sits on the floor with him and drives a toy truck back and forth across the mat on which she's sitting. She says, "Let's play cars." After watching for a moment, Brandon starts pushing the car he has been holding back and forth on the mat. "Good job, Brandon," Miss Peters says, adding, "We're playing cars." Later Miss Peters says, "Brandon, Beth is playing baby. Look, (pointing) she's rocking the baby." Brandon watches Beth closely but doesn't know what to do. Miss Peters hands Brandon another doll, and says, "Brandon, play baby with Beth," pointing to Beth. Brandon approaches Beth, sits on the floor beside her, and begins rocking the baby doll he is holding similar to the way Beth is rocking her baby doll. After a moment Beth says, "Rock the baby," a phrase that Brandon repeats. Encouraging children with ASDs to first observe and then indicate through their own actions that they are interested in what others are doing by imitating them will help them with the first steps of socializing.

Figure 6.1. By capturing Greg's attention with her hand and drawing her finger to her eyes, Greg learns to look at his teacher's eyes when she greets him. Once he looks at her eyes she praises him and gives him a tangible treat. Over successive repetitions, the tangible reward is phased out and praise followed by additional conversation is sufficient to maintain his eye contact.

Robin is 5 years old and in an integrated kindergarten class in which one third of the children have a developmental disability and two thirds are typically developing. She is diagnosed with PDD-NOS. She engages primarily in parallel play, so her teacher is working with her on learning to share her achievements or things she finds interesting with others. Mr. Greeley, the paraprofessional is seated next to Robin at a table. Robin is stacking colored plastic rings on a pole. When she places the last ring on the pole, Mr. Greeley says, "Wow, that's great! Show it to Miss Levine," pointing to the teacher. Robin walks over to Miss Levine and stands holding the stacking toy up to the teacher. "That's wonderful," Miss Levine says, clapping her hands together. "You stacked the rings," she adds. By creating opportunities for children with ASDs to share their achievements, they eventually learn to do so spontaneously.

Show-and-tell is another great vehicle for teaching children with ASDs to share their interests with others and is an ideal opportunity for school–home collaboration. Miss Levine sends a note home to parents of children in her class explaining that on Tuesdays each child is invited to bring one thing to school with them that they wish to share with the other students. The teacher provides ground rules for what types of things are most appropriate. Sunday afternoon Max and his family go for a walk around the lake and collect acorns and broken cattails from stalks along the shore. When he returns home from his walk, Max's father talks with him about what they found. Max sorts the items into boxes and learns the names of each item: *acorn, leaf,* and *cattail*. Monday evening Max's father asks him, "Which would you like to bring for show-and-tell?" Max doesn't understand. Max's father explains that the next day he can bring one thing and show it to the other children. Max points to a cattail, and his father says, "Great! What is its name?" Max replies, "Cattail." "Right," says his father. His father rehearses with Max what he will say when he shows his classmates the cattail. "This is a cattail. It was by the lake," Max repeats after his father. The next morning when Miss Levine calls on Max, he takes the cattail out of a bag and holds it up so the children can see it and proudly says, "This is a cattail by the lake." The other children say, "Wow!" "Cool!" and crowd around and try to touch it. Max finds this disturbing and tries to retreat, but Miss Levine tells Max it's okay and encourages the children touch the cattail gently. Then she says, "Max brought a cattail. That's wonderful you've shared it with us." Many repetitions of this kind of sequence are required before children with ASDs will begin spontaneously sharing their interests.

Incidental Learning Opportunities

There are many opportunities nearly every day for young children with ASDs to learn to show their interests to others. When a child is playing with a toy dog on the floor, his mother can say, "Show Grandma the dog," who is seated nearby. That will elicit a natural response from the child's grandmother, "Does he bark?" she might ask, followed by a "woof, woof" sound. When a child is helping with a household chore, such as setting the table, her mother might say, "Show Daddy what a good helper you are," pointing to the silverware on the table. The child points to the silverware and his father says, "That's great! You're being a good helper." With some planning, parents and teachers realize there are numerous opportunities to incidentally teach children to show their accomplishments and interests in the course of normal daily routines.

SHOWING INTEREST IN OTHERS

It is usually easier to teach young children with ASDs to show others what they have done than to spontaneously recognize opportunities to show interest in other people. Like all children, young children with ASDs are mainly interested in themselves and what they are doing. Commenting about others and asking questions of others can be taught with patience and planning.

Recruiting Spontaneous Comments

Parents and teachers can stimulate the child's interest by wearing an unusual article of clothing, such as a shirt with images of animals on it or a brightly colored hair band. When a child notices animals on the shirt, his or her father can say, "What do you see?" The child may name the animals he or she recognizes. That will provide an opportunity for the child's father to make follow-up comments and ask additional questions (e.g., "What does the cow say?"). Teachers and therapists often carry a surprise bag containing interesting objects that captivate the child, such as brightly colored finger puppets, a colorful ball, a pine cone, or a plastic prism. When the therapist arrives at the child's home, Max immediately wants to see what is in the surprise bag. The therapist waits until Max looks up at his face and says, "Okay, Max, let's see what's in the bag" and takes out a finger puppet. In school, the child's paraprofessional points to her headband and asks what color it is. When Robert, another child, arrives at school with freshly cut hair, the child with an ASD might be asked what is different about Robert. That teaches the child with an ASD to become observant about others.

As noted in Chapter 4, children with ASDs are often interested in adults' activities that are out of the ordinary, such as replacing a light bulb or quilting. When Robin approaches and seems to be interested in what her father is doing, he may say, "I'm changing a light bulb. Do you want to help?" "Help, light bulb" Robin might reply. After he has removed the burned out light bulb, Robin's father might say, "Put the bulb in the trash" handing her the bulb and pointing to the trash. By keeping the child engaged, it increases the likelihood the child will continue being interested.

Ben's mother, who is quilting, might attract her son's attention.

"Doing?" Ben might ask.

"Making a quilt. It is like a blanket," his mother continues. Next she says, "It has lots of little pieces (pointing to the pieces making up the quilt)."

"Red, purple, green," Ben says in response, as his mother points to each piece.

"That's right," she replies. "Do you like the quilt?"

"It's red and purple," the child may reply.

"Is it pretty?" the mother asks, following up.

"Pretty, red and purple," may come the reply.

Practicing this type of exchange, though initially seeming scripted, eventually takes on a more natural character as the child learns how to express genuine interest in others and their activities, and as his vocabulary increases.

Planning Ahead

It is important in identifying opportunities to teach a child with an ASD to show interest in others. In the evening before bedtime, jot down what you have planned for the next day (e.g., dropping off Sarah's brother Keith at school, taking your mother to the doctor, picking up some groceries on the way home, having coffee with your friend Anne, preparing lunch, going to the library to pick up a book for the book club, making after-school brownies). For each activity that you will be doing while Sarah will be present, think of opportunities to teach her to show interest in others. Perhaps Sarah could say something to her brother about his new jacket (e.g., "blue jacket"). She could comment about the flowers at Grandma's house (e.g., "pretty flowers"). She could comment to your friend Anne that her sweater is green. She could ask the librarian where the CDs are located. She could ask to help make brownies. On each occasion, Sarah's mother prompts her to look at the face of the person to whom she is talking before speaking. Such everyday exchanges are opportunities to learn how to show interest in other people and their activities.

Asking Questions and Joining in

As youngsters approach adolescence they are taught to show interest by asking questions and offering to participate. "What is that?" an 11-year-old might ask his father who is slicing ingredients for a salad. "Those are olives. Would you like an olive?" his father replies. When a 13-year-old's mother is sorting and folding laundry, her daughter might ask, "Can I help?" Her mother may reply, "Sure, you can fold shirts" and shows her how to fold a shirt. A 15-year-old observing his brother play a video game may ask, "Can I play?" Parents can create scenarios in which these skills are practiced so when the actual situation arises it is more likely the youth will respond appropriately. It is helpful to prepare communication partners so they understand the plan and will reinforce the child's communication attempts. It is a good idea to create a list of opportunities and post them in a prominent place you are likely to see, such as the refrigerator door as a reminder or in school on top of the child's desk.

RECIPROCITY AND TAKING TURNS

Reciprocity involves give and take, a teamwork relationship. Learning reciprocity begins with taking turns. Galmmeltoft and Nordenhof's (2007) *Autism, Play, and Social Interaction* contains a wealth of ideas for using a game-based approach to teaching reciprocity and promoting more complex play skills. It begins with very simple two-person games, transitions to more complex games including make-believe activities, and concludes with games with more complex social rules for highest-functioning older children.

Rolling a Ball and Building a Puzzle

The prototypic situation involves a caregiver and a child seated on the floor facing one another with their legs spread apart. The adult rolls a ball to the child and says, "Sam, roll the ball," holding hands outstretched to receive the ball when it is rolled. Many children will roll the ball back, some require a second adult behind him or her manually guiding him or her through pushing the ball back to the first adult. As soon as the adult receives the ball Sam has rolled, he is praised for doing a good job. This activity is repeated for several minutes or until the child begins to lose interest. By repeating this exercise several times over the course of the day, the child will soon reciprocate by rolling the ball back and forth. Placing wooden pieces in a puzzle is another activity useful in teaching turn-taking. A teacher's aide places a circle in the appropriate place on the puzzle board, hands the child a square, and says, "Sam, do it" or "It's your turn." The adult and child alternate until the puzzle pieces are all in place.

Spinner Board Games

A child who has sufficient skills to play a board game can usually be taught to take turns. A spinner is made with the circle divided into three segments corresponding to numbers *1, 2,* and *3.* Kang is encouraged to select a game piece from a selection of four animals. He chooses the giraffe and his mother selects the lion. Kang's mother waits until he is looking at her and then says, "It's my turn" and spins the spinner. It stops on the number 2. She says, "Two, I jump two spaces," and with animated movements jumps her lion game piece two squares. Then she waits until Kang is oriented toward her and says, "It's Kang's turn to spin," pointing at the spinner. Kang spins and the pointer stops at the number 3. She asks what number it is. Kang replies, "3." "Great," she replies. Kang jumps three spaces pointing at his giraffe game piece. With each jump she counts, "1, 2, 3." Most children quickly come to repeat the numbers as their parent says them. After 3–4 repetitions of the game, Kang's mother stops counting for him and says, "Kang, count." After Kang has mastered a two-person board game, his father or older sibling can join with three people taking turns. Regardless of which person reaches the goal first, everyone should receive a treat.

Stacking Games

A variation on this strategy involves a stacking game in which each family member (or other student) has a turn to add one block to a tower, which will eventually fall down when it becomes too high and unsteady. This game is exciting to young children because of the suspense involved in when the blocks are going to fall. Instead of taking turns in succession around a table, for example, the person who stacks the next block is determined by spinning a spinner. Family members' (or other students') photos are substituted for numbers on the face of the spinner circle. The last person who stacks a block spins the spinner and wherever it stops determines who places the next block on the stack. This is an especially good activity because it encourages a child with an ASD to look from person to person to see facial reactions when the spinner stops on each picture (a matching-to-sample task) and how everyone reacts when the blocks fall down.

CREATING MOTIVATION TO COMMUNICATE

Promoting social interactions between children with ASDs and adults or peers often begins by engineering the desire to interact.

Placing Desired Materials out of Reach

Alexis's teacher is working with her to promote greater interest in communicating. Mrs. Olson places a red plastic stacking pole on the table in front of Alexis and gives her the first (largest) ring to place on the pole. Alexis does so and is praised. Mrs. Olson has placed two rings each in two clear plastic containers on a shelf behind her in the direction Alexis is looking. After Alexis placed the first ring on the pole, Mrs. Olson says, "Alexis (pause), what do you want?" She gestures with her raised hands turned upward and raised eyebrows and widely opened eyes. Alexis looks at the pole and then at Mrs. Olson's face. She glances at the shelf behind Mrs. Olson where one of the clear plastic containers containing two colored rings has been placed. Mrs. Olson repeats, "What do you want?" Alexis points to the container and makes an "mmm" sound. Mrs. Olson says, "Great, I'll get you more rings," and takes the container from the shelf and places two additional rings in front of Alexis. Alexis quickly adds them to the first ring already on the pole, which requires two more rings to be complete. Alexis seems to be catching on to how this game works. She rises and walks over to the shelf where there is another clear plastic container holding the last two rings. She looks at Mrs. Olson, points at the rings, and says, "mmur." "Terrific," Mrs. Olson replies, "I'll get more rings." She deposits the final two rings on the table in front of Alexis, and she quickly places them on top of the others to complete the task.

Cooperative Activities

Children with ASDs are initially not attuned to coordinating their actions with those of other children. A variety of gross and fine motor activities can strengthen such skills.

Gross Motor Cooperation

Adriana, who is 5 years old, is diagnosed with an ASD. She has good receptive language but limited expressive language. She has participated in several games involving turn taking, so she is able to participate in a 2–4 person activity without exhibiting behavior problems. Mr. Romero is about to initiate a gross motor activity during adaptive physical education. He asks Adriana and another child to roll out a mat on the floor by having each child push one end of the rolled up mat until it is lying flat on the floor. This is a very simple gross motor activity that requires a child with an ASD to coordinate his or her responses with another child.

Making a snowman can be a another effective gross motor activity in which most children with ASDs can participate with siblings or peers regardless of their cognitive level. In warmer climates, digging a hole in the sand at the beach and taking turns pouring water in the hole can serve a similar purpose.

Adriana's mother asks her and her brother to fold towels. The towels are too long for one child to fold alone, so she demonstrates how each child holds the corners of one end of the towel, brings the two corners together, and then hands the half-folded towel to the other child to fold again. This is a slightly more complex version of the mat rolling activity.

Tao's family is on a picnic in a park. They are preparing to make a fire and roast marshmallows. His father, Neng, asks his three children to find small pieces of firewood and place them in the center of a circle of rocks so he can build a fire. Tao watches his siblings and imitates them by retrieving pieces of wood from a nearby wooded area with numerous fallen branches, and he takes turns placing them on top of one another within the circle of rocks. Neng lights the fire and soon the family is roasting and enjoying marshmallows. This activity involves a combination of imitating and coordinating placement of pieces of wood on the fire and has an enjoyable natural consequence.

Fine Motor Cooperation

Arts-and-crafts projects are often excellent vehicles for fine motor cooperation. A popular cooperative activity involves covering a balloon with pieces of tissue paper. The activity begins by tearing up pieces of tissue paper and then gluing them onto a blown up balloon to make a pâpier mâché sphere. The materials needed include Elmer's glue, several sheets of tissue paper of various colors, a balloon, a large plastic bowl or container, a tin can (3 inches or so in diameter) on which the balloon will be propped up, and aprons for each child. The teacher or a parent blows up the balloon and ties off the end so the air doesn't escape and places it on top of a tin can with the balloon's end inside the tin can. It is helpful to fix the bottom of the balloon to the tin can with masking tape so it doesn't fall off. The children, one of whom has Asperger syndrome, are shown how to tear the tissue paper into various sized irregular pieces. The teacher then pours some glue into the plastic container and adds some water to dilute the glue. The water and glue are mixed and then the teacher demonstrates how to dip pieces of tissue paper into the glue and then place them on the balloon. As more and more pieces of paper are placed on the balloon, the teacher (or parent) points out places where the balloon remains uncovered, and encourages the child with Asperger syndrome to dip another piece of paper into the glue mixture and cover up any uncovered areas. The balloon covered with pâpier mâché is allowed to dry. The portion of the balloon that was resting inside the can is carefully removed with scissors and the pâpier mâché sphere can be hung in the classroom or in the child's home with the opening pointing upward suspended by pieces of string. This activity has numerous advantages. It is an activity that does not involve right and wrong responses; it is very forgiving. Children usually enjoy dipping the paper in the glue mixture. They often like the feeling on their fingers. It requires that each child responds to what another child has done (e.g., placing a piece of paper on the balloon alongside another child's). The activity has an endpoint when the balloon is entirely covered with tissue paper and there is a concrete product of their cooperative activity that they can all enjoy. Like previous activities, it requires coordinating responses with those of others. Peers or members of a family may participate in carving a Halloween pumpkin, in which the child with an ASD may scoop out the seeds but lack sufficient skills to carve the facial features, which may be done by a sibling or friend (see Figure 6.2).

Game Cooperation

Older and higher-functioning children can participate in more academically oriented cooperative play. In one version of this activity, one child places a cardboard square with a number written on it on the table and the child next to him or her places a second card with a number that adds up to a given number (e.g., *7*). The first child looks at his or her cards and selects the number *3* and places it on the table. The adjacent child who has PDD-NOS looks at his or her cards and finds one that will add up to the number *7*, so he or she selects *4* and places it on the table alongside his or her peer's card, and they both receive a star or checkmark. Frequently, typical children will become excited during the game and prompt the child with an ASD, "Emma, look for a *4*" which promotes interactions among the children. At the end of the game everyone receives a prize.

For the highest-functioning older children, games similar to Clue are often effective. With each new problem to solve, a stack of cards is placed upside down in the center of the table. When each card is turned over it presents a printed clue. The youngsters turn over the cards one at time from left to right around the table. Clues such as, "It's brown," "It has a tail," "It barks," and so forth might be used with younger children. This is an obvious example, but the

Figure 6.2. Carving a Halloween pumpkin can be an effective activity for a child with autism and members of his family to participate. Michael, who has autism, is scraping out the seeds and pulp inside the pumpkin, and then his older sister and brother will help him carve out the eyes, nose, and mouth. Few fine motor skills are involved, and many children with ASDs enjoy the feeling of mushy pulp on their hands, which is reminiscent of water table activities in preschool.

puzzles to be solved can be made more challenging based on the children's cognitive level. The group's task is to place all of their clues on the table one at a time to see who can guess the correct answer based on the collective clues. In this case, the answer was the family's pet dog, Brownie. The first child to guess the correct answer wins; however, all participants receive a small prize.

For elementary or middle school children with Asperger syndrome, PDD-NOS, or high-functioning autism, a shared storytelling activity is often enjoyable and very effective in promoting interactions. A teacher or parent starts the story to create the context and provides a leading sentence. For example, Mrs. Gross may start the story by saying, "Bobby was walking in the dark forest, which was very scary. When he came upon a clearing, he saw a big green monster." The first child to the teacher's left (or right) is expected to add another sentence to the story. Abigail might say, "The monster growled and chased Bobby." Each child adds another sentence until everyone has had an opportunity to contribute to the story. If another adult is available, he or she can transcribe what each child says and then write or keyboard the story and print it out for all of the children in the group. Most children find that this is an amusing and enjoyable social activity that requires practice of language skills as well as attending to social cues from others in the group.

Playing with Siblings

Part of being a sibling involves learning how to play with your brother or sister. Siblings of children with ASDs attempt to engage their sibling with a disability from a very early age, and they quickly learn that he or she does not respond as other children do. Children with ASDs often unwittingly disrupt their typical sibling's toys or activities leading to conflict between them. By the time a child with an ASD is 3–4 years of age, predictable patterns of interactions between them emerge with the typical sibling making accommodations for their sibling with an ASD. The extent and type of interactions depend on the cognitive ability of the child with an ASD and whether she has received effective early intervention services. In families in which a child with an ASD has received intensive early behavior therapy, part of the intervention usually involves teaching the child how to play with another child. Communication and imitation learning are usually emphasized early in therapy, so the child with an ASD has learned how to imitate his sister or brother and how to communicate basic needs and wants.

Although it is a good idea to encourage play between siblings, it is often a mistake to insist that the typical sibling incorporate the child with an ASD into most of his or her play activities. Siblings need times to themselves, free from disruptions and the need to accommodate a brother or sister who usually has significant limitations in his or her ability to play interactively and cooperatively. Enforcing too much togetherness between a typical sibling and his or her brother or sister with an ASD can lead to resentment and aggression directed toward the child with an ASD. As much as visual schedules are used at school to help organize children's educational activities, parents can create visual schedules at home with designated interactive play times. Photographs of the two children playing together can be used to signal such play times on a daily schedule. Using the strategies outlined in the previous sections, parents can teach the child with an ASD how to be a more enjoyable play partner for his or her sibling.

Social Skills Groups and Video Modeling

There is growing evidence that group social skills training can be effective in improving skills of both younger children (4–6 years) (Kroger, Schultz, & Newsom, 2007) as well as teenagers with high-functioning ASDs (Tse, Strulovitch, Tagalakis, Meng, & Fombonne, 2007). Although participation in relatively unstructured play and activity groups may yield some gains, groups that practice specific skills and role-play social scenarios appear to lead to greater gains. Used in conjunction with video modeling, this strategy holds promise for making substantial gains in social skills. Nikopoulos and Keenan (2007) had children with ASDs view a short video of two people engaging in a simple sequence of activities. Then each child's behavior was assessed in the same room. Video modeling enhanced the social initiation skills of all the children and facilitated reciprocal play. These social skill changes generalized across peers and were maintained after a 1- and 2-month follow-up period.

PLAY DATES

Many children with ASDs have no siblings with whom to play. Others live in rural areas some distance from other families or in cities where it may not be safe to play outdoors without close supervision. That can make it difficult to create opportunities for some children with ASDs to acquire play skills.

Identifying Potential Playmates

During one of my first meetings with parents of an only child who has an ASD, I asked them to think about children near their child's age who could be invited to their house or apartment for play dates. It is not unusual for parents of children with ASDs to become isolated from neighbors and friends because of their child's behavior problems. Parents will often initially say they are unaware of children who are the same age living in their neighborhood. But with additional probing, they usually begin recalling the names of children they have seen shopping with a parent, reading at the library, or walking through the neighborhood. At times I encourage parents to think about peers who are children of parents who attend the same church or mosque who could serve as playmates.

Educating Playmates

It is important for parents who are seeking playmates for their child with an ASD to educate the peer's parents about the nature of autism, what it is and isn't and what to expect. Parents who may have witnessed bizarre-looking hand flapping or other stereotypical movements or perhaps a meltdown are often initially wary. But after spending a half hour over coffee at the home of the family in question having and observing the child, they realize that many of his or her interests and activities are similar to those of their own child. This is especially true of younger children. It is also important that parents prepare both children for their first play date. The child with an ASD should be provided with practice sharing, taking turns, and if possible engaging in cooperative play with his or her parents. The peer's parents should try to avoid saying negative things (e.g., he or she flaps his or her hands, screams) focusing instead on positive things that may interest their child (e.g., he likes to play cars, she has a toy house with dolls). It is wise to limit initial play periods to between 30 and 45 minutes and always end on a positive activity, such as having milk and cookies together before the playmate leaves. One family with whom I worked had a housekeeper who visited once a week with her daughter who was the same age as the child with autism. Each child had a box with their own toys in a closet, so when they played that avoided competition for the same play materials. Both children were rewarded for playing nicely, and they greatly enjoyed their time together.

SMALL-GROUP ACTIVITIES

Social life for children with ASDs is more comfortable when it resembles singing in a quartet rather than being part of a choir.

Small-group activities are appealing because there aren't so many unexpected social demands. As children enter elementary schools, it often becomes possible for children with autism to participate with typical peers in groups such as Girl or Boy Scouts, YWCA, or Jewish Community Center activities. They have the advantages that group membership is fairly constant and the groups are small. In addition, a specific activity is planned for each meeting.

Acquaint Group Leaders with Features of Autism

It is very important that the parents of a child with an ASD talk with the adult group leader to make certain he or she welcomes children with special needs and explain how their child behaves and functions. The group leader may request that the child's parents attend the first meeting or two to help with their child, if the need arise. In most instances, once group leaders better understand the child with an ASD, they gladly incorporate him or her into the activities and quickly learn how to make accommodations for language and social limitations.

Identify Supportive Organizations

Numerous other community organizations such as children's art organizations, athletic groups (e.g., Special Olympics), clubs and groups attached to schools or libraries, and church groups welcome children with special needs. Some children and youth with Asperger syndrome reject participating in organizations that include numerous individuals with distinctive physical features or disabilities, such as Down syndrome or cerebral palsy. They do not think of themselves as being like those individuals and much prefer organizations primarily involving typical children. Hiking clubs and other outdoor organizations (e.g., ecology or rock collecting clubs) can be appealing to youth with Asperger syndrome or PDD-NOS. For older children, participating in outreach activities that benefit older adults who are shut in and seldom see visitors can be very rewarding for a child with an ASD and the older adult. A 15-year-old with high-functioning autism with whom I worked volunteered through his church to help deliver meals to elderly people in assisted living. The older people were very accepting of his differences and often enjoyed his company, and the young man expressed pleasure that he was doing something to help others. Some community organizations, such as local autism societies or ARCs provide social groups for high school–age and young adult individuals that include those with ASDs. Dances and other social events are often regularly scheduled that provide young adult individuals with developmental disabilities to socialize and practice skills they have learned at school or home.

LARGE-GROUP ACTIVITIES

Larger-group activities are more difficult for many children with ASDs. Youth with ASDs are often very anxious in a room full of people, many of whom seem like strangers to them. The more structured the activity, the easier it is for youths with ASDs to be comfortable and assimilated.

Music and Sports

Larger choral groups can be an excellent large-group socialization activity for children with ASDs who enjoy music and who are not bothered by large groups of people. Rehearsals are structured and provide clear cues regarding what to expect. Charitable and religious organizations often provide such opportunities. Team sports are usually more difficult because typical peers are motivated by winning and are less prone to make allowances for youths with disabilities. Some school athletic teams welcome a student with an ASD as an assistant trainer, helping with uniforms and sports equipment and otherwise playing a supportive role. It is essential that a parent and the team's coach explain the youth's disability and make it clear that teasing or otherwise taking advantage of the vulnerable student with an ASD will not be tolerated.

Devising Accommodations

The reactions of children and youth while attending sporting events, movies, and concerts are unpredictable and depend on the individual's interests and tolerance for the characteristics of the setting. Loud music and raucous crowd noise at sporting events may be alarming to many children and youth with autism. The mother of a 9-year-old with high-functioning autism told him that he and his typical older brother and sister were going to attend a Harry Potter movie. The movie featured battle scenes with a bombastic soundtrack replete with loud music and ear-popping sound effects. He had seen the previews and was initially resistant to attending the movie, but after thinking about it for a minute he said, "If it gets too loud I can cover my ears." Children and youth who have learned such adaptive skills can often get along very well in a wider variety of large- group settings but that has to be evaluated on a case-by-case basis. It is also important to accept the fact that a youth with an ASD may need to leave in the middle of a movie or sporting event, which may create a backlash with others who are enjoying the event. Parents are wise to develop an alternative plan before going to such events (i.e., what they will do if the child urgently needs to leave) to avoid disrupting the experience for others who are enjoying the experience, while honoring the youngster's need for relief from an intolerable situation.

A young adult with autism and a significant cognitive and language disability indicated to his mother that he wanted to attend an IMAX movie about volcanoes. As he and his mother approached the entrance to the theater, he became very agitated and refused to enter. Because they were early, his mother asked the usher if they could look inside the theater. As they entered the empty theater, he appeared alarmed as he stared intently toward the middle of theater at the empty rows of seats. His mother asked him if he was afraid he couldn't leave the theater once it started, and he nodded vigorously. She pointed at an empty seat adjacent to the entrance to the theater, and asked him if he could sit in that seat would he like to see the movie. With great relief he nodded and said, "yes." He was terrified of feeling trapped and unable to escape if he felt an urgent need to leave. It isn't always easy divining exactly what it is about a given large-group setting that is disturbing to individuals with ASDs, but with patience and perceptiveness, one can often make an educated guess as to what it is, as did the mother of this young man.

SUMMARY

Social skills do not come as naturally for children with ASDs as they do for other children. Younger children with ASDs usually must be taught to observe, imitate, and show their interests to others. Gross and fine motor turn-taking and cooperative activities can lay the foundation for later more complex social activities. Sibling play can be supplemented by play dates with same-age peers. As children become more socially comfortable, small-group activities, such as scouts, and larger-group activities, such as choir, can be very appropriate socialization opportunities for many children with ASDs. Older, higher-functioning children may enjoy belonging to topical clubs (e.g., rock collecting, photography, art) that provide an opportunity to embed social activities within a substantive context that appeals to the youngster.

7

Nothing Is Easy

Overcoming Stimulus Intolerance

Many of us experience discomfort when peering down from the railing of a tall building or into a deep pool of swirling water, inborn forms of acrophobia. These reactions are believed to be an evolved adaptation to a prehistory in which falls from high places posed a genuine danger to our ancient ancestors. But people with ASDs often experience discomfort when experiencing a variety of common situations that are benign or even positive to others. In a personal communication on June 7, 2007, Ruth Elaine Hane, a well-educated professional with an ASD, reported

> As a child I had avoided looking at people's faces and into a person's eyes. Faces were frightening to me. In the act of glancing or gazing into a face, I felt a loss of my very self, my identity, and where I was in time and space. The intensity of the energy from a pair of eyes burned through me like a beam of yellow light. When I did look, the features were not separate—eyes, nose, mouth—but a meaningless blob of flesh that moved. I noticed that the movement I observed usually occurred more around the lower portion of the face, called *mouth*, than around the upper portion of the face, called *eyes*.

Although few children with ASDs report such unusual responses to faces, many display exaggerated responses to stimuli that are unexpected. Amy, a 5-year-old who has autism, is screaming and crying, sobbing inconsolably. Her mother tries to comfort her but it doesn't seem to help. The episode was set off when her mother gave her peanut butter instead of her usual bologna sandwich for lunch. Parents and teachers who witness such puzzling and disturbing behavior invariably wonder what is going on inside a child to cause her to act in such disproportionately emotional ways. How can parents and teachers cope with these outbursts? In this chapter, stimulus intolerance and overselectivity will be discussed along with ways of intervening to prevent and overcome these problems.

OVERCOMING NOVEL STIMULUS INTOLERANCE

During dinner at a conference in Portofino, Italy, a city overlooking the Gulf of Genoa known for its seafood, the appetizer consisted of tiny baby squid in a savory tomato, basil, and garlic sauce. The half-inch long cephalopods with their diminutive tentacles floating in the fragrant mixture had a troublingly exotic appearance. To an American who had grown up in the Midwest, the appetizer looked strange. As I peered at the wee creatures, a fleeting sense of distaste came over me at the idea of swallowing the little beasts whole with their legs flailing on their way down my esophagus. Fortunately, I overcame my initial hesitance and tried the seafood starter and discovered, to my delight, that it was delicious. My gustatory horizon had been correspondingly expanded. Many adults and children alike share my initial diffidence when encountering food that is unfamiliar or has an unusual appearance, but with children with ASDs, rejection of unfamiliar foods is a much greater problem.

Neophobia and Food Preferences

Nearly all toddlers and young children are neophobic; they refuse to eat unfamiliar-tasting foods or food items with novel textures. This is an important biological adaptation that protects them from eating foods that might be harmful to them before they have developed the ability to distinguish dangerous from safe things to put in their mouths. As children grow older, they are gradually exposed to a range of food and beverage tastes and textures that are part of their family's diet, thereby accepting and enjoying an increasing array of foods. In a survey of food preferences by children with autism reported by their parents, Schreck and Williams (2005) found that children with ASDs preferred fewer types of food items within groups than their families; however, family food preferences appeared to influence food selection more than the diagnostic characteristics of autism.

Broad Intolerances for New Stimuli

Food taste and texture preferences are only one of an array of stimulus intolerances displayed by children with ASDs. Parent surveys nearly universally indicate that their children with ASDs have strong negative reactions to some textures, tastes, sounds, or appearances of different foods. (Baranek, Foster, & Berkson, 1997; Rogers, Hepburn, & Wehner, 2003). Evaluations using Dunn's sensory profile manual (Dunn, 1999) yield similar results (Kientz & Dunn, 1997). Although several studies have indicated some children with ASDs may be more responsive to the loudness and pitch of pure tones (Bonnel et al., 2003; Khaifa et al., 2004), in a review of 48 laboratory studies processing of sensory information by Ozonoff and Rogers (2006) found that there is not good evidence that these symptoms differentiate autism from other developmental disorders or that there are significant sensory processing differences. They found that there was very little support for hyperarousal and failure to habituate to novel stimuli in autism as had been proposed, but there may be more evidence that children with autism are underresponsive to some sensory stimuli.

How Important Is the Child's Stimulus Intolerance?

An initial question parents, teachers, and therapists might ask when encountering a child with an ASD who exhibits stimulus intolerance is, "Is there a good reason the child should have to learn to tolerate the disliked taste, texture, or sound?" In some cases there may not be. Sometimes parents are fearful that their child will be malnourished if he or she doesn't eat all of the various foods on his or her plate. Malnutrition among children with autism is very uncommon. Taking a moment to realistically look at the need for the child to tolerate what it is that is giving rise to behavior problems can avoid unnecessary worry. At times it may be best to focus efforts on other issues that may be more important. Secondly, "How much does the child's intolerance interfere with her or his daily life?" Finally, "How disruptive is the child's stimulus intolerance to others around him or her?" Sometimes children with ASDs "outgrow" specific stimulus intolerances in the course of normal daily life. Because they are incidentally exposed to the disliked stimuli and nothing bad happens, many children eventually tolerate them with equanimity. At other times, children may devote a considerable part of their day at school trying to avoid particular sounds, or they may refuse to eat meals at home, breaking down into sobbing and throwing tantrums. Under the latter circumstances, caregivers have little choice but to intervene to overcome the child's intolerance to those specific stimuli.

Do Children with Autism Have Sensory Issues?

A comment commonly heard during a discussion of a child with an ASD is that "he or she has sensory issues." The *American Heritage Dictionary* refers to *issues* as an informal (i.e., slang) term referring to a personal problem. The expression *sensory issues* obfuscates the child's behavior and its circumstances rather than accurately characterizing them. We may think we understand what the speaker means, but often we don't appreciate its implications. Those of us who spend our lives in the world of people with ASDs are well aware that they often react in unorthodox ways to certain kinds of stimulation, textures, sounds, or tastes. But does that mean that they have sensory processing differences, which is usually implied by the phrase *sensory issues*? I prefer bee-bop jazz to funk. I doubt one would conclude that I have sensory processing differences if I quickly turned off the radio when a song by the funk group The Soul Destroyers unexpectedly erupted from my car's speakers. People with ASDs are intolerant of unexpected stimuli that are different from those with which they are familiar. The implication of the concept of *sensory issues* is that the person with an ASD has a dysfunction in the way his or her brain processes sensory information or perhaps the way he or she perceives stimuli. In the following section this notion will be examined.

Sensory Integration

In *Making Sense of Autism* (Thompson, 2007), I reviewed what is known about the effectiveness of *sensory integration,* a term coined by Jean Ayres (1979), which is summarized here. Ayres hypothesized that because intact, efficient sensory processing leads to a child's adaptations across changing environments, dysfunction in one or more senses can lead to deficient or maladaptive adjustment. Ayres assumed that specific sensorimotor interventions would correct the sensory processing dysfunction. A variety of sensory integration therapy techniques have been employed by occupational therapists based on Ayres's theory and Dunn's *The Sensory Profile* (1999), but there are no well-controlled clinical trials among children with autism. In its 2001 report, the National Research Council-National Academy of Sciences Committee (Lord & McGee, 2001) reviewed educational methods for young children with autism and found that there was very little research concerning sensory integration treatments in autism.

Therapies based on sensory integration theory include the sensory diet, in which the environment is filled with sensory-based activities that are hypothesized to satisfy a child's sensory needs. Few, if any, empirical studies of these techniques have been published. Sensory stimulation techniques vary but usually involve passive sensory stimulation; they are incorporated within the broader sensory integration programs or used in isolation. Examples include use of deep pressure to provide calming input by massage or joint compression or use of an apparatus such as a weighted vest. Vestibular stimulation, another example, is often used in an attempt to modulate hypothesized arousal abnormalities, facilitate postural tone, or increase vocalizations. These interventions have also not yet been supported by empirical studies.

Auditory Integration Therapy

Auditory integration therapy is a type of sensory integration for autism that has received considerable media attention. Proponents of auditory integration therapy suggest that music can "massage" the middle ear, reduce hypersensitivities, and improve overall auditory processing ability. From a review of available studies, it appears that there is no empirical evidence from controlled investigations that auditory integration therapy has any effect on children with autism. The underlying assumptions behind the method have been considered questionable on scientific grounds (Lord & McGee, 2001).

In short, there is no consistent evidence that sensory-based treatments have specific lasting effects on the behavior of children with ASDs (Dawson & Watling, 2000; Goldstein, 1999). Although a lack of empirical data does not necessarily prove that a treatment is ineffective, it does indicate that there is no evidence to date demonstrating that such treatments have significant practical benefit for children with ASDs. Rather than undergoing a major difference in the way children with ASDs process sensory information, it appears that the problem is intolerance for stimulus change or novelty, a more general characteristic of children with ASDs as originally noted by Kanner (1943). Any sensory experience that deviates from what children with ASDs expect and what they are accustomed to tends to be rejected and may create a strongly negative reaction. An alternative strategy involves attempting to increase tolerance of novel stimuli by children with ASDs by desensitizing them to new stimuli.

Desensitization and Reinforcement for Increased Stimulus Tolerance

A small percentage of children with ASDs are found to have food allergies similar to those of other young children, the most common are to cow's milk followed by eggs and peanuts. Less common food allergies include wheat, tree nuts, fish, and shellfish. True food allergies involve an interaction between the body's immune system and the protein in a particular food. The allergy antibody involved in food allergy is called immunoglobulin E (IgE). It is important to distinguish true food allergies from other reactions, such as constipation or diarrhea, because true allergies can lead to severe or potentially fatal reactions called anaphylactic shock. Between 30 and 50 million Americans are lactose intolerant, and certain ethnic and racial populations are more affected than others. Up to 80% of African Americans, 80%–100% of American Indians, and 90%–100% of Asian Americans are lactose intolerant (National Institute of Child Health and Human Development [NICHD], 2007). Lactose is milk sugar that can cause bloating, cramps, and diarrhea when milk products are consumed by intolerant individuals. If parents are concerned about the possibility that their child has a true food allergy or is lactose intolerant they should have their child seen by a pediatric allergist or immunologist. The names of pediatricians who are specialists in Allergy and Immunology can be obtained from the American Academy of Pediatrics or your state pediatric society.

An age-old method used by parents of typical children as well as those with ASDs involves encouraging the child to take a bite of broccoli so he or she can then have a spoonful of applesauce. Eventually, most children will accept an initially rejected food item and the applesauce reward is phased out. Although some food items will continue to be favored over others, the less preferred foods are usually accepted to some degree. Reports by parents that this approach has been effective with their own children with ASDs are supported by clinical studies as well. Levin and Carr (2001) studied effects of positive reinforcement applied to consuming a nonpreferred food item. Participants initially displayed significantly more problematic behavior during the nonpreferred foods condition. During treatment they consumed nonpreferred target food items only when prior access to preferred foods was limited and was made available only after consuming a small amount of the nonpreferred food. Careful analysis indicated the children's problematic behavior (e.g., crying, throwing tantrums) was maintained by their avoidance of nonpreferred food and gaining access to preferred food. Gradually fading in the nonpreferred food in small steps was more effective than simply trying to induce the child to accept the nonpreferred food and ignoring behavior outbursts. Piazza, Patel, Santana, Goh, Delia, and Lancaster (2002) used either simultaneous or sequential presentation of a preferred food along with a nonpreferred food with three children with ASDs. For two of the children, presenting both foods concurrently increased consumption of the nonpreferred food. For one child, consumption of the nonpreferred food increased only when the preferred food was provided after eating the nonpreferred food.

Children with ASDs won't easily give up their tried and proven whining and crying that has worked for them in the past to avoid the nonpreferred food and gain access to preferred food items. Behavioral outbursts inevitably lead to adult attention in the process. Children with ASDs may persist for some time trying to avoid nonpreferred stimuli by crying and exhibiting meltdowns. Scolding or coaxing usually makes matters worse. If a child becomes unmanageable, it is best to end the desensitization session even if it is mealtime. After a child has calmed down, repeat the same procedure. In most cases, after the second or third desensitization attempt, a child will accept minimal exposure to the nonpreferred item and be rewarded for tolerating the nonpreferred stimulus. On successive repetitions, fussing diminishes, and a child usually accepts exposure to the previously avoided stimulus. Perhaps most importantly, children learn that nothing terrible will happen when they eat the previously rejected food, tolerate the fabric that they had resisted, or are exposed to a humming sound in their classroom that initially disturbed them. As a result, they will become less agitated and more at ease in situations that were very disturbing in the past.

Depending on how the child is being rewarded, it may be useful to provide the highly desired food or other item *only* after exposure to the nonpreferred item and at no other time during the rest of the day. For some children, as in the Piazza et al. (2002) study, simultaneous presentation of nonpreferred and preferred items can also be effective. This capitalizes upon the child's need for control. Having a choice may make some stimuli more tolerable. Although there is some evidence that these procedures can produce a generalization to natural environments when implemented in clinical settings, as a general rule of thumb they are usually most effective when carried out in the course of normal daily routines.

Tactile and Fabric Desensitization

Before beginning tactile or fabric desensitization, it is wise to consult your child's pediatrician to determine whether the youngster may have specific contact allergies. If so, you should avoid exposing the child to the allergen (e.g., specific type of fabric, soap, lotion). If there is no indication of an allergy, this general strategy is effective. Ellis, Ala'i-Rosales, Glenn, Rosales-Ruiz, and Greenspoon (2006) treated two children with ASDs who refused to tolerate the application of lotion, ointments, or other substances to their skin. The researchers used a combination of providing a graduated exposure to the substances, modeling, and paying attention when the children accepted the skin products. Behavior problems gradually decreased and acceptance of skin care products increased.

In fabric desensitization, the technique is slightly modified but involves the same principles. It is very common for children with ASDs to dislike and avoid coarse or scratchy fabrics, such as some wool sweaters, caps, or scarves. By spending an hour or two shopping, parents can usually identify blouses or shirts that have different fabric compositions, ranging from rayon or acrylic blends to rayon–cotton blends, fine cotton, coarser cotton, fine wool, or coarser wool. There are two aspects of desensitization to fabrics: 1) a hierarchy of texture from smooth to coarse in numerous gradations, and 2) a progressively longer duration of exposure to the fabric. A good time to introduce a new fabric texture is immediately before the child is going to do something he enjoys and which is time-limited. For example, your daughter may love to go to the pet store and look at the hamsters. Just before you leave the house, ask her put on a new blouse made of the next step in the fabric sequence, say fine cotton (you have just succeeded in getting her to wear rayon–cotton blends). The visit to the pet store won't last more than 15–20 minutes and then you'll come home. Tell your daughter, "Melissa, put on your new blouse so we can go to the pet store. When we come home you can wear your red shirt" (which you know is her favorite shirt). The next time you go on a somewhat longer outing, perhaps shopping at the grocery store, repeat the same instruction. On each successive exposure to the new fabric, extend the amount of time she wears the blouse until it becomes apparent that she has forgotten she's wearing it, usually no more than 4–6 times. At that point you can ask her to put on the blouse before school in the morning, and she should be comfortable doing so. You are now ready to move to the next step in the fabric coarseness hierarchy: coarser cotton. By very gradually exposing a child to progressively coarser fabrics for gradually longer time periods, most children with ASDs learn to accept a wide range of fabrics against their skin with ease. Some children may never feel comfortable wearing coarser fabrics, which is not at all unusual. Many typical adults feel the same way.

Overcoming Sensory Intolerance Summary

Brief exposures (e.g., 15–30 minutes) to unrelated novel stimuli several times per week (e.g., tones, music through headphones, sand, water, weights, tactile stimulation, pressure), especially out of the natural environment, doesn't appear to have any effect on a highly specific stimulus intolerance among children with ASDs. To be effective, desensitization must be carried out with the specific avoided stimulus (e.g., food item, fabric texture, sound) and preferably in the course of typical daily routines. This eliminates the need for overcoming a lack of generalization. Remember, children with ASDs thrive on consistency. If parents or teachers are inconsistent in the way they implement these methods (i.e., one parent follows the agreed-upon method and the other doesn't), the child's stimulus intolerance may grow worse and become much more difficult to overcome.

The main elements of these various desensitization procedures are 1) gradually exposing the child to the avoided or nonpreferred stimulus in a series of very small steps in a procedure called *desensitization* (e.g., fabric texture, sounds, food) and 2) increasing the incentive for tolerating the nonpreferred stimulus. By using small steps the child's distress and strong resistance are prevented. Most children with ASDs have had experience avoiding nonpreferred items by whining, fussing, or using other expressions of refusal. Parents and teachers are encouraged to avoid reacting to a child's negative behavior that he or she has used in the past to avoid the nonpreferred stimulus. When a child fusses, look away and appear to be attending to something else. If the child begins to cry, turn away and talk with another child and only return your attention to the child who was crying when he or she stops. Because children with ASDs often appear disinterested in social interactions, it is easy for adults to make the mistake of assuming that adult attention isn't as important. It usually is. Attempting to be reassuring (e.g., "It isn't so bad. You will like it") reinforces the whining and resistance and perpetuates the problem.

If done well, you can avoid a great deal of resistance or signs of distress from a child when implementing desensitization procedures. The first time or two a child is presented with a spoonful of the nonpreferred food he or she may pucker up and turn away, but usually by the second or third practice session he or she consumes a small amount of the food with little or no resistance or sign of unhappiness. After he or she has done so for three or four sessions, very gradually increase the amount to be consumed before providing the desired reward (praise and a preferred food item). Increase the amount of exposure to the nonpreferred stimulus only after several sessions with no resistance. With sufficient experience, many children actually come to enjoy the food they initially rejected. The goal is to help the child tolerate exposure to a wider range of stimuli he or she will encounter in his or her day-to-day natural environment without experiencing distress.

STIMULUS OVERSELECTIVITY

Figure 7.1. A child with autism selectively attends to one aspect of complex stimulus.

Related to the tendency for children with ASDs to overreact to novel stimuli is an attention problem called *stimulus overselectivity*. Lovaas and Schreibman (1971) first reported this phenomenon, which has important practical implications because in most daily situations, combinations of auditory, visual, and tactile stimuli are presented to children simultaneously. If children with autism are learning to respond to a complex cue, say a spoken instruction and a visual stimulus simultaneously (e.g., a picture), they tend to respond only to one or the other stimulus and not both.

Multimodal Overselectivity

Schreibman, Koegel, and Craig (1977) worked with 19 children with autism on a discrimination task with a complex cue composed of two visual cues. After the children mastered the task when both cues were presented, they were exposed to a testing phase with probe trials in which the cue components were presented singly. Sixteen of the children initially showed overselectivity (i.e., they responded to one cue but not the other) and three responded to both cues. Of the 16 children who showed overselectivity, 13 decreased their level of overselectivity with continued exposure to the combined visual stimuli, suggesting that overselectivity is not an immutable feature of sensory processing in autism. Kolko, Anderson, and Campbell (1980) studied the relationship between stimulus preference and overselectivity in five children with autism and five matched typical children. The children were first given an opportunity to indicate a sensory modality preference by selecting whether they wanted to either view slides or listen to music. The children were then taught a discrimination between the presence or absence of a compound auditory-visual stimulus (a sound and light). Testing for stimulus overselectivity revealed that the children with autism attended to only one aspect of the compound stimulus (see Figure 7.1). In all cases this was the sensory modality that was selected during the preference test. Typical children indicated equal preference for music and slides and displayed no overselectivity. Ploog and Kim (2006) investigated overselective combinations of tactile stimuli. They found that the children with autism responded overselectively to tactile stimuli as well, suggesting this phenomenon is not limited to visual and auditory cues.

Overselectivity in School and at Home

Teachers and parents who are attempting to teach children with ASDs to respond to common, everyday experiences should be attuned to the fact that it is likely that the child may only be learning about the importance of one aspect of a complex stimulus that is involved in teaching. For example, a teacher is working on phonemic awareness with a child with an ASD. In phonemic awareness instruction, children are shown exactly how to sound out words and how to divide spoken words into individual sounds and how to blend spoken sounds into words. Children must also learn that sounds can be represented by letters and learn to recognize sound–letter relationships. The teacher holds up a card that has the word *cat* on it. He points to each component and says, "kuh-aaa-tuh." A child must attend to the printed letters, the sound of the teacher's voice and the way his or her mouth looks as he's saying the phonemic components of *cat*. That is an extremely complex task for many children with ASDs who will likely require many more repetitions than a typical peer to learn, even one with a similar IQ. Most children with ASDs show preference for visual cues, so they may focus first on the printed letters, next on the spoken phonemes, and last on the appearance of the teacher's mouth as he or she is producing the sounds. A child's mother says, "It's time to put away your toys. Put the Legos in the blue box and the Lincoln Logs in the red box." The child must discriminate Legos, Lincoln Logs, red, and blue and be able to connect the spoken sounds of those words with the actual objects and retain all of that information at the same moment in time. It should come as no surprise that many children with ASDs will simply sit on the floor and continue to play with their Legos, which may be the only word they heard as their mother spoke.

SUMMARY

Few are less willing to tolerate exposure to new tastes, textures, sounds, and sights than individuals with ASDs. Life is not easy for children with ASDs. Unusual and exaggerated emotional responses of children with ASDs to sights, sounds, tastes, smells, and tactile stimuli that differ from those with which they are familiar is nearly universal. This may be not only in part due to the child's generalized intolerance for novel stimuli of any kind but may also relate to stimulus overselectivity, the tendency to respond to only one aspect of a stimulus situation at time. A novel stimulus may be far more salient and be selectively attended to, or perhaps excluded from attention than other familiar background stimulation. Some stimulation may be inherently aversive and therefore avoided whereas others receive selective attention, such as parts of complex stimuli. Ruth Elaine Hane, who was discussed earlier in the chapter, reported that she wasn't totally aware of her inability to perceive faces until adulthood:

> There had been clues in my life that I was not reading and comprehending faces. For example, in the earlier years of my career, I was, quite remarkably, chosen to be an apprentice in a famous designers' Atelier (workroom) in New York City: Koos Van den Akker. At the conclusion of my training, Koos gave me one final assignment to test my visual and auditory recall: I was to attend several of his friend's fashion shows and then report back to him what I had observed without taking notes. When I returned to make my report, I could easily describe the clothing in exquisite detail—the fabric choices and styles, the colors and lengths of pants and skirts. What I could not recall was detail about the models themselves—hairstyles, ethnicity, or facial expressions. I could recall the hair color, but not the style. I remembered every belt and shoe style in the shows, but retained nothing about the faces. The background music was also a blur. I could remember the kind of music: Jazz, Rock, Disco, but could not recognize the song titles or artists.

Ruth Elaine reported another incident that forcefully brought home her lack of facility at perceiving faces.

> The first time I understood that I was not gathering what others apparently were when I looked at faces was at the airport on a mild spring afternoon. Susan and I were seated at the Minneapolis terminal waiting to meet our husbands, both of whom would arrive on the same flight. Later we chatted at the baggage area as the passengers from their flight began arriving to claim their luggage. I scanned the

crowd of people, searching for my husband, Jay. I didn't see him. Suddenly my friend jumped to her feet, rushing forward to greet her husband, confident that she recognized him from among the group of mostly look-alike travelers who were at least 30 feet away. I watched and waited, but I felt unsure which of these many men might be my husband. Then I noticed a familiar gait and the angle of very square shoulders. I was sure: That was Jay. It was when he reached out to give me a hug that I realized, however, that in looking for our husbands, Susan had seen something I had not seen. I had not recognized my husband's face from far away, and I did not see his face as an integrated whole.

At that moment, then, I understood a vitally important piece of information about myself: I understood that I did not "read" faces. And since I did not read faces, i.e., receive significant information from faces, I did not have the capacity to, at some future time, recall the face. I'd not been able to recognize Jay's face because there was, in essence, a lack of order in my memory that would induce such a recall. And there was no face called 'Jay' that I could conveniently reassemble from the bits and pieces stored there. I later discovered a name for my particular inability: it is called *visual facial agnosia*. This condition had been brought to public attention years ago largely through the writing of Oliver Sacks in his book *The Man Who Mistook His Wife for a Hat (1998).* Visual agnosia is the inability of the brain to make sense of or to use visual stimuli effectively; it is the inability to recognize familiar faces, or objects, even though vision is otherwise normal.

Ruth Elaine's approach to overcoming this limitation involved systematically studying how she looked at faces as compared with other people.

Like an anthropologist, I noted what other people looked at, where they looked, and for how long they looked. And I sought also to impartially observe my own behavior: How did I look, where did I look, and for how long did I look? What would it take to "read" a face? After studying my situation for 2 years, I had developed a system that would help me. I discovered that I could look at people better if I stood at a window, looking through a small, framed windowpane. By building on the geometric shape of a rectangle, a specific object, I created a face shape with rectangular windows cut out, each opening placed to define the fields of interest, delineating the organic fields of eyes, nose, and mouth. The geometric shapes, a familiar object, outlined the hard-to-recall portions of a face like a window frame. By using this technique, I'd learned about faces, about how to remember faces, and about how to read faces "in real

> time" while a person is speaking. I developed new "neural pathways" in my brain. Faces are no longer frightening. And I recognize Jay from a distance by the features of his face, not only by his build or his walk or his clothing. What an amazing achievement!

Ruth Elaine Hane's story of developing a strategy for overcoming a specific type of stimulus overselectivity (visual facial agnosia) is quite remarkable and reminds us that many, perhaps most, people with ASDs develop unique coping strategies that are generally unknown to others. Caregivers can help by using a combination of desensitization and reinforcement for tolerating novel stimuli in a series of gradual steps, usually overcoming stimulus intolerance. Repetition of complex stimuli with periodic probes to make certain the child is attending to each component of the stimulus is required to overcome stimulus overselectivity. Although all children with autism profit from the desensitization procedure for stimulus intolerance, children with moderate- to high-functioning ASDs seem to learn to attend to most components of complex stimuli more readily, and, like Ruth Elaine Hane, develop novel solutions to their lack of ability to perceive relevant aspects of complex stimuli.

8

Putting Out Fires

Coping with Behavioral Challenges

Jennifer knew it was going to be one of those days as soon as Alex entered her classroom. It was like watching a looming black cloud rapidly approaching on the horizon with flickers of lightning in the distance, the kind that spawns tornados. Alex's face was tense, and his jaw was clenched. He stared straight ahead, saying nothing. After throwing his jacket on the floor instead of hanging it up, as he usually does, he headed directly toward Jack, who was seated in Alex's favorite place at the table. Alex's legs were widely spaced and his gait uneven as he propelled himself across the room. He screamed something at Jack who jumped up in fear. Alex grabbed Jack and began hitting him, screaming and shouting as he pummeled him. Mr. Blakely, the classroom aide, grabbed Alex and dragged him off Jack, but, despite being only 9 years old, Alex was strong and managed to bite Mr. Blakely. Alex's face was red, his pupils were dilated, and he was taking rapid gulps of air. Alex's screaming and flailing continued for another 15 minutes while Mr. Blakely tried to calm him down. Perspiration was running off of Alex's face and his shirt was soaked. Gradually the storm passed and little by little Alex's body began to relax. He appeared exhausted and confused, and he began crying and then sobbing. Jennifer took Alex's hand and led him to a quiet area behind a screen across the room. "You were really upset, Alex. What happened? Why were you so mad?" she asked. Alex sobbed more loudly and said, "I don't know. Go away!" and he pushed her away adding, "I don't know why. I was just bad."

Most teachers and many parents of children with ASDs have experiences like Jennifer's incident with Alex. A severe emotional storm appears to erupt out of nowhere, runs its course, and then gradually subsides. During a debriefing after the episode, the teaching staff or child's parents ask one another, "Where in the world did that come from, and why did it happen?" Most of the time, such severe outbursts of aggression or self-injury occur for good reasons, but it is often very difficult at the time to discover the basis for any given episode. In this chapter, strategies for uncovering the causes of aggressive and SIB are discussed in relation to compulsivity. Once the causes and contributing factors are identified, methods for intervening to prevent future recurrence of similar outbursts are explored.

CRISIS INTERVENTION VERSUS PREVENTION AND TREATMENT

Most of us go through life putting out fires instead of preventing them. We wait until a crisis erupts and then we figuratively call the fire department to put out the blaze. In reality, it is rare that severe behavioral challenges of children with ASDs emerge out of the blue. Warning signs have usually been becoming progressively worse over several weeks, and parents or teachers try various palliative measures on their own, and then one day an acute crisis occurs. The youngster is seriously hurting him- or herself or others. But instead of calling for crisis intervention assistance, parents and teachers often call a psychologist or behavior analyst and ask for help. In most instances, such professionals aren't equipped to contain violent situations. They cannot subdue or contain a youngster who is seriously out of control. When families are in the midst of a serious physical crisis with their child with an ASD, their options are to call a crisis intervention service that works in people's homes or to have their youngster hospitalized. Once the immediate crisis has been contained, it is very likely an experienced therapist can work with the family to plan a longer-term solution to preventing similar recurrences.

Controlling a dangerously out of control youth in a classroom is a matter of school policy and planning for such crisis-management situations. It is not a matter for behavioral intervention, which requires days and weeks to be effective. It is the difference between giving a person with diabetes orange juice to treat severe hypoglycemia and long-term dietary and medication management of a patient's blood sugar. Schools have specific crisis management teams whose job it is to intervene in such situations. A behavioral crisis calls for a different type of intervention from long-term intervention and prevention programs, which is the subject of this chapter. Fouse and Wheeler's (1997) *A Treasure Chest of Behavioral Strategies for Individuals with Autism* includes a section on crisis management in autism, which is a good starting point. In addition, there are numerous books available through commercial book dealers on mental health crisis management for schools.

FUNCTIONAL BEHAVIORAL ASSESSMENT

The reasons behind people's actions can be confusing and can lead to incorrect conclusions about their causes. Parents and teachers often ask me what the best intervention for aggression in autism is. Others ask the same question about self-injury. What they usually mean is, "What should I do to my child once he or she has been aggressive or has injured him- or herself?" That would be like asking what the best treatment for dizziness is. The short answer is that there isn't any best intervention for either behavioral challenge, any more than there is a single best treatment for dizziness. Much as the child's doctor would want to investigate what is causing dizziness (e.g., ear infection, hypertension, medication side effect) before treating it, the most appropriate intervention depends on the reasons why the person is displaying aggression, self-injury, tantrums, or meltdowns. A functional behavioral assessment can help identify the social and health factors contributing to challenging behavior (Carr et al., 1999; Carr, Reeve, & Magito-McLaughlin, 1995; Horner et al., 1990; Kennedy & Thompson, 2000; O'Neill, Horner, Albin, Sprague, Storey, & Newton, 1997).

History

The first step in developing an intervention strategy for a behavioral challenge in autism is to explore the history of its development.

When Did It First Occur?

If the behavior problem emerged suddenly and very recently, that suggests an environmental or health condition that recently changed may be the root of the problem. Has there been a major change in the family (e.g., the death of a relative or pet)? Has the child shown signs of illness, such as an earache, toothache, gastrointestinal (GI) problem, or seizure? The child should be seen by his pediatrician to explore possible health reasons contributing to behavior problems. If the behavior problem first emerged 6 months ago or longer but has grown progressively worse in a series of episodes, it suggests the problem is a learned adaptation to being unable to communicate or otherwise control his or her environment.

Has the Problem Been Better in Some Situations and Worse in Others in the Past?

If the problem is clearly situational, that generally rules out a health condition as the major cause. If the problem tends to occur in the presence of some people but not others, it suggests that there are important social reasons for the behavioral challenge.

Have Any Treatments Seemed to Be Associated with Improvement or Worsening of the Condition?

For example, have any medications, educational, behavioral, or speech-language interventions seemed to make the problem better or worse? Important clues can be obtained when the problem seemed to temporarily improve when a particular therapy was in place (e.g., using PECS in communication intervention or being on a high-bulk diet).

Setting Sleep Events

For at least 1 week, parents are urged to record the approximate number of hours (e.g., 6.5 hours) the child sleeps each night and whether the child awakened during the night (and how many times). Sleep deprivation is associated with increased problem behavior (Kennedy & Meyer, 1996). Parents are also asked to keep a record of bowel movements and stool consistency. Constipation is common among children with ASDs and causes irritability and increases susceptibility to behavior problems. Teachers and parents are asked to keep a record of any event that occurred early in the day, which seemed to predispose the child to having problems throughout the remainder of the day. Becky got in a fight with a boy on the bus on her way to school and was irritable and difficult the remainder of the day. Mrs. Robinson was ill and a substitute teacher took over her class. Ramon refused to participate in activities for most of the day, and when he did, he had tantrums. Did the child exhibit any signs of other health problems on some days but not others such as sleepiness, complaints of stomachache, and so forth that seem to be associated with more challenging behavior? If so, a visit to the doctor may be helpful in resolving any health setting events.

Gastrointestinal Problems as Setting Events

Parents of children with ASDs often report that their children have bowel or stomach problems, usually constipation, loose stools, or bloating and gas (Gurney, McPheeters, & Davis, 2006; Mercer Creighton, Holden, & Lewis, 2006).

Diet

In attempting to determine whether gastrointestinal problems may contribute to problematic behavior, parents can begin by looking at their child's diet. Children with ASDs are often finicky eaters and may be consuming insufficient fiber in their diet. If a child has chronic problems with constipation, adding high-fiber breakfast cereals can be helpful. Encouraging children to eat apples or pears with the skin on or prunes can also assist with loosening stools. Make changes gradually. Don't add 2–3 high-fiber foods at the same time because that may lead to cramping and diarrhea. Children who frequently have loose stools may be suffering from toddler's diarrhea, which many pediatricians think is caused by drinking too much juice. Toddler's diarrhea usually begins between the ages of 6 and 30 months and goes away by the time children are about 4 years old. They may have 2–6 loose stools each day but otherwise seem well and are gaining weight normally. Reducing the amount of juice consumed usually resolves the problem.

Lactose Intolerance

Lactose intolerance is common among children of all kinds, even those who do not have disabilities. Lactose intolerance is the inability to digest significant amounts of lactose, the major sugar found in milk. Lactose intolerance is caused by a shortage of the enzyme lactase, which is produced by the cells that line the small intestine. If a child is lactose intolerant, he or she will often experience cramps or nausea and need to have a bowel movement within 2 hours of consuming food containing lactose. Some children have to stop consuming milk products, but many others do very well by drinking low-fat or fat-free milk in servings of no more than one cup. If possible, the milk should be used on cereal to reduce the likelihood of discomfort (NICHD, 2007). Your child's doctor will conduct tests to determine whether he or she is actually lactose intolerant.

Dietary Supplements and Special Diets

Many parents of children with ASDs provide their children with special diets and high doses of vitamins, minerals, Omega-3 fatty acids, amino acids, enzymes, probiotics, and other supplements, as well as chelating agents, believing they might reverse autism symptoms. Some of those substances can produce nausea, diarrhea, or constipation. Some parents of children with ASDs follow part or all of the Defeat Autism Now (DAN) Protocol, which involves 20 different substances, many of which include combinations of individual agents (Jang, 2003). In addition, many children with ASDs are receiving psychotropic drugs that can cause constipation as a side effect (e.g., atypical antipsychotic drugs, cyclic antidepressants), and antidepressants with antianxiety properties (e.g., SSRIs), which may cause nausea, abdominal discomfort, and diarrhea. If a child is taking St. John's Wort along with an SSRI, the GI problems will be made much worse and may cause other very serious side effects. St. John's Wort should never be taken with antidepressant drugs.

Fecal Contamination

Children who attend preschool are particularly vulnerable to contracting intestinal infections that are spread from feces to hands and then to the mouth due to poor hand washing. Some children may not have symptoms but can spread the infection, whereas others develop intermittent diarrhea and still others become very ill. Parents may misinterpret such episodic symptoms as being indications that their child has an underlying GI or immune disorder, which in turn, they believe has an important link to the cause of their child's ASD. There is little evidence for such a link. Parents should consult their child's doctor who may want to culture stool samples to determine whether overgrowth of certain bacteria has occurred.

Trigger Events

Many teachers and parents initially say that a child's outbursts show no pattern and no rhyme or reason. That is very rare. In most instances, specific things happen around the child before an outburst sets him or her off. Things that happen immediately before and provoke an outburst are called *trigger events*. Parents and teachers are asked to keep a record for one week of each outburst (e.g., aggression, tantrum, meltdown, self-injury) and what happened immediately before each occurrence. In recording trigger events, caregivers should be specific, such as, "Clinton was asked to get ready for bed" or "Ashley's brother teased her." By reviewing a week's worth of episodes with a behavior analyst, special education specialist, or psychologist, it usually becomes apparent that there are two or three types of trigger events. The most common is interrupting or otherwise preventing a child from engaging in a highly preferred routine or self-stimulatory activity. Peter likes to flip the light switch on and off repeatedly, which is disruptive to the other children in the classroom. Mr. Green, the classroom paraprofessional, approaches Peter and says, "Peter, stop flipping the switch" and tries to lead him away from the light switch, at which point Peter hits the aide and screams at him, "No! No! Go away!" Mattie is on the playground swinging, when a boy in her class approaches her and calls her stupid. She looks away, but he walks up close to her and puts his hand on the swing to stop it, and says, "What's the matter stupid, cat's got your tongue?" Mattie jumps off the swing and hits the boy and grabs him and tries to choke him but is interrupted by Mrs. Jamison, the playground aide. Sometimes trigger events are more subtle. Fatin's mother says a neighbor is coming with her two children for tea. Fatin begins to whimper, which his mother ignores. A few moments later, Fatin is lying on the floor sobbing. Fatin is afraid of the two older boys because they make too much noise.

Problem Behavior Description

Kenny exhibits several problem behaviors. He grabs items off shelves and throws them on the floor, sometimes breaking them. He screams very loudly and threatens to hit himself in the head with his fists, though he seldom actually does so. He occasionally hits his sister, Madeline. His parents see these three things as different problems, but when they are analyzed carefully, it is discovered that he does all three things for the same reason. They all lead to attention from one of his parents. They all belong in the same *response class*. By carefully recording each behavioral outburst and exactly what the child does, that sets the stage for the final step of determining the purpose or function. Functional behavioral assessments are used to discover all of the different behaviors a child exhibits that serve the same purpose or function and identify other behavior that serves a different function. Kenny also cries and sobs inconsolably when he sees the credits appear on the screen at the end of his favorite video. This behavior doesn't serve the same purpose of obtaining his parents' attention. Its function is to avoid the end of the video.

Identifying Consequences

Keeping track of what happens following a child's behavioral outburst can begin to more adequately determine the behavior's function. In Kenny's case, there were two functions: 1) procuring his parents' attention and 2) avoiding the end of his preferred video. Timmy, who is nonverbal and has limited skills, is a student in Anna's classroom. Anna is concerned because over the first 2 weeks of school, Timmy has been increasingly hitting his head with his fist and biting his wrist. She keeps a record of these episodes, what triggered them, and the usual consequence. When she asked Timmy to match colors he bit his wrist, and she stopped asking him to match colors, redirecting him to another activity. When she read a story to him he didn't hit his head until she asked him to point to the picture of the dog. Then he hit his forehead and she stopped asking him to point to pictures. When he was playing at the sand table and she asked him to pour sand in the pail, he did so without hitting or biting himself. When Anna surveyed her week's worth of data, it appeared that the trigger events always involved asking him to do something he didn't want to do or know how to do, and the consequence was always discontinuing the task demand. The function of Timmy's SIB was to remove unwelcome task demands. Intervention involved teaching him the prerequisite skills so he could successfully complete some of the activities that were initially too difficult for him and teaching him to use PECS symbols to request a break from activities he didn't like. By permitting him short breaks from tasks that were too difficult, self-injury was no longer necessary.

Antecedent Behavior Consequence Charts

Parents and teachers can learn to use Antecedent Behavior Consequence (ABC) charts to keep track of antecedent triggers, behavior, and consequences (see Figure 8.1). A computer program can be used to make a generic table with days of the week down the left column and the words *Setting events, Antecedent triggers, Behavior,*

ABC Summary Table

Directions: In the behavioral challenge column, list the three most troubling behavior problems in order of importance. For each behavior challenge, list in order the most common setting events, antecedent triggers, behavior, and consequence that is associated with each behavioral challenge.

Setting events	Antecedent triggers	Behavior	Consequence

Figure 8.1. Antecedent Behavior Consequence (ABC) summary table.

and *Consequence* across the top row. A month's worth of charts can be printed out in advance and stapled together. Many parents find it easiest to post the chart on the refrigerator door where it will be easily accessible. If the chart is placed in a drawer, parents are more likely to forget to record what happened. In classrooms, teachers often keep a notebook at their desk for each student, and the ABC chart can be placed on the first page so it is easily found. In other cases they tape the chart to the child's desk.

Sample Antecedent Behavior Consequence Chart

An example of an ABC chart is shown in Figure 8.2. This is a record of Max's outburst for a 1-week period, complete with triggers, a

Day	Antecedent trigger	Behavior	Consequence
Monday	"Put away your shoes." "Don't hit your brother."	Screamed and hit Hit Billy again	I put his shoes away for him. I scolded him and made him stop.
Tuesday	"It's time for bed."	Cried and had a meltdown	I let him stay up 15 minutes longer.
Wednesday	"Eat your oatmeal."	Threw dish on floor.	I gave him cereal.
Thursday	"Stop hitting your brother."	Hit Billy harder	I scolded him and made him go to his room.
Friday	Billy's friend Aaron came over. "It's time for bed."	Cried and tried to push Aaron down Kept banging his spoon on the table	I made him stop and sent him to his room. I made him stop banging, read him a story, and sent him to bed.
Saturday	We arrived at swimming class. I gave him pizza.	Sobbed and refused to go in pool Cried and pushed the plate away	I let him sit on the side of the pool and watch the other kids. I made him a peanut butter sandwich.
Sunday	Grandma Alice tried to pick him up and give him a hug. The dog barked loudly at a cat by the window.	Screamed, stiffened, and hit her Covered ears and cried	I scolded him and sent him to his room. I held him and comforted him.

Figure 8.2. Max's Antecedent Behavior Consequence chart: Week of February 11, 2008.

description of his behavior, and the consequence that followed. Max's ABC chart provides the basis for making hypotheses about the reasons for his problem behavior. These hunches will need to be tested by implementing interventions addressing each reason for his problem behavior, but the connections are evident. Of nine behavioral outbursts over the week, Max received parental attention each time. His parents thought "scolding" would discourage his outbursts, but from Max's vantage point, scolding is just another form of attention that is helping maintain his behavior problems. Six occasions involved escape from nonpreferred activities. That raises the question, "Why does Max feel a need to escape from these particular situations?" This will involve further assessment to determine whether he lacks skills, or whether desensitization to some stimuli may be required. His parents are also differentially rewarding him for food refusals by giving him alternative foods when he cries and carries on and at bedtime by allowing him to stay up longer to avoid going to bed. These observations provide a starting point for the next step: devising an intervention plan.

Antecedent Behavior Consequence Analysis of Alex's Outburst

Let's return to Alex's severe aggressive outburst in Jennifer's classroom. When we explore Alex's history, we realize he has had similar but less severe outbursts over the past several months. That suggests that this is a learned behavior pattern and not a sudden health or environmental problem. Aggression had usually gotten him what he wanted in the past, when he had no way to verbally request what he wanted or didn't want to do specific activities. But there may be more to Alex's outbursts than that. We ask Alex's mother how he slept the night before, and she reports that he had trouble falling asleep, not really sleeping until nearly 11 p.m. He awakened several times during the night crying. He was irritable in the morning when he came down for breakfast. He refused to eat his cereal, and his father told him he had to eat his cereal or there would be no TV after school. Alex angrily threw his cereal bowl on the floor. His father lost his temper and harshly said, "Alex, you pick up the bowl and clean up the mess right now, or you're not going to see a movie on Saturday afternoon!" Alex became enraged and tried to hit his father, at which point his father carried him to his room and slammed the door and said loudly, "You can come out when you're ready to behave yourself." Alex didn't really understand what that meant, but he realized his father was very angry with him and that he wouldn't be able to see his favorite movie on Saturday. So the setting events were 1) lack of sleep which increased his irritability and 2) an altercation with his father that involved losing something that was very important to him. Those setting events, combined with a history of having successfully used aggression to achieve outcomes that he wanted in the past, created the context for the events that would follow. When Alex walked into Jennifer's classroom he was ready to explode and required only the slightest trigger (i.e., Jack sitting in his preferred seat) to set off a severe aggressive outburst. If that hadn't been the trigger, there very likely would have been another.

How could the situation have been handled differently? It would be helpful to try to discover why Alex is having sleep problems. Is it a health issue, such as nighttime breathing problems or indigestion, or is he experiencing pain? Is he drinking caffeinated soda in the evening that makes it difficult for him to sleep? Is he suffering from anxiety about a problem he is unable to express to his parents?

Next, it is unwise to progress through a series of escalating threats to a child or youth with an ASD. That nearly always backfires and leads to an outburst. Had Alex's father given him a choice of what he wanted for breakfast, it is likely the escalating sequence would have stopped at that point. In the future, it will be important to make certain Alex has ways to request *not* to do some things, or at least delay them, or request a choice. For example, if Alex said, "No cereal. Toast and peanut butter," the altercation would have been avoided if his father had accepted the requested alternative. Remember, control and choice are everything to children with ASDs. An alternative approach would have been to announce to Alex that breakfast was over when he threw the cereal bowl on the floor. His father could have said, preferably calmly, "All done. Brush your teeth for school." If Alex said, "I'm hungry" and requested an alternative food, his father could have said, "Okay, you can have toast and peanut butter when you're ready for school." In that way his inappropriate behavior is not being rewarded, but he is permitted some choice in the situation. It is likely any of these alternatives would have prevented the altercation. Unfortunately, once Alex arrived at school an outburst was going to happen no matter what occurred. The slightest irritation would have set him off.

ANXIETY AND COMPULSIVE RITUALS

Anxiety and autism go hand in hand. A recent national survey revealed that children with autism had a significantly higher prevalence of depression or anxiety problems than typical children of the same age (38.9% versus 4.2%) (Gurney, McPheeters, & Davis, 2006). Children with ASDs are more prone to fears and phobias. Evans, Canavera, Kleinpeter, Maccubin, and Taga (2005) studied anxiety symptoms among children with ASDs compared with matched typical children and children with Down syndrome. Children with ASDs had more situational phobias and medical fears but fewer fears of harm or injury compared with the other groups. For children with ASDs, fears, phobias, and anxieties were closely related to problematic behaviors, whereas fears, phobias, and anxieties were less related to behavioral symptoms for the other groups of children. As children with ASDs grow older, they devote an increasing amount of time and energy to anticipating bad things that might happen in the future. The last time Karl was taken to see his doctor he received an immunization shot that was painful. Today when his mother asks him to take a shower in preparation for going to the doctor, Karl screams and falls to the floor sobbing. The shower isn't the problem, it is seeing the doctor who may give him another injection that terrifies him.

A Balanced Approach to Children's Fears

Although it is important that parents and teachers take a child's fears seriously, it is equally important that they don't allow their lives to be governed by them. I have known parents who literally plan their entire day in advance so they avoid any situation that might cause their child to be even slightly anxious. Avoiding unnecessarily alarming situations makes sense, but changing the lives of all members of a family so a 4-year-old with autism isn't occasionally uncomfortable is unreasonable. It sometimes takes detective work to determine what it is about a situation that is upsetting to a child, but in most cases the problem can be found and rectified.

Coping with Specific Fears

One child disliked loud sounds, so he placed cotton in his ears when the family went to the shopping mall where there were a lot of people talking and loud music playing. He gradually removed the cotton for progressively longer periods until the noise no longer bothered him. Another young man feared attending a motion picture. In the past he occasionally felt the urge to leave the theater in the middle of a movie, and discovered that if he was seated in the middle of a long row of seats he felt trapped. The solution was to allow him to sit at the end of the row near the aisle. A boy with high-functioning autism feared going to the barber for a haircut. Starting several weeks before his appointment with the barber, his father helped desensitize him to the sound and feeling of the barber's razor. He bought an inexpensive electric barber razor and desensitized his son to the sound and vibrating sensation of the razor through a series of steps. Before each session he asked his son to select a treat that he would receive for cooperating. At first he had his son hold the razor when it was turned off. Next he turned the razor on and encouraged his son to briefly hold it. The following day the razor was turned on and held against the palm of his hand so he could feel it vibrate. The last step involved turning on the razor and running it up and down the back of his neck, which simulated how it would feel when the barber actually cut his hair.

Leave-Taking Requests

Children with strong fears can be helped by being taught to make a "stop" or "leave" request, which are called *leave-taking requests*. When confronted with a fear-provoking situation, such as riding an escalator, and the child is beginning to become upset, a parent or teacher can say, "Do you want to stop?" and the child is urged to say, "Stop, please" or hand the adult a card with a picture of a stop sign on it. Immediately when the child has requested to stop, the adult should honor the request for a minute or two. Once the child began to calm down, the adult continues, "When we get off the escalator you can have a treat" and points to an ice cream stand at the top of the escalator. It is best to step on the escalator when few other people surround the child. Ideally one adult should hold the child's hand and another stand behind him with their hands on his shoulders, making reassuring comments, such as, "What a brave boy" and "We're almost there." As soon as the child steps off the escalator, the promised reward should be provided. Typically 3–5 repetitions of this type are sufficient to overcome the child's fear.

A young man with autism had a history of severe self-injury when he was upset. He was very interested in animals, so the staff who worked with him took him to the zoo. As he approached one of the caged areas, he began to breathe very rapidly and deeply, and rocked from back to front. The staff member said, "Roger, would you like to leave?" Roger vigorously shook his head "yes," so they turned around and began to walk away from the area. Roger's agitation subsided. Subsequently, Roger was taught to use picture icons to communicate, which he carried with him in a communication wallet. One of the icons had the word *leave* printed on it with a photograph of Roger walking away from the camera. Once Roger learned to use icons to make requests, such as to leave a situation that was disturbing to him, his self-injury stopped.

Compulsive Rituals

Children with ASDs often engage in compulsive rituals that can drive teachers and parents to distraction. The type of ritualistic behavior varies to some degree with the child's cognitive level. Higher-functioning children collect and hoard objects, line up toys, repeatedly turn the TV on and off, and some very verbal children engage in repetitive verbal routines. Every morning when a 7-year-old boy with PPD-NOS arrived at school, he insisted on reading the nametags on each student's desk. At other times he read all of the words posted on his classroom's bulletin board. If he was interrupted he became very agitated and cried and then started over reading the names. Weather is a favorite topic for higher-functioning children. A young man who regularly used the computer printed out the National Weather Service's daily forecasts and kept copies in a notebook. When he had nothing else to do he paged through the weather forecasts, poring over them in great detail and commenting on the day's weather forecast. Children with the least cognitive skills often engage in ritualistic movements and routines such as twirling in circles, hand flapping, holding water or saliva in their mouth and spitting, tearing up pieces of paper, or picking pieces of thread from their clothing. A young nonverbal man with very limited skills whom I visited repeatedly picked at his sweater until he found a loose piece of yarn, and then unraveled the yarn until his sweater had been destroyed.

Limiting Ritual Times

As noted in Chapter 2, it is often possible to provide specific times during the day when higher-functioning people can engage in preferred rituals, and to limit their availability at other times. This strategy is more difficult to implement with nonverbal children who are less cognitively capable.

Medications for Compulsive Rituals

At times, children and youth with ASDs who have very severe compulsive rituals who have not been responsive to environmental interventions profit from medication. With children, the most widely used medicines are SSRIs, such as fluoxetine (Prozac), paroxetine (Paxil), sertraline (Zoloft), and citalopram (Celexa). With teenagers and young adults, some doctors prescribe clomipramine (Anafranil), which has more side effects.

MELTDOWNS AND TANTRUMS

The distinction between a meltdown and a tantrum, is, at times, in the eye of the beholder. In both cases the child has an emotional and behavioral outburst. The main difference is that in a tantrum, the child typically behaves aggressively or engages in property destruction. He or she may strike out at teachers or parents or throw objects, such as toys or other nearby objects. The child usually has an angry appearance. In older children who are verbal, they may shout obscenities or threats. A meltdown is a pure expression of anxiety and emotional distress. The child may scream, cry, sob, and flail his or her arms, but those actions are not directed at others. As a practical matter, a tantrum often ends up being a meltdown. The child's outburst may begin with striking out at others but transitions to sobbing and expressing great distress. The most common triggers for both types of outbursts are changes in routines from what the child expects. The change may involve providing a child with a different food at mealtime, switching the order of activities in school, or driving a different route to Grandma's house. Tantrums with aggression are most often precipitated by the disruption of a highly preferred self-stimulatory activity or other daily routine. The child usually appears frustrated and angry. He or she doesn't understand why the teacher has stopped him or her in the midst of twirling in circles or why his or her father turns off a video game. Meltdowns without aggression most often occur when the child is fearful of something, such as entering a classroom, encountering a dog while out for a walk, or hearing an ambulance or fire truck. Rational reassurance does little good to assuage the child's fears. Parents logically look for something in the immediate environment that is triggering an outburst, but the problem may be in the future. Because children with ASDs are usually ineffective in discussing future events, even those with reasonably good language skills are often incapable of explaining that they are concerned about going to the shopping mall after dinner, which may be 2 hours in the future.

AGGRESSION

Aggressive outbursts often occur for social reasons that may vary from child to child. The task is to identify the main reasons for a given child.

Caregiver Attention

The most common reason for aggressive outbursts is that they are very effective in demanding teachers' or parents' attention, which usually leads adults to try to figure out the source of the problem. The most common immediate trigger for aggressive outbursts is failure of the caregivers to provide a child with what he or she wants, often access to a highly preferred self-stimulatory activity, a food or beverage, or attention. Occasionally, a caregiver has changed a typical daily routine. The parents of a 4-year-old with high-functioning autism were puzzled about why their son was hitting and shoving his baby brother, often many times a day. The reason was fairly simple. Whenever he hit his brother or pushed him down, his brother cried and his mother or father came running to resolve the problem. His aggression was 100% effective in procuring his parents' attention. The solution was to help the boy learn another way to gain his parents' attention without hurting his brother.

Obtaining Access to Commodities or Activities

The other reason he behaved aggressively was that it was very effective in leading his mother to try to figure out what he wanted, such as a preferred food item from the refrigerator. The solution we suggested involved encouraging his mother to selectively pay attention to him at times when he was appropriately engaged in activities and ignoring minor aggressions that didn't involve a risk to his brother. The second step involved teaching him a communication system that he could use to more appropriately request help or attention. When both were in place, his aggression stopped.

Antecedent Behavior Consequence Charts to Identify Functions of Aggression

In each case, teachers and parents will nearly always find it helpful to conduct an ABC analysis of setting events predisposing to aggression (e.g., poor sleep), triggers (e.g., interrupting a preferred ritual), and consequences (e.g., "scolding" and paying attention to the child following the aggressive act). Some parents have said that their child should know better than to behave a certain way. Children with ASDs seldom assimilate such notions until they are much older, and even then, may have difficulty accepting their parents' or teachers' notions of appropriate behavior. Caregivers who contend that the child with an ASD "ought to know better" are in for a lot of frustration.

Barry: A Case of Excruciating Self-Injury

Barry was 23 years old when I first met him. He had a diagnosis of autistic disorder and moderate intellectual disability. One psychiatrist suspected that he may have a mood disorder, and a neurologist thought he may have a partial seizure disorder, but there was no confirmatory evidence indicating either diagnosis was correct.

When Barry first came into my office accompanied by two staff members holding his arms, he had a tightly twisted terry cloth towel between his teeth and tied behind his head so he was unable to bite himself. Despite his numerous scars where he had injured himself over many years, he was a good-looking young man. His previous caregivers described appalling instances of self-injury, including pulling out seven teeth with his fingers; biting off a piece of his lip; jamming pencils, pens, and other pointed objects into his chest; mashing his nose against his face with his hand until the cartilage broke, which produced profuse nosebleeds; and running and smashing his shoulders and head into concrete block walls. On one occasion he ran his head through a plate glass window in a furniture store apparently attempting to escape and suffered severe lacerations. Barry had been in and out of three large public state institutions, had been refused services by numerous residential treatment programs, and had made many visits to community hospital emergency departments for treatment of his SIB episodes. He had nearly annual hospitalizations in acute psychiatric units during especially excruciating self-injury episodes in which he was treated with high dosages of antipsychotic medications. Over the months following his hospitalization, the doses of antipsychotic drugs were gradually reduced and discontinued. Over many years he had been treated with numerous psychotherapeutic and seizure medications, which did not seem to help his self-injury. When we first began working with Barry, he had been in leather restraints 20 out of 24 hours per day for some time.

Barry moved into a house by himself with two staff members working under our supervision. We removed his leather restraints, which were never used again. Lithium (for hypothesized mood disorder) and chloral hydrate (for sedation) medications were discontinued. We were warned never to take Barry to the YMCA to go swimming or to a shopping mall or any other setting that was noisy. We were told he had a history of severely hurting himself in these settings. For the next 3 weeks, trained staff members took Barry into a wide variety of community settings to observe how he reacted. It was important to understand what caused him alarm, what seemed to interest him, and whether he enjoyed specific settings and activities. We used this period to conduct a very detailed ABC analysis.

We noticed that shortly before Barry showed signs of impending self-injury, he began hyperventilating and rocking back and forth from front to back. Barry had some speech, but because of his tongue injury and missing teeth, he was very difficult to understand when he spoke. On one occasion, Barry was in a shopping mall with two staff members when he appeared agitated and began hyperventilating and rocking. One staff member asked him, "Barry, would you like to leave?" He vigorously nodded "yes." As soon as they were headed for the exit, Barry began calming down and hyperventilation stopped. Over the next week, Barry was taught to use an "all done" manual sign (both hands with palms downward crossing in front of his body) to indicate when he wanted to leave. Over ensuing weeks, Barry visited the YMCA and went swimming (at 10 a.m. on a Tuesday morning when there were few people present), went to the zoo (again on a weekday morning when the zoo was largely empty), went shopping at a convenience store (which he loved, except the waiting in line), played Bocce Ball with some older men in a park, ate at McDonalds, and went to a pinball arcade (his favorite activity). In each instance, when the noise level became too great or too many strangers crowded near him, he became agitated and began hyperventilating and he signed that he wanted to leave. Staff honored his request immediately. Those were the triggers. Barry had social phobia and claustrophobia. He feared strangers being near him and being trapped and unable to leave. Once we understood situations that bothered him and honored his requests to leave by making a manual sign, most of his SIB stopped.

Because Barry had no communication system, we developed a pictorial icon system in which activities and rewards were shown in pictures. Photos were taken of him engaging in nearly every conceivable activity throughout his day from arising in the morning until climbing into bed at night. The photos were reduced in size and laminated between sheets of plastic and a Velcro tab was placed on the back. Each morning when Barry arose to get ready for work, he looked through the icons (there were ultimately 125) and selected those that represented his planned schedule activities for the day (e.g., eating breakfast, riding to work in the van, working, playing pinball at lunchtime, stopping in the park on the way home for a walk, helping make dinner, washing dishes, playing cards, taking a shower, making his lunch for the next day, having a bedtime snack, and going to bed). He removed the icons he planned to use from a large poster board and placed them on Velcro strips in order in his wallet, which represented his activity schedule for the day. When he was unable to articulate a word clearly, he pointed to an icon in his communication wallet and showed it to the person with whom he was attempting to communicate. The bottom icon was always "Leave, please."

Over the first 6 months of intervention, Barry learned to do his own laundry, vacuum his room, assist with meal preparation, make his own lunch for work, bathe and shave with an electric razor, and make his bed. His recreation–leisure schedule of community activities during evenings and weekends included more activities than most adults without disabilities, including exercising at the YMCA, playing Bocce Ball in the park, playing pinball in an arcade, and playing cards with friends. Three other young men with autism moved into his residence and became his roommates. All of Barry's psychotropic medications were gradually phased out except for Prozac. His SIB dropped sharply and then stopped and did not resume over a 14 year follow-up, with one exception when he developed a bladder infection. After the infection was treated, he had no further episodes of self-injury.

SELF-STIMULATION AND SELF-INJURY

Self-stimulation refers to nonfunctional movements that serve no other purpose than generating sensory feedback. Self-stimulatory behaviors are also called *stereotypies*. Common forms of self-stimulation include rocking, hand flapping, twirling, weaving the head from side to side, and holding up objects (e.g., pencil, long-handled spoon) and waving them back and forth while staring intently at them. All children engage in such stereotypic movements as babies, but by the time they begin developing language, the nonfunctional stereotypic movements are gradually replaced by communicative gestures and speech. No one knows for certain why children with ASDs frequently engage in pervasive stereotypic movements well beyond the age other children have stopped doing so. Shiny objects that twirl or swing are appealing sources of visual self-stimulation. The poet Lorine Niedecker wrote "There's a better shine / on the pendulum / than is on my hair / and many times / I've seen it there" (Niedecker, 2002, p. 1), which to a child with an ASD may provoke visual self-stimulation.

In children with more severe disabilities, such repetitive movements often gradually take on a different form. Instead of merely rocking back to front repeatedly, the child periodically hits his head against the crib or a wall as he rocks. In other cases, instead of repeatedly licking objects, the child begins to repeatedly press the object against his tongue and gums until they bleed. Flapping hands in the air gradually becomes flapping his hands so it strikes the side of his face. When a repetitive, nonfunctional movement occurs with sufficient intensity or frequency and is directed at a body part that it is capable of causing tissue damage, it is referred to as *self-injury*.

Self-injury is the most excruciating behavioral challenge parents of children with autism, their teachers, and doctors encounter. SIB is a repetitive, intentional act by the individual that may inflict tissue damage to him- or herself. SIB in autism is different from self-inflicted harm by individuals who have major mental disorders, such as schizophrenia, bipolar disorder, or borderline personality disorder. In the latter cases, the self-inflicted harm is usually infrequent (e.g., weekly, monthly), and it occurs during a psychotic episode (in schizophrenia or bipolar disorder) or a conscious ritual (e.g., self-cutting in borderline personality disorder). Among individuals with ASDs, SIB occurs daily and sometimes many times per day. On each occasion, the appearance of the self-injurious act may appear nearly identical to the last.

Self-Injurious Behavior Types

The most common SIBs in autism are head-hitting and self-biting. The child may strike his own face, arms, or legs with his or her hands or fists, or strike body parts against hard surfaces (e.g., the floor, walls, tables, door frames, bathroom fixtures). SIB may also involve self-biting, at times causing serious damage to fingers, wrists, or hands. A third type of SIB involves self-scratching or pinching causing abrasions, sores, or bruises, which can become infected if not treated and bandaged. It is not uncommon for individuals to poke or strike at their eyes, nose, or ears, which is particularly dangerous.

Health Problems

If the child has other health problems, such as an earache or toothache, it is important the source of the illness be identified and treated. A child who is in pain will be irritable and more easily trigger a bout of SIB. Children in preschool and kindergarten who engage in SIB can usually be helped by using the foregoing techniques alone, or in some cases, with minimal medication treatment. If a child is easily upset and has poor ability to self-calm once he or she loses control, sometimes the blood pressure medications Catapres or Tenormin can help reduce this overarousal.

Bouts of Self-Injurious Behavior

SIB occurs in bouts. An environmental event usually triggers the beginning of a bout of SIB, but once started, it may continue independently of what triggered the SIB. A bout may last a minute or less, with repeated face slaps, head hits, or attempts at self-biting, but at times may occur on and off over several hours. Factors that are associated with more severe SIB are low IQ and lack of communication skills (spoken or augmentative). Children with physical disabilities and frequent illnesses are also more prone to bouts of SIB (e.g., earaches, toothaches, GI problems). The combination of the inability to communicate, lack of basic skills, and irritability caused by physical illness are predisposing factors.

Social Functions of Self-Injurious Behavior

Over the course of my career, I have worked with scores of children and adults with self-injury, at times severely disfiguring. Between one half and two thirds of episodes of SIB are attempts to escape or avoid a situation (Kahng, Iwata, & Lewin, 2002). Many times it is a situation that a child finds intolerable. The most common trigger events are thwarting a preferred activity (e.g., watching a preferred video), a change in expected routine (e.g., giving the child pieces of fresh apple instead of ice cream), asking the child to do something he or she is unable to do (e.g., put on shoes), or asking the child to do something he or she doesn't understand or finds alarming (e.g., enter a room crowded with strangers). Adult caregivers, understandably, stop making the request in order to terminate the SIB episode, which teaches the child that SIB is an effective way of stopping adult demands. About one third of the time, children with ASDs who engage in SIB do so to produce adult caregiver attention (Kahng, Iwata, & Lewin, 2002). Naturally, parents, teachers, and therapists quickly intervene by restraining the child so he or she won't further harm him- or herself. That teaches the child that if he or she wants adult attention an effective way to obtain it is by hurting him- or herself.

Preventing Self-Injurious Behavior

The most effective treatment for SIB is to prevent it from happening in the first place. Parents and teachers occasionally scoff when I say this, but it is true. If one attempts to "treat" an instance of SIB after it has begun to occur, it is already too late. There are two reasons. First, once SIB has begun caregivers have no choice. They must attend to the behavior, which reinforces it and makes it more likely to occur in the future. Second, once a serious bout of SIB has been initiated it feeds on itself and continues largely independently of what is going on around the child. This appears to be an internal chemical response to the self-inflicted pain.

Preventing SIB requires determining what triggers the problem and teaching the child alternative skills that will achieve the same purpose. For example, a child needs to be able to make a request for what he or she wants rather than biting his or her hand until a caregiver figures out what he or she wants. If a caregiver asks a child to do something he or she doesn't know how to do, the child needs to be taught to ask for help. If giving attention to the target child's sibling or another student in the classroom triggers SIB, the child should be taught a legitimate method for requesting attention other than self-injuring.

Functional Behavioral Assessment for Self-Injurious Behavior

When a functional behavioral assessment is conducted, the majority of the time clear patterns emerge. Constipation, indigestion, and lack of sleep are among the most common setting events that lower the threshold for self-injury. Correcting these basic health problems is a prerequisite for implementing a behavioral intervention treatment plan. When the child's ABC chart is studied for 7 days, including at least 3 weekdays and one weekend day, usually other patterns are discovered. Six of the 10 severe instances of SIB over the past week were preceded by the parent asking the child to do something he or she didn't want to do, wasn't able to do, or involved stopping a preferred activity. And when the child self-injured, in each case his or her parent stopped making the demand, restrained him or her, and tried to comfort him or her. On four occasions, the parents were playing with his or her sibling and were ignoring him. When he or she began hitting him- or herself (not as severely as following demands), the parents turned to the child and said, "Stop! No hitting! Be nice, now" (or something similar). Overcoming the child's self-injury involves discovering which parental demands trigger SIB, and how to teach the child to make an alternative response instead of hurting him- or herself, such as asking for help. Teaching the child legitimate ways to ask to do the requested task after a delay can also reduce SIB. Differentially attending to the child prior to beginning to play with the sibling is likely to reduce jealousy-triggered SIB. In addition, parents might engineer opportunities to play games with both children and lavishly praise the child with SIB for his participation.

Medications for Self-Injurious Behavior

Antidepressant medications are not FDA approved for younger children, though some doctors prescribe them in off-label low doses. School-age children are more frequently treated with Prozac, Paxil, or one of the other SSRI antidepressants in dosages adjusted for their lower body weights (Kolevzon, Mathewson, & Hollander, 2006). Older children with severe self-injury may be treated with an atypical antipsychotic medication such as Risperdal (Zarcone et al., 2004) or Abilify (Hellings, 2002). Some physicians treat older children with antiepileptic medications that are also used for treating mood disorder, such as Tegretol or Depakote (Hellings, 2002). Children with ASDs who also meet the diagnostic criteria for ADHD may be treated with stimulants, such as Ritalin, Adderall, Concerta, or Focalin (Santosh, Baird, Pityaratstian, Tavare, & Gringras, 2006). With rare exceptions, these medications will not alone stop self-injury.

Between one third and one half of individuals with severe chronic self-injury are responsive to the opiate antagonist medication naltrexone which is sold under the trade name Revia (Sandman, Barron, & Coman, 1990; Thompson, Hackenberg, Cerutti, Baker, & Axtell, 1994). Individuals who have benefited from naltrexone have tended to engage in numerous episodes of SIB per day that most often involved hand or finger biting and/or head hitting. Again, a combination of behavioral intervention and naltrexone tends to be most beneficial (Symons, Fox, & Thompson, 1998).

SUMMARY

All children with ASDs exhibit behavioral challenges to some degree. The primary reasons parents and teachers seek professional assistance with their child or student is usually because of their disturbing, and, at times, alarming behavior. Although it may initially seem that a child's outburst occurs willy-nilly and for no apparent reason, from the child's perspective there is almost always a good reason. Graduated exposure to novel stimuli combined with increased motivation for tolerating them can overcome most intolerance to tastes, textures, or sounds that initially create a very negative response from the child. Tantrums involve destructive behavior and are more akin to aggressive outbursts. By their very nature, tantrums are coercive, leading parents or teachers to do whatever is necessary to end the outburst. This establishes a pattern in which the child uses the tantrums to solve problems rather than more appropriate communication methods. Sometimes tantrums and aggression occur because access to a highly preferred self-stimulatory activity or preferred food item is restricted. Limiting access to self-stimulatory materials while teaching the child more adaptive ways of requesting what he or she wants usually reduces outbursts. So-called meltdowns are usually an expression of anxiety or anguish at exposure to a frightening or otherwise disturbing situation. A child feels he or she has no control over the situation and has no other coping skills. Teaching a child to communicate needs and wants usually reduces meltdowns. In each case, discovering the functions of behavior can be greatly aided by conducting an ABC analysis (i.e., antecedent triggers, the exact nature of the behavior, and the consequence that usually follows).

9

Daily Freedoms and Responsibilities

Freedom is an abstract idea we often associate with Constitutional rights. But for children and youth with autism, the opportunity to make practical daily choices is often the most compelling form of freedom they experience. In this chapter, strategies for enabling young people with ASDs to gain the skills that make it possible to make such choices and participate more fully in a range of daily activities are examined. In addition, I explore how a concept of responsibility can be instilled in young people with ASDs through practical daily experiences.

DAILY LIVING SKILLS

A child who is able to eat with a spoon and fork has more choices at mealtimes. He or she can select food items that would otherwise be difficult or impossible to eat. Learning to select clothing and dressing appropriately for the weather or planned activity provides more choice and control over a wardrobe for a child with an ASD. Daily living skills are a portal to greater freedom, though young children with ASDs may not initially see it that way. They tend to interpret these daily living skill requests by their parents as additional demands that may be seen as unwelcome intrusions. Our job as parents and teachers is to help them develop important skills without causing undue distress in the process.

Mealtime

Of daily living skills, mealtime activities are usually the first and easiest to teach because there is a built-in reward. Teaching self-feeding to a child with an ASD is the same as any other toddler, except it requires more patience and planning. A 3-year-old child has recently been diagnosed with autism and his parents are wondering how to deal with mealtimes, which are a struggle. He has been a finicky eater since he began consuming solid food. He rejected some foods and seemed never to get enough of others. Though most typical 3-year-olds eat at least some of their food with a spoon, it is very common for children with ASDs of the same age to insist on eating finger foods. Some mealtime rules of thumb will prevent problems and help promote appropriate mealtime skills.

Rule 1: Eat with Your Child

It is important to model appropriate mealtime behavior. Children are less likely to perceive eating as being another chore if their parents sit with them when they eat their meals. Creating a regular routine and positive atmosphere reduces problems. Even if you are only having a cup of coffee and a piece of fruit or a cookie, you should sit with your child while he or she is eating and calmly make conversation. Make positive comments about what he or she is eating, such as, "Mmm, that tastes good" or "Beans are yummy." It assists in establishing mealtime as an enjoyable family experience.

Rule 2: Sit at the Dining Room or Kitchen Table to Eat

Do not allow your child to eat while standing or walking. I worked with an elementary school–age boy with autism several years ago who never sat during mealtime. Instead, he walked through his house in a circular pattern passing from room to room, and each time he walked through the kitchen where his parents and siblings were having dinner he grabbed a Pop-Tart from a kitchen cabinet and continued walking, eating as he walked. His parents permitted this behavior to avoid a tantrum. It is best to require the child be seated as soon as he or she is having meals with the family. If the child gets up and leaves the table, his or her food should be removed from the table until he or she returns and is seated. If the food becomes cold, it can usually be reheated in a microwave oven.

Rule 3: Frequently Vary the Appearance, Texture, and Taste of Foods that Are Offered

As soon as a child is diagnosed, begin varying the type of bread for sandwiches or the luncheon meat or cheese or fruits and vegetables at each meal. Offer at least three items from different food categories (i.e., meat, starch, vegetables, and fruit). Instead of always serving the same type of macaroni, offer your child multicolored macaroni alternating with typical white-colored macaroni. By varying food appearance, texture, and flavor from an early age, your child's tendency to accept only a single food item will be reduced.

Rule 4: Give Small Servings

Many children see what they perceive to be too much food on their dish and they push it away and refuse to eat. Spoon a tablespoon each of three items on your child's dish, place it in front of him or her and say cheerfully, "It's time to eat." If the child consumes everything on his or her dish, offer a choice of more. If he or she eats only one item and requests more of the same item, say, "Finish your lunch" pointing at the other items. Wait for a few minutes to see if he or she eats some of the other food. As soon as he or she does, offer a small amount of the requested item. Avoid giving your child more of a single item he or she has eaten when he or she is whining or crying.

Rule 5: Don't Coax, Plead, Beg, or Otherwise Try to Convince Your Child to Eat

In most cases, the more you coax, the more your child will resist. Children will eat when they are hungry. Even if your child only eats a small portion at one meal, by the next meal he or she will be hungrier and is likely to eat a larger portion. It is very rare for children with ASDs to be truly malnourished due to finicky eating. If you are concerned about nutrition, consult your child's nutritionist about adding vitamin or mineral supplements to his or her diet.

Rule 6: Avoid High-Calorie, Sweet Snacks Between Meals

Most commercial snack foods marketed for children are high in sugar, fat, and salt. Small cups of apple juice, small slices of a cooked vegetable that have been cooled (e.g., carrot, zucchini), gelatin cubes, or an orange segment are good snacks. Other healthy options are Fig Newtons, frozen fruit bars, frozen grapes, and raisins. Give your child a small portion for a snack, and then encourage him or her to resume another activity. Snacks shouldn't substitute for meals. Don't worry, your child isn't going to starve.

Eating with a Spoon

Offer your child something to eat that he or she especially likes that has a consistency thick and sticky enough to remain on a spoon but that can be easily scooped onto the spoon, such as applesauce. Hand him or her a child-sized spoon with a plastic grip that is easily grasped, and say, "Eat with your spoon" pointing at the applesauce in the dish. Orient the spoon correctly and place your hand over the child's hand and gently guide the spoon to the food, scooping up a small portion. As you bring the spoon toward his or her mouth, release your hand just before it reaches his or her mouth. Let him or her place the spoon in his or her mouth as you say, "Yum, that's good!" or a similar phrase. Wait until he or she has swallowed the applesauce. If you are fortunate, this procedure will work the first time you try, but children often resist, cry, or try to grab the dish of applesauce. If your child does so, push the dish across the table where it can't be reached and wait until the fussing stops. As soon as he or she stops protesting, place the applesauce in front of your child and repeat the procedure until he or she accepts your manual guidance. After successive repetitions, usually over several days, as you are guiding your child's hand toward his or her mouth, release your hand sooner (i.e., halfway to his or her mouth), and let him or her do the rest. Most children spill some food. Say something reassuring, such as, "That's okay. We'll get some more." With most 3–4-year-olds, within a week or so they are scooping the applesauce by themselves and bringing the spoon to their mouth.

Once this method has worked successfully over several occasions, have the child feed him- or herself using mashed potatoes or finely chopped meat or vegetables. The food needs to be in small enough pieces that it can be easily scooped on the spoon. On the first few occasions that meat or vegetables are consumed, mix a little bit of mashed potato in with the other food item so it sticks together and doesn't fall off the spoon. Many children become frustrated, spilling food and throwing their spoon or grabbing their dish. Simply move the dish away from them and say, "When you're ready, we'll have some more." Try to remain calm because if you become upset, your child will also become more upset. The child is likely to cry, scream, and try to do whatever is necessary to make you return the food. Wait until he or she stops the tirade, and as soon as this happens, return the dish of food.

At some point, many children will say, "I do it" or "Jimmy do it" referring to themselves. That is a good time to stop manual guidance. When a new type of food or the fork is introduced, manual guidance may be temporarily required; however, it is wise to encourage independence as soon as the child has the skill to feed him- or herself. Spilling food is usually self-limiting. Although spilling is likely to occur over the first few weeks, that gradually improves because the child wants to get the food into his or her mouth rather than seeing it drop on the table. Many children scream and cry when they drop food on the floor and insist they be given the food. Under no circumstance should the child be allowed to consume food that has dropped on the floor. It is unsanitary and can cause disease. It also teaches the child that it is safe to eat things off the floor.

Occasionally, younger children or those with coordination problems (e.g., some children with Asperger syndrome) have more difficulty managing typical spoons, bowls, and plates. Several companies sell adaptive or assistive eating utensils and dishes that make it easier for such children to negotiate scooping with their spoons, eating off of a plate, and drinking from a cup. Spoons with larger grips and plates or bowls with raised bumper edges can be purchased from numerous suppliers. Parents or teachers can consult with an occupational therapist who can evaluate the child's grip and motor coordination. After having done so, the therapist can advise parents on appropriate adaptive utensils and dishes.

Toothbrushing: A Daily Aggravation

Toothbrushing is a daily crisis for many families who have a child with an ASD. A mother of a 4-year-old told me she dreaded brushing her child's teeth more than any other daily activity. Her son cried, screamed, and fought the toothbrush. He clamped his mouth shut, turned his head sideways, and refused to cooperate. Another told me that her daughter "had a conniption" as soon as she saw her putting the toothpaste on the brush. But toothbrushing can become an accepted daily routine like any other activity if approached the right way.

Create a Daily Toothbrushing Routine

According to the American Dental Association (ADA), toothbrushing should be a regular, daily routine by the time a child is 2 years old, and by 6 or 7 children should be able to brush their own teeth twice a day with supervision (ADA, 2002). Children with ASDs are creatures of habit and are more likely to cooperate if toothbrushing is always done at the same time and if the same routine is followed. Brushing after breakfast and before bedtime are usually good times because they are invariable parts of every day's routine.

A Child's Perspective

If one considers toothbrushing from the child's vantage point, the activity makes no sense. Why would he or she put something in his or her mouth, move it around, and then spit it out? The only things the child puts in their mouth are food or beverages, which they swallow, or their thumb or pacifier, which they suck. Toothpaste doesn't taste like food and a toothbrush isn't like a pacifier. To the child, it is a weird activity that doesn't feel right, and we all know how children with ASDs react to things that don't feel right.

The Initial Goal

The initial goal is to help the child accept placing a toothbrush with a small amount of an appealing-flavored toothpaste in his or her mouth, swish it around, and then spit it out in the bathroom sink.

Use a Soft Toothbrush

Children who resist toothbrushing either dislike the feeling of the brush on their teeth and gums, or they dislike the taste of the toothpaste. Several companies manufacture soft or ultra-soft toothbrushes. The Amazing Products Store (http://www.pacwestserv.com/) sells ultra-soft toothbrushes and flavored toothpastes and gels for children. Soft toothbrushes have nylon bristles that are 0.007

inches in diameter or less. These bristles are hard enough to remove sticky plaque but are not so hard that they cause damage to the soft tissues of the gum. The Biotene Toothbrush SuperSoft with bristles that are 0.003 inches in diameter is even softer, mostly due to the toothbrush's narrower, more flexible bristles. All bristles should be end-rounded, which means that the toothbrush producer has run the bristle tips through a polishing machine to round the rough cut ends of the filaments. Some companies advertise their toothbrushes as being soft, but they aren't, so consumers must check with the company to make certain the bristles are under 0.007 inches (preferably smaller).

Use Flavored Toothpaste

For 2- to 3-year-old children, a pea-sized amount of toothpaste is sufficient. Flavored toothpastes are usually preferred over the stringent mint taste of most toothpastes. Although several toothpastes sold by the Amazing Products Store are mint-flavored, the company also offers strawberry, strawberry-banana, cherry, herbal bubblegum, and mango-flavored toothpastes or gels. The online store Breath Palette sells a variety of flavored toothpastes, such as fresh yogurt, monkey banana, kiwi fruit, strawberry, and blueberry, at least one of which is likely to be appealing to your child.

Reward Progress

Before beginning toothbrushing training, figure out how you are going to reward your child for cooperating. If your child has a favorite short video, allow him or her to watch it immediately after breakfast toothbrushing. In the evening, if he or she enjoys playing a specific game, plan to play the game as soon as the bedtime brushing routine is complete. If you are inconsistent, the procedure won't work.

Desensitize to Brushing

Begin by placing a very small amount of flavored toothpaste on your child's finger and encourage him or her to taste it by placing it in his or her mouth. Because your child has control over what is put in his or her own mouth, this tends to work better than if being placed there by a parent. Once the child discovers he or she likes the taste, the next step is to place a small amount on a child-sized soft bristle toothbrush, and allow your child to place the brush in his or her own mouth with manual guidance. Say, "Brush your teeth." Your child will usually suck or chew on the bristles. That is okay for now. This should be repeated for at least 3–4 days.

The next step is to manually guide your child's hand so the bristles brush lightly across his or her tongue once or twice. Encourage your child to spit out the toothpaste rather than swallowing it, but that is often difficult to manage with younger children with ASDs. Next, guide your child's hand so he or she feels the bristles brushing lightly once over the outside of upper teeth and lower teeth. If he or she resists, say, "Okay. We're almost done," and stop as soon as possible. Remember, always reward him or her immediately after he or she has spit out the toothpaste and wiped his or her face. Within a week or two, most children will tolerate brushing upper and lower teeth on the inside and outside surfaces. Over the next 2 weeks, gradually increase the length of time your child brushes, from 15 seconds to 30 seconds to 60 seconds, and so forth.

Fade to Normal Toothpaste

Parents may decide to continue using the exotically flavored toothpaste or eventually phase in the more conventional toothpastes, selecting one with the least flavoring. Specialty stores often sell mildly mint-flavored toothpastes that can be gradually mixed with one of the fruit-flavored toothpastes or gels and then phase out the exotic flavors to a standard flavor, which most children will accept over several weeks.

Encourage Self-Sufficiency

At some point, most children indicate that they want to brush their own teeth, and all you have to do as a parent is observe and assist with rinsing the toothbrush and making certain they have wiped the excess toothpaste off their face. Children should be able to brush alone by age 7.

Promote Hygiene

Do not allow your child to share her or his toothbrush with a sibling. Sharing a toothbrush can result in risk for transferring colds or other infections. Thoroughly rinse toothbrushes with a strong stream of tap water after brushing to remove any remaining toothpaste and debris. Store the brush in an upright position and allow the toothbrush to air-dry until used again. Do not cover toothbrushes or store them in closed containers. A moist environment, such as a closed container, is more likely to lead to the growth of microorganisms than the open air. Replace toothbrushes every few months. Some of the softer toothbrushes need to be replaced more frequently, especially if a child chews on the bristles during the first few weeks of learning to brush.

Toothbrushing Summary

Toothbrushing is one of those daily activities that can be an ongoing struggle or merely another predictable routine that your child accepts depending on how you approach the activity. By trying to understand your child's perspective, employing a soft toothbrush and flavored toothpaste, and desensitizing your child to the feeling or taste, most youngsters with ASDs become independent at brushing their teeth.

Toileting

Every family has their own unique terms relating to their children's toileting. Some say, "Going pee pee" others, "wee wee" and still others, "piddle." When referring to bowel movements, some parents say, "going poo" or "poopy." Whatever terms are most comfortable for parents, its is important that they decide what words they will use before beginning toilet training and stick with them so they are able to consistently communicate what they mean to the child with an ASD.

Bladder Training

Most parents begin with bladder training. Before beginning bladder training make sure your child is producing normal-smelling urine and shows no sign of discomfort when he or she urinates. Strong- or unusual-smelling urine or signs of pain when urinating may mean the child has a urinary tract infection or a mechanical problem with his or her urethra. Those will require that he or she be seen by a pediatrician. If he or she has been developing a diaper rash on and off or has urine of an unusual odor, have your child checked by a pediatrician before beginning bladder training.

When to Begin

Many children with ASDs start bladder training between 3 and 4 years of age, though some parents attempt earlier bladder training. Before introducing the toilet or potty, it helps if parents have an established daily routine. This way the new activity of using the potty can be inserted into your normal routine. Children are usually ready for bladder training when they have dry diapers for at least two hours, which usually occurs between 2 and 3 years of age. That means the youngster is able to store urine in the bladder, which empties automatically in younger children. Another sign your son or daughter might be ready for bladder training is his or her interest in seeing other people use the bathroom. If a child with an ASD wants to watch his brother or sister use the toilet and wants to be in the bathroom when his mother or father urinates that is also an indication he or she may be ready. One of the surest signs is that your child dislikes wearing wet diapers. He or she may try to pull them off when they are wet.

Equipment and Reward for Sitting on the Potty

Before beginning, make sure you have decided whether you are going to use a potty or a seat placed on the adult toilet. There are clear advantages of the potty. It is portable and less intimidating than climbing up onto the adult-sized toilet. Next, keep track of when your child wets his or her diaper by checking it every hour or two for several days. Most children urinate 15–30 minutes after drinking a glass of milk or juice or after eating a meal. Once you have a record of the most frequent times your child's diapers are wet, you are ready to begin. Check out a video from the library about bladder training. Show your child the video, and talk about what the child on the video is doing. Next, show the child the potty and have him or her sit on it. Reward the child for sitting, even for 15–30 seconds. Repeat this a few times and gradually lengthen the amount of time he or she sits. On each occasion tell him or her what a big boy or girl he or she is. Select a day when one parent can spend the entire day with the child and the child is in a good mood. Don't begin bladder training during a period when the child has a cold or has been fussy for several days. Wait until he or she is in good spirits and when one parent has time to devote to training the child to use the toilet.

Select Clothing and Practice Patience

Dress the child in elastic waistband pants, or if the weather is warm, let him or her wear pull-up diapers and no pants. When the child gets up in the morning, instead of changing the diaper, put on pull-up underpants and then go to breakfast. Give the child extra milk or juice during breakfast and encourage him or her to drink it. Between 5 and 10 minutes after breakfast, take the child into the bathroom and pull down the pull-up underpants. Say, "It's time to go potty" and seat him or her on the potty. Set a cooking timer for 5 minutes and say, "When the bell rings, you can get up and we'll have a treat." Look at the chart of the times the child has most often had wet pants over the previous 2–3 days. Repeat the above procedure, placing him or her on the potty chair 10–15 minutes before the next time he or she is likely to wet his or her pants. It safe to assume that any time the child is given a cup of juice over the course of the day, it is likely he or she will need to urinate shortly thereafter. By repeating this over the course of the day, it is likely the child will eventually urinate in the potty. When he or she does, praise him or her lavishly and provide a special treat, one that hasn't been previously offered. If the child cries, throws tantrums, or refuses to sit on the potty chair, walk away and say nothing. Wait for 15–30 minutes and repeat the "go potty" request. Occasionally, the child will repeatedly refuse, in which case it is usually better to discontinue that day's attempt and then to begin again the following day. It is best to avoid making bladder training a war of wills (i.e., forcing the child to sit on the chair while he or she screams and attempts to get off). That is nearly always counterproductive.

Coping with Resistance

Using the foregoing procedure, many children will be urinating in the potty at least intermittently by the end of a week. Over time you will learn what times your child seldom needs to urinate and eliminate those times from the potty schedule. If he or she cries, fusses, and insists on getting up from the potty, allow him or her to do so, but give him or her no attention. Pull up the pull-up underpants and walk away and say nothing. Scolding and coaxing generally backfire. Wait for 30–60 minutes and repeat the "go potty" request. In most instances, the child may fuss a little and then sit on the potty chair because he or she wants the treat.

Strive for Independence

Over the next few weeks, the child will likely show anticipatory signs of having to urinate by squirming, holding his or her genital area, and looking preoccupied. When you see these signs say, "It's time to go potty," and lead him or her to the potty chair. Most children walk to the potty chair, pull down their own underpants, and sit on the potty unassisted by this point. For children who are verbal, it is very common for them to begin saying *potty* during these anticipatory periods. Say, "Good boy. Let's go potty!" When this occurs, you're 90% of the way to the goal. Now it's only a matter of time until the child begins spontaneously saying, "Go potty," and runs off to the potty chair.

Bowel Training

Teaching children to have bowel movements in the potty or toilet is usually somewhat easier because the child has already learned to sit on the potty chair. For 3–4 days before beginning, provide your child with a high-fiber diet and adequate liquids. Don't give him or her too much apple juice, or his or her stools will be loose and watery, which is incompatible with bowel training. The child's stools should be well-formed but not hard with constipation. Each morning for a week when the child is awakened, take him or her to the bathroom, unfasten the diaper, and say, "Let's put the poop in the toilet."

Chart Bowel Movements

As with bladder training, for several days keep track of the times during the day when your child has bowel movements, usually 30 minutes or so after meals. Passing gas is a sign of an impending bowel movement. Your child may also suddenly sit very still, hunch over forward slightly, and become silent. He or she is likely to have a preoccupied expression on his or her face as a bowel movement is about to happen. Quickly take the child to the potty and say, "It's time to go poop." You are likely to be too late on the first few occasions as you are in the process of learning the signs that the child is about to have a bowel movement. But with patience, you will learn to predict the times your child is going to have a bowel movement. Don't require the child to sit for more than 5 minutes. It can help to read them a book, such as *Potty Time* by James Patterson (1993) or *The Potty Book for Boys* and *The Potty Book for Girls* by Capucilli and Stott (2000a, 2000b).

Reward Progress

Because they have had experience with a similar procedure for bladder training, most children catch on to using the potty or toilet for bowel movements more easily, unless they are having problems with loose stools or constipation. Use praise and tangible rewards, such as favorite treats, following using the toilet. *Potty Training Chart & Stickers by Potty Patty* and *Potty Training Chart & Stickers by Potty Scotty* (Parpia, 2007a, 2007b) can help with bladder training.

Hygiene

It is important to teach children to wipe properly after urinating and having a bowel movement. They should always wipe from front to back. This is particularly important with girls, in which wiping back to front can lead to bladder infections. After wiping, have the child stand on a stool in front of the sink and wash his or her hands. Liquid soaps are available with cartoon characters inside the bottles, which make washing hands more interesting. Parents may find *Toilet Training for Individuals with Autism and Related Disorders* by Maria Wheeler (1998) especially helpful.

Hand Washing and Bathing

Children with ASDs who resist bathing and washing their hands often do so for somewhat different reasons. Children who dislike hand washing usually have an aversion to the feeling of water on their hands. In some cases, they may have experienced water that has been too cold or too hot, but generally they simply dislike the feeling of water on their hands. The second reason is that they may have gotten shampoo or soap in their eyes when their hair was washed in the past.

Densensitizing to Water on the Hands

Overcoming a child's resistance to water involves desensitizing him or her to the feeling of water while making the experience enjoyable. One of the more effective strategies begins by spreading a heavy towel on the kitchen table, then placing a plastic bin or tub that holds 1–2 gallons of warm water. Place several plastic tub toys and a small bucket in the bin along with the water. Add a small amount of baby shampoo to the water so it creates a small amount of bubbles. Invite the child to sit on a booster chair at the table facing the bin, and begin pouring water from the small plastic bucket on top of the floating toys. Comment on how much fun that is. If the child has a sibling, invite the sibling to participate as well. When the child with an ASD sees how much fun it is, especially if his or her sibling is participating, he or she will often join in, at first very cautiously but often within a matter of minutes he or she will be actively engaged. After 15–20 minutes, say, "It's time to put the toys away," and take the floating toys and small bucket out of the bin and drying them on a towel. Then dry the child's hands and arms and remove them from the table and empty the large bin into the sink. Repeat this procedure for 2–3 evenings. On the next evening, run comfortably warm water in the bathroom sink and add a few squirts of baby shampoo into the water. Place the same floating toys and small bucket in the sink. Place a stepstool in front of the sink and encourage the child with an ASD to stand on the stool in front of the sink and play with the toys in the sink, pouring water and using the plastic toys for pretend play. After 15 minutes, say, "All done," drain the sink, and dry the child's hands and the toys. The following evening as you are running water in the sink, encourage the child to place his or her hands under the running water coming from the faucet before placing the toys in the sink. Most children will do so because they have become desensitized to putting their hands in the water. The next step is simply to ask him or her to put his or her hands under the running water, squirt liquid soap on his or her hands, and wash and rinse his or her hands. After doing so, the child is allowed to play with toys in the sink for a few minutes before drying his or her hands.

Bathing and Washing Hair

Having been desensitized to water on his or her hands and arms, teaching bathing is now much easier.

Bathing

Place the child's sibling in a bathtub that has been filled with 3–6 inches of warm water where he or she can splash and play with the same toys that were used in the sink. Have the child with an ASD kneel alongside the tub and encourage him or her to reach into the tub and play with the toys as before, but without getting into the tub. Dry the toys and the child's sibling as before and empty the tub. By the next evening, it should be possible to induce the child with an ASD to sit in the tub along with his or her sibling and play with the toys in the tub. At this point, the child with an ASD has become accustomed to being in the tub with water and finds the experience enjoyable.

Washing Hair

Children often resist bathing because it has been associated with washing their hair, which they usually dislike. They fear the feeling of water being poured over their head and may have had the experience of getting shampoo in their eyes, which often stings. After the child is seated in the tub, use the small plastic bucket in the tub to pour a very small amount of water over the back of his or her head, so it doesn't run down his or her face or get in his or her eyes. Use no shampoo at this point. Comment on how much fun it is. Do the same with his or her sibling. After successfully pouring small amounts of water over the child's head, say, "Shut your eyes," and then pour water (with no shampoo) over his or her entire head, so some runs down his or her face. Say, "Wow, that was fun!" and immediately dry his or her face so no water can run in his or her eyes. After the child has tolerated having water poured over his or her entire head, it's time to introduce shampoo. Several brands that produce little or no stinging if they get in the child's eyes are available. Johnson and Johnson's No More Tears baby shampoo has a balanced pH similar to the eyes' natural acid/base balance. Parents who are looking for more exotic shampoos may consider Mustela Bebe Foam Shampoo for Newborns or Bebe brand baby shampoo, which are more expensive, but will not sting when washing your child's hair. Make certain you dry the child's face immediately after rinsing to ensure that no soap remains that might get in his or her eyes. Although the child may fuss or resist slightly when you first rinse the shampoo from his or her hair, in most instances resistance will be minimal and will quickly dissipate. After the child's hair is washed, allow him or her to play and splash in the tub for several minutes before getting out. After he or she is out of the tub, dried, and in his or her pajamas, it's time for a treat. Repeating this regular routine for a week or two will usually make it possible for most children to bathe before bedtime without problems.

Video Modeling

For children who are extremely resistant to placing their hands in water, video modeling can be successful. In video modeling, a short video is shot of a sibling or adult displaying a specific response, then the child with an ASD is asked to reproduce that response. Video modeling has an advantage because the child isn't distracted by irrelevant nearby stimuli, permitting him or her to focus only on the specific response that is to be copied. Begin by teaching the child to reproduce other simple movements, such as driving a car across a table or placing a block in a box. Videotape the sample to be used to teach the child, and then edit so it is no longer than 5–8 seconds. It is a good idea to tape 3–4 examples of the same response (e.g., pushing a car across a table) so the child doesn't think there is only a single way to accomplish the task. After showing the video sample, say, "Do this" pointing to the video sample. After several repetitions, most children with ASDs will try to copy the videotaped sample (e.g., pushing a car across the table). Use a lot of praise and tangible reward, especially in the beginning. Expose the child to at least three different responses that he or she is supposed to copy before introducing placing hands in water (e.g., pushing a car, placing a block in a box, rubbing his or her hands together). Next, videotape an adult or sibling inserting his or her hands into a plastic tub with water and moving his or her hands around in the water. Place the video monitor on a table 3 feet or so from the child who is seated at a separate, child-sized table. Place a plastic bin on the table and pour a gallon or so of warm water in the bin. Seat the child at the table and then turn on the video of a parent or sibling inserting his or her hand into the same plastic but with water in it. Point to the video sample and say, "Do this." As soon as the child begins to place his or her hands in the tub of water say, "Great job!" and allow him or her to remove his or her hands. Repeat the video and ask him to "do this" again. After 3–4 repetitions, most children will copy the response shown on the video.

As an intermediate step to actually washing his or her hands, place the bin in the kitchen sink, set the video monitor on a nearby kitchen counter top far enough away so water won't splash on it, and have the child stand on a stool facing the bin in the sink. Play the same video sample, and say, "Do this" pointing to the video sample. When the child is successfully performing the task (i.e., placing his or her hands in the water while standing in front of the sink), it's time to show him or her a video of your hands in the water playing with a plastic toy or pouring water from a pail. Although he or she may not initially understand what is expected, by using gentle manual guidance it is likely he or she will catch on and begin playing with a plastic tub toy and pouring water in the tub, as shown on the video model. In most cases, children will immediately transfer this skill to the bathroom sink without further use of the video model. Have the child stand on a stool in front of the bathroom sink, fill the sink part way with water, and model what you want him or her to do (e.g., pour water from a small pail into the sink). If he or she does so, you are now ready to use the procedures described above to teach hand washing and bathing.

Overcoming Sleep Problems

Parent reports and clinical studies indicate that individuals with ASDs often have sleep problems. In one study, 64% of parents reported that their child had sleeping problems, and in another clinical study, 80–85% of children and youth with ASDs had trouble falling asleep or remaining asleep (Polimeni et. al., 2005; Schreck & Mulick, 2000). Not surprisingly, children with ASDs who sleep poorly also have daytime behavior problems.

Sleep Stages

When your child curls up under a favorite blanket with his or her head on a pillow that is scrunched just so it conforms to the shape of his or her head, falling asleep is a gradual process divided into two broad phases: rapid eye movement (REM) sleep, and non-REM sleep (Dan & Boyd, 2006; Fuller, Gooley, & Saper, 2006; Markov & Goldman, 2006). The first phase is non-REM sleep lasting about 80 minutes, and the second is REM sleep, lasting about 10 minutes. When children first close their eyes, they are drowsy and start dozing off but are easily aroused if their name is called quietly or they hear a sound outside their room. During the next stage, they breathe very regularly, make few movements, and are more difficult to arouse. Later, a loud sound may be required to awaken them, and some children may even need to be physically shaken to awaken. During the 10 minutes of REM sleep, eye muscles are moving rapidly and children are often dreaming. REM and non-REM sleep alternate in roughly 90-minute cycles throughout the night.

Parents report that most children with ASDs who have sleeping difficulties either have difficulty falling asleep (non-REM sleep) or they wake up during the night and can't fall asleep again. Problems with initially falling asleep can be due to medications being taken during the day or foods or beverages consumed, usually from around dinnertime to bedtime. Caffeinated drinks are also a problem for sleep (Erman, 2004). Coke and Mountain Dew contain large amounts of caffeine and should be avoided beginning in the mid-afternoon. Similarly, coffee, cappuccino, ice cream, and yogurt contain substantial amounts of caffeine, as do many chocolate candy products. Hot cocoa or hot chocolate contains smaller amounts of caffeine.

Over-the-counter medicines that contain caffeine can cause difficulty falling asleep, such as Anacin and Excedrin, and nasal spray decongestants should be avoided. Prescription medications such as Ritalin or Adderall and other stimulants, Prozac and related selective serotonin reuptake inhibitors (SSRIs), beta blockers (e.g., Tenormin, Inderal), and some steroids can prevent children from falling asleep (Morin, Jarvis, & Lynch, 2007).

Avoid Naps

Difficulty falling asleep can also be due to the child's daily schedule or behavioral factors. An average 2-year-old naps about 90 minutes during the day. A child who is 4–5 years old or older usually doesn't require a nap. Allowing an older child to regularly nap during the day will decrease his or her ability to fall asleep and remain asleep at night (Davis, Parker, & Montgomery, 2004).

Daily Routines

Children with ASDs respond favorably to regular routines and have difficulty when daily routines are unpredictable. All children need regular, specific bedtimes, but children with ASDs need a more regular schedule (Hoban, 2004). A dinner that includes foods high in glucose (e.g., baked potato, jasmine rice, white bread, Chinese or Japanese white rice) can promote sleep onset several hours later (Afaghi, O'Connor, & Chow 2007). Forty-five minutes to an hour before bedtime, the child should be bathed and begin settling for sleep. Large snacks should be avoided within 2 hours of bedtime, and those that are permitted should not include high-fat or spicy ingredients (e.g., pizza) that cause nighttime indigestion. After a child takes a bath and has pajamas on, he or she can be given a light snack consisting of a small beverage (4 ounces) or food that is high in tryptophan content, such as cottage cheese, cheese, soy milk, tofu, a chicken breast, an oatmeal cookie with milk, half of a slice of whole-wheat bread with peanut butter, or a 4-ounce glass of passion fruit juice. These foods will not cause a child to fall asleep, but they will prepare a child for falling asleep by making him or her relaxed and slightly sleepy.

Behavioral Factors

During the last 15–20 minutes or so before putting a child down for the night, read him or her an age-appropriate book or picture book, and if the child enjoys music, put on a CD with calming instrumental music (avoid prominent rhythms or loud music with lyrics). Encourage the child to sit quietly and look at the pictures in the book and relax. It is a great time for expressing warmth and affection. Once it is time for bed, turn down the volume on the TV in the other rooms, avoid loud conversations anywhere near the child's room, and turn off the rap music coming from his or her older brother's bedroom. In other words, keep things quiet for the first half-hour or so once the child has been put down for the night. When the child is placed in bed, make certain he or she has a favorite blanket and stuffed animal and turn on a CD of quiet, calming music that shuts itself off automatically after 15 minutes. To do this, plug the CD power cord into an inexpensive timer (purchased in an electronics or home supply store) that automatically shuts off a power source after a specified time. Turn on a nightlight, cover the child with a blanket, kiss him or her goodnight, turn off the light, and leave the room. The music will provide a transition cue beginning a minute or two before the bedroom light is turned off until 10–12 minutes after the light has been turned off.

Is He Afraid?

Many parents are convinced the reason their child is crying at bedtime is because he or she is terrified of being alone in the darkened bedroom, so the child coaxes and cajoles parents to sit alongside the bed talking with the child attempting to reassure him or her. Occasionally, children have general separation problems, including going to bed at night. Providing them with a favorite cuddly blanket or stuffed animal, reading a story, and then tucking them into bed with the cuddly item usually facilitates the transition. In most instances, however, children aren't really afraid, they prefer to stay up rather than go to bed. They employ whatever behavioral measures have been effective for them in past, from meltdowns to screaming to threats of self-injury (e.g., they may slap their face or bump their head against the headboard) to convince their parents to allow them to stay up rather than going to bed. Parental coaxing and cajoling will nearly always make matters worse. If the child fusses, cries, or calls for Mommy, it is best to ignore him or her. It is common for children with ASDs who strongly resist going to bed to cry for 30–45 minutes the first night. Occasionally, some children cry longer. This is extremely difficult for parents and siblings. It is important that parents agree before beginning this procedure that they will not allow their child to get up no matter how much he or she carries on. If one parent begins to feel he or she has to "give in" to the child, that parent should go for a walk or take the car out for a drive and allow the other parent to handle the situation. Parents need to support one another through this difficult and trying experience, and taking turns sitting through the child's crying is a good way to do that. In most instances, by the second night the child's crying is only one half to two thirds of the duration of the first night. By the fourth or fifth night, most children fuss a little and then fall asleep. Within 7–10 days most children fall asleep within a few minutes of turning off the light in their room. If parents go into the child's room "to make certain the child is really alright" in the midst of a crying outburst, even once, the whole cycle will resume and then the procedure will have to start over again, beginning with 45 minutes of crying or possibly longer.

Remaining Asleep: Nighttime Awakening

Many children with ASDs not only have problems falling asleep, but they often awaken during the night and have difficulty falling asleep again. Sometimes they play quietly in their bed until they become drowsy and fall asleep. One mother reported peeking in her son's bedroom late at night and seeing him rocking with his eyes closed for nearly 10 minutes then slumping to one side and resuming sleep. At other times children begin crying and screaming in the middle of the night until a parent comes to their room to see what is wrong, and they usually promptly stop crying. The problem from the child's vantage point is that he or she doesn't understand how long it will be until morning and he or she dislikes being alone in the room. Children with ASDs have little sense of time. They have no idea how long it will be until the next event happens, such as when their mother is going to come into their room and get them up for breakfast.

Awakening During Light Sleep Periods

During the first stage of each 90 minute cycle the child's sleep is light, and the slightest noise or discomfort is likely to awaken him or her. A dog barking next door, discomfort caused by sleeping in an awkward position, or indigestion may be sufficient to awaken the child. If a child falls asleep at 9 p.m., the next sleep cycle is likely to begin around 10:30 p.m. when he or she is especially likely to awaken. This happens repeatedly throughout the night, so a child will experience several light sleep periods per night when he or she is particularly likely to awaken.

Music Transition Cue to Fall Asleep Again

The main problem is not so much whether a child arouses briefly but how to help him or her to fall asleep again. Most typical children are able to fall asleep again on their own. Older children who have problems awakening can be taught to turn on the CD player that was used for initially falling asleep, which will provide the falling asleep cue that facilitates resuming sleep. Another aid is a Progression Wake-Up Clock sold by Hammacher and Schlemmer that can also be set to operate in reverse with gradually diminishing light and producing a distinctive scent and sound to transition the child into a relaxed slumber. Several nature sounds can be selected that become softer and turn off after 15 minutes. Either of these approaches will usually work, but the child needs to be taught how to turn the music or the clock on so the sequence begins. Most 4–6-year-old children can learn to do this with several repetitions.

Behavioral Approaches for Sleeping

Some therapists conduct falling asleep exercises with 3–6-year-olds to teach self-quieting. It is often difficult for children with ASDs to engage in pretend play, but some children enjoy playing with dolls or action figures, which can be a vehicle for "putting the baby to bed" exercises. Sleep preparation may be more effective if used in conjunction with one of the commercially available heartbeat musical CDs, such as that available from BabyGoto-Sleep.com, which superimposes calming children's songs on top of the rhythm of the human heartbeat. Controlled research has demonstrated the heartbeat–music combination effectively calms infants in nurseries and promotes restful sleep (Joyce, Keck, & Gerkensmeyer, 2001).

By practicing "putting the baby to bed" and then asking the child to lie down as well and listen to the CD, the music becomes a cue associated with falling asleep. Once the child has had 3–4 practice sessions preparing for naptime using the "putting the baby to bed" routine while listening to the CD, he or she can be asked to turn on the CD player when going to bed at night. After several repetitions demonstrating that he or she can turn on the CD player, the child can then be encouraged to push the button if awakened during the night. Though the music is very quiet, if parents are concerned about awakening a sibling who shares the same bedroom, under-the-pillow speakers are available so only the child with an ASD hears the music and heartbeat.

Relaxation Exercises

Older, high-functioning children can take advantage of relaxation therapy exercises similar to those used with typical children. Books and CDs are available from commercial distributors. A child who successfully sleeps through the night or awakens but does not cry or scream should be rewarded in the morning with a favorite treat for breakfast.

Sleep Medications

Most sleep medications are designed to encourage falling asleep but are not intended to maintain sleep throughout the night. A recent study by Dr. Giannotti and colleagues in Rome examined effectiveness of controlled-release melatonin for children with autism with chronic sleep disorders and found it effective with minimal side effects (Giannotti, Cortesi, Cerquiglini, & Bernabel, 2006). Atarax (hydroxyzine), an antihistamine, is often prescribed to promote sleep (in 0.5–2 mg doses) for children with ASDs, though it is not specifically recommended by the FDA for this purpose. Catapres (clonidine), a blood pressure medicine, has mild sedation as a side effect and is also used to assist with sleep. Occasionally, children may have other emotional or health problems that interfere with sleep, and an overall sleep-hygiene strategy may require targeted treatments for those conditions as well. After several months, many pediatricians taper or discontinue sleep medications for young children assuming they have established more regular sleep patterns. Occasionally, children may have other emotional or health problem that interfere with sleep, and an overall sleep-hygiene strategy may require targeted treatments for those conditions as well.

TEACHING RESPONSIBILITY

The Yiddish word *mensch* refers to a person of character, trustworthiness, and responsibility (Rosten, 1968, p. 237). We all strive to be worthy of that term, and from time to time we genuinely succeed. But that is a very high standard to set for most children with ASDs, though it is certainly a commendable goal. The extent to which children with ASDs are capable of understanding what it means to behave responsibly is generally different from that of their peers. When we say someone is responsible, we usually mean that person is accountable for something that is within his or her power or control. Legal meanings of responsibility incorporate the idea that the person has the capacity for moral decisions and implies the person is capable of rational thought and action. Though many individuals with ASDs have limitations in their ability to grasp the latter meaning of responsibility (i.e., capable of rational, moral decisions), they are nonetheless capable of learning to be reliable, accountable members of their families in much of their daily life.

When we say our child is responsible for his or her own room, we mean that he or she will keep it clean and tidy, put soiled clothing in the laundry basket, and make his or her own bed. If the child fails to do so, his or her parents may say he or she isn't taking the responsibility seriously. Similarly, if a typical teenager who is out with friends says, "I'll be home at 9 o'clock" but returns at 9:30 instead, we say he or she wasn't behaving responsibly. Often when a child demonstrates that he or she can be responsible, he or she is praised or is recognized in other positive ways. But more often, failure to do so produces negative sanctions, such as not being allowed to go out in the evening for a week. The child who doesn't miss a day of school over the course of the year is considered especially meritorious and is awarded a certificate for his or her responsibility by the school's principal at the end-of-the-year ceremony. More often, behaving responsibly in daily life yields no immediate rewards, though parents may relax rules when a youngster has been especially responsible, such as allowing a youngster to stay out later in the evening.

Daily and Weekly Chores

A good place to begin is to assign children age-appropriate tasks for which they are responsible. Encourage the child to do whatever he or she is capable of doing and don't to it for him or her. As soon as a child is able to wash or dress him- or herself, encourage him or her to do so. If he or she needs assistance learning specific steps, spend a few days teaching him or her to complete them with minimal prompts, and then leave it up to him or her. Many children with ASDs are capable of learning this type of responsibility through doing daily chores. Being responsible means doing your part like

Figure 9.1. Sister of a child with an autism spectrum disorder taking turns with baking tasks.

other members of your family. Add new things to the list as the child is able, such as making the bed, washing his or her own plate, or helping with cooking and baking (see Figure 9.1). Let him or her know (in a pleasant way) that everyone is expected to pull his or her weight in the family, and provide plenty of praise for any help you do receive.

Start Small and Provide Prompts

Opportunities for teaching children with ASDs to behave responsibly usually begins with doing household chores and completing homework and similar concrete tasks. But don't overwhelm a child with too many tasks. Take into consideration the child's ability and temperament and give him or her tasks at which he or she can be successful. Success and praise will motivate him or her to do more. Too many tasks can result in failure and undermine motivation. Simple daily activities, such as hanging up their coat in the closet and placing their boots on the mat by the door, can be the beginning of teaching responsibility. Because children with ASDs thrive on structure, it is usually fairly easy to teach them to carry out these chores if you begin with small steps. Younger children with ASDs usually require a visual schedule to prompt them through the sequence of activities they are expected to complete. By posting the visual schedule in a prominent place that is frequently seen, such as on the refrigerator door or on a bulletin board in the family room, the child sees the schedule each time he or she passes through the area.

Sharing Family Chores

Other responsibilities might include helping set the table for dinner or placing dishes in the dishwasher after dinner or taking out the trash. Try to provide the child with latitude about exactly how to perform the task. Too much guidance and too many corrections frustrate any child and especially one with an ASD who usually has very definite ideas about how he or she wants to carry out the chore. Rather than employing negative sanctions for failing to comply, it is usually more effective to build in reinforcement for completing tasks.

It is important that all children in a family have assigned chores, not just the child with an ASD. Some families place a chart in a prominent location that lists chores for each child that are crossed out when completed. As children grow older, the entire week's worth of tasks can be listed by day of the week. On Sundays, the children's mother or father assigns chores for the week by printing their names on the day and the chores for which they are responsible. In Figure 9.2, Ben, who has PDD-NOS, shares some of the chores with his typical brother, Mike, and sister, Sarah. Each day as they complete their chores they mark an *X* on completed tasks.

Not only does this teach Ben that he shares responsibilities with everyone else in the family, it also teaches that there is fairness in task assignments. Every child does the same tasks on different days, creating a sense of equity. That tends to make the child with an ASD see him- or herself as being like his or her siblings, and the converse is true as well. Parents periodically praise each child for doing an especially good job in completing one of the assigned chores as a means of conveying the importance they place on being responsible.

	Monday	Tuesday	Wednesday	Thursday	Friday	Saturday	Sunday
Feed Fluffy	**Ben**	Sarah	Mike	**Ben**	Sarah	Mike	**Ben**
Take out trash	Mike	**Ben**	Sarah	Mike	**Ben**	Sarah	Mike
Water the plants		Mike		Sarah		Mike	
Set the table	Sarah	Mike	**Ben**	**Ben**	Sarah	**Ben**	Sarah
Dishes in dishwasher	Mike	Sarah	Mike	Sarah	Mike	Sarah	**Ben**
Fold laundry						Mike	
Wash Fluffy's dish	**Ben**	Sarah		Mike		Mike	

Figure 9.2. Daily task schedule for Ben.

Planning and Doing What You Say

An integral part of responsibility is doing what you say you are going to do. That is called *say–do consistency.* Children with ASDs have language problems and difficulties dealing with future events, which make it difficult to make meaningful commitments and then follow through. Youngsters with ASDs are often unable to accurately anticipate when some future event will be.

Say–Do Consistency in Younger Children

Teaching say–do consistency begins with very short time intervals. For example, a child might say, "I'll put away my toys later," which has little meaning because it could be in a few minutes or next week. Children can be taught to say, "I'll put away my toys after (name a preferred activity)," in which a concrete activity or event fills in the blank. The time that the task is to be done can be indicated by the bell of a cooking timer. The child's mother says, "You need to put away your toys," and the child is taught to say, "I'll put away my toys when the bell rings" and is rewarded for doing so. Initially, the timer can be set at one minute, and the duration gradually increases to 30 minutes. A child may be asked to get ready for bed and may reply, "Can I get ready for bed as soon as the TV program is over?" The child's father replies, "Okay, but as soon as the show is over you need to get ready for bed." If the child does as he or she said he or she was going to do without fussing or resisting, he or she receives a special treat. As the child gains skill in doing what he or she said he or she is going to do at a future time, the time interval is lengthened. For example, after school a child's mother says, "When are you going to do your homework?" and the child replies, "After dinner." After dinner the child's mother says, "It's time to do your homework" and if he or she does so promptly, the child receives praise and a star on the weekly chores chart.

Adolescent Say–Do Consistency

By teenage years, say–do consistency often revolves around coming home on time and completing homework assignments. Though a child may be high functioning in many respects, he or she often lacks organizational skills. Helping the child plan how he or she will carry out his or her homework will reduce task avoidance and increase success. That may involve helping the child decide what materials he or she will need (e.g., notebook, ruler, pencil, eraser) and how to organize them so they will be where he or she needs them in order to successfully complete an assignment. With older children, that may involve helping them plan for and decide what book they need from the library or any special materials, such as construction paper, paste, or felt-tip pens that will be required.

Weekly Chore Chart Revisited

It may be difficult for some children with ASDs to plan ahead for more than a day at a time. They can be taught to write on their weekly chore chart (i.e., "to do" list) when a specific activity is to be completed. By providing them with a choice of day and time, they will be more likely to do what they say they will do. If they say they will complete a task on Friday and today is Monday, it is likely they will need to be reminded on Thursday to look at the schedule for Friday as a prompt that the promised task will be due the next day. If a child forgets a chore for which he or she is responsible, avoid chastising or making negative remarks, such as, "You're being irresponsible." It is better to rephrase the statement, "How are you going to be more responsible next time?" By guiding the child through the steps that went wrong and discussing what he or she can do next time, he or she will more likely do what he or she said he or she was going to do in the future.

ALLOWANCES AND BUDGETING

Some high-functioning youth with autism are given allowances by their parents, which provide practice with budgeting. Others earn money doing chores around the neighborhood, such as walking the neighbor's dog, shoveling snow, and raking leaves.

OVERCOMING RESISTANCE AND ACCEPTING ASSIGNED TASKS

A child with an ASD, like any other child, may object to a chore assigned to him or her. Before responding to the complaint, make certain the task is one he or she is capable of understanding and doing. Perhaps the child didn't completely understand what you asked him or her to do. The child may lack skills in carrying out a portion of a multistep task, in which case it may be necessary to teach him or her the missing step before expecting him or her to do the chore. William was asked to take the family's dog, Ginger, for a walk after school. He began to fuss and cry and said he wouldn't do so. His mother asked his older sister if she knew why William didn't want to take Ginger for a walk, and his sister explained that the last time he did so, a neighbor's dog growled and chased Ginger. The teacher asks Abbey to walk around the classroom and collect the students' spelling papers. Abbey looks around the classroom, slumps down in her seat, and begins to whimper. The task looks too overwhelming to her. The teacher says, "Abbey, you collect the papers in rows 1 and 2, and Sam will collect them from rows 3 and 4." Abbey gets up and begins collecting the children's spelling worksheets. Most of the time, when children with ASDs resist doing assigned tasks or chores it is because they aren't sure they know how to do the assigned task, they are afraid of some aspect of the task, something about the activity is inconsistent with one of their rigid rules or preferences, or it looks too large and daunting to them. Taking time to determine the source of a child's resistance is nearly always preferable to trying to force him or her to do the task.

ENCOURAGING SOCIAL RESPONSIBILITY

Children with ASDs often lack altruism. They don't implicitly take satisfaction in doing things for others. But many can learn to enjoy altruistic activities through a combination of modeling and practice. I worked with a teenage boy with high-functioning autism whose parents wanted him to learn that doing things for others was a worthwhile activity. In their own lives, they very generously donated their time through their church and other organizations to help less fortunate people. Their son joined them on some of these activities, at first reluctantly and then increasingly enjoying visits to nursing homes and interacting with elders. He said he wanted a job, so his mother arranged for him to work with an organization that delivered meals to older adults who were needy. He learned to take great satisfaction in delivering meals to elderly people who had few visitors and who, as a result, enjoyed chatting with him. They understood he was different from other boys his age and admired his generosity.

Charitable organizations often show photographs of children who are poor in far away lands that will directly profit from donations by American television viewers. They have learned that people are more likely to give generously if they know the actual person who will benefit. People with autism are similar; however, the most appropriate vehicles for expressing altruism involve activities making it possible to see the concrete consequences of their good deeds, not only a photograph of the person. During the holiday season, wrapping gifts for children who are poor and then delivering them in person can be an effective activity because a youngster with an ASD sees the excitement of the children when the packages arrive. Serving Thanksgiving dinner in a homeless shelter makes it very clear to a teenager with an ASD that specific people benefit from his or her altruism. As youngsters with ASDs have increasing experience with such acts of generosity, they should be encouraged to volunteer through their synagogue, YMCA, or other organization to assume additional responsibilities. Parents and teachers naturally praise youngsters who volunteer to help others, and often schools have special recognition events for children who have gone out of their way to make other people's lives better, which can be a terrific opportunity for a youngster with an ASD. It is wonderful to watch a youngster with an ASD rise and walk down the aisle of the school auditorium to receive a certificate of appreciation from the school principal in recognition of his or her selflessness. It conveys important messages, both for the young person receiving the recognition as well as all of his or her peers, who may often see him or her as only being different.

Although many children with ASDs don't appear to assimilate empathy into their own thinking and feeling, some do. An 8-year-old boy with high-functioning autism was finishing dinner at his grandmother's house. His grandmother placed the piece of pie on his dish. He stared at it for a moment and said, "No" and pushed it away. She assumed he didn't like apple pie and said, "Mickey, don't you like apple?" He replied, "Yes, but then Esther won't have any. Apple pie is her favorite." Esther was his sister seated nearby. His grandmother said, "Should we give half to Esther?" He nodded affirmatively and said, "Yes, give it to Esther." Mickey wasn't sure why his grandmother gave him such a big hug, but that was okay because Esther had apple pie, too.

MORAL AND LEGAL RESPONSIBILITY

Whether children with ASDs can be responsible in the legal sense is unclear. To be legally responsible, a person must have the capacity for moral decisions, and it implies the person is capable of rational thought and action. There is considerable evidence from neuroscience research that important brain areas involved in thinking, reasoning, and planning (frontal cortex) and in empathizing (amygdala and orbitofrontal cortex) are often dysfunctional in ASDs. There has been very little research on moral reasoning and judgment among individuals with ASDs. In tasks requiring the understanding of pretext, children with ASDs often fail to understand deception, or why another person would engage in deception. Grant, Boucher, Riggs, and Grayson (2005) compared the abilities of children with autism and matched controls to make moral judgments. Participants were presented with pairs of vignettes in which actions were either deliberate or accidental and caused injury to a person or damage to property. Participants were asked to judge which protagonist was naughtier and to verbally justify this judgment. The children with autism were as likely as controls to judge culpability on the basis of intentionality and to judge injury to persons as worse than damage to property. It is unclear, however, whether these judgments involved merely following rules they had been taught (e.g., it is bad to intentionally hurt someone), or whether the children actually empathized with the individuals who were harmed and grasped the longer-term consequences of that harm. Because children and youth with ASDs generally have impaired ability to clearly anticipate the consequences of various courses of action and to empathize with others, it is possible that having learned a rule, such as it's bad to hurt other people, may not mean the child understands the reasons behind the rule, which is basic to assigning moral responsibility.

Responsibility Summary

Taking responsibility for day-to-day concrete tasks and chores can be taught to many children with autism, which integrates them within their family and among their peers at school. As a result, they are seen as being more like others. It also prepares them for later vocational and residential options (i.e., taking responsibility for work and living space). Whether most people with ASDs are capable of learning to exercise more complex moral judgments is doubtful.

SUMMARY

When children enter kindergarten or first grade, teachers are more concerned about their ability to perform dialing tasks, such as eating appropriately, toileting, and washing their hands, than about whether they know the letters of the alphabet. Assisting a child with an ASD in learning these basic skills before entering school will prevent many problems later on and can permit teachers and other personnel to focus on academic, language, and social skills in school. A combination of careful planning, use of evidence-based procedures, and patience generally pays off in teaching children the necessary skills that are a foundation for later learning.

10

The Importance of Leisure

The anthropologist Margaret Mead wrote, "Leisure and the cultivation of human capacities are inextricably interdependent" (1967). But, to our detriment, we Americans have increasingly lost leisure and recreational skills. We often feel we don't have time for leisure activities with the multiple demands of our jobs and household and family responsibilities. But one in every four or five Americans finds time for sedentary pursuits. We hone our couch-potato skills by watching television, an escape from daily pressures. For some people, their most active pastime when not working or managing their family responsibilities involves sitting in front of their computer surfing the Web or answering e-mail. Fewer than 5% of us play board games or cards and only about 3% paint, draw, or take photographs. And just more than 3% of us entertain friends or relatives at home (U.S. Census Bureau, 2007). Too few of us go for walks on the beach or along the creek, and only one in four of us enjoy outdoor activities, such as hiking, playing sports, swimming, or engaging in other physical exercise, according to the CDC (2004). Compared with our European counterparts, Americans are recreationally challenged. It shouldn't be surprising that our children, including those with ASDs, are also lacking in leisure skills.

WHAT IS LEISURE?

Some people think of leisure as a way to spend time when there is nothing else to do. But leisure is much more than that.

Leisure Is an End in Itself

Leisure is the engagement in discretionary, enjoyable nonwork and nonschool activities, in which the following conditions are met: 1) the activity is freely chosen as one cannot be forced to engage in leisure activities; 2) the activity is experienced as enjoyable by the individual engaging in it; and 3) the activity is not simply a form of required maintenance work or as a way to meet basic needs; doing unpaid chores or getting a normal night's sleep are not leisure activities. There is a difference between *having leisure time* and *engaging in a leisure activity*. Leisure time may be filled with dysfunctional activities providing little enjoyment.

Most children with ASDs over 6 years of age spend approximately 6 hours at school and 8 hours sleeping and the rest of their time is devoted to daily living skills, play, and leisure activities, which averages about 10 hours per day of play and leisure with twice as much time on weekends. In this chapter I will discuss the reasons why leisure skills are so important and strategies for engaging youngsters with ASDs in constructive leisure activities.

LEISURE AND PLAY

Children devote much of their leisure time to play, but leisure activity is not necessarily always a form of play. Although most play involves expenditure of at least some effort and may often be imaginative, leisure can involve the absence of mental effort, and it often does. Leisure can be walking through a garden, wading through the surf on a beach, or collecting rocks and organizing them after returning home. Some theories suggest leisure consists of activities that meet needs not met at school, or, in adults, at work. When I'm feeling mentally exhausted, I enjoy visiting an art museum, strolling through galleries until I find a painting I find especially captivating. I sit down on a bench in front of the artwork for a half hour or so soaking up the image. I am engrossed in the colors, composition, and textures, pondering what the artist had in mind when creating the work. Nothing else enters my mind. When I get up to leave, I invariably feel refreshed. A child with an ASD who finds school especially socially demanding may need quiet time with a parent. A youngster with a high-functioning ASD may find the opportunity to go for a walk in a park or around a lake with his or her father and take photographs a very enjoyable leisure activity. Perhaps the child can learn how to download the images on a computer and select several to be printed and displayed in his or her room. The important aspect of such leisure activities is that they are enjoyable to the child and meet a need that would not otherwise be fulfilled.

LEISURE ACTIVITIES FOR CHILDREN WITH AUTISM SPECTRUM DISORDERS

Leisure activities for children with ASDs have specific characteristics that distinguish them from similar activities for other children or adults. In this section some of the key features of leisure activities for children with ASDs are examined.

Key Features of Leisure Activities for Children with Autism Spectrum Disorders

In their book *Developing Leisure-Time Skills for Persons with Autism,* Coyne, Nyberg, and Vandenburg (1998) outlined several important features of leisure activities for individuals with ASDs.

Leisure Activities Should Be Understandable

Leisure activities need to be clear and have predictable rules and well-defined beginning and end points. They often have a repetitive quality and involve steps that can be represented visually. They require minimal verbal instruction and are inherently structured.

Leisure Activities Should Be Reactive

Play activities for children with ASDs that provide sensory feedback are usually more appealing. Games such as Spirograph, Lacing Cards, View-Master, and Simon provide immediate feedback and are often engaging for children with ASDs. For higher-functioning children, collecting and sorting specimens or pasting pictures in albums by category can also be enjoyable.

Leisure Activities Should Be Comfortable

Activities that are challenging without being overly stimulating and are within the child's ability level are usually effective. Ideally, activities that have minimal demands for complex social interactions are better than those that require considerable use of language and follow social rules (e.g., Simon Says). Activities that provide an opportunity for a sense of mastery and control over materials are often more engaging to children with ASDs (e.g., completing a puzzle) than those that are open-ended or ambiguous.

Leisure Activities Should Be Active

Children with ASDs often have difficulties remaining seated and focusing their attention for long periods of time or waiting their turn while several other people take turns. For younger children or those with more cognitive limitations, games that involve physical activity, such as hiking, climbing, swinging, or swimming, are often suitable.

Leisure Activities Should Involve Visual–Spatial Organization

Activities that involve organizing, manipulating, and sorting objects into categories, fitting objects into places, or pasting objects into albums are often especially enjoyable.

DOWNTIME IS SELF-STIMULATION TIME

Leisure activities are especially important for children with ASDs because when left to their own devices for prolonged periods, they often revert to self-stimulatory activities or compulsive rituals.

Toys that Promote Self-Stimulation

For many, downtime becomes self-stimulation time. Video games and toys that produce repeated sounds or visual stimulation (e.g., Lite-Brite) can become forms of self-stimulation. Many children with ASDs are drawn to television remote controls, repeatedly switching between channels, or short segments of computer videos that can be repeatedly played, reversed, and replayed, sometimes dozens of times. Some parents mistakenly conclude that these actions reveal unusual intelligence, when, in fact, they indicate intense compulsiveness. These activities serve the same purpose for the child as flicking his or her fingers before his or her eyes or weaving his or her head from side to side. If left uninterrupted, such self-stimulatory activities may eventually consume most of a child's leisure time, and any attempt to interrupt this will trigger a tantrum. It is wise to limit access to self-stimulatory toys, even if a child insists on playing with them.

Self-Stimulation Can Become Self-Injury

For children with ASDs and more severe intellectual disabilities, there is a greater risk because they are less skilled at becoming involved in more appropriate leisure activities. I once observed a 4-year-old with autism seated with his eyes closed in front of a television that was blaring out the sound of a children's cartoon. He bounced against the sofa cushion repeatedly until he was redirected. His mother reported that he engaged in this type of stereotypical rocking throughout an entire half-hour television cartoon if allowed to do so. When interrupted, he cried and occasionally had tantrums. If allowed to continue, repetitive self-stimulatory activities of this type can gradually transform into self-injury, such as head-hitting or face-slapping, which can be extremely difficult to stop once it has become ingrained. The risk of that happening is greater among children with no speech and lower cognitive abilities. It is important to structure children's leisure time as much as other aspects of their day. That doesn't mean a youngster is required to do a specific activity during every waking moment but should have options of constructive leisure activities rather than being left to entertain him- or herself.

LEISURE ASSESSMENT: OVERCOMING NARROW INTERESTS AND EXPERIENCES

Narrow interests are a major factor limiting leisure activities in ASDs and usually correspond to limited leisure skills. A child cannot enjoy an activity if he or she doesn't know how to engage in that activity. Children often possess the ability to do some of the components making up a given leisure activity, such as climbing on monkey bars in the park or catching fireflies and placing them in a jar, but they may lack others. A youngster might very much enjoy a new activity if he or she developed more skills and competence in that activity, but until that happens, the child is likely to avoid participating. Planning leisure activities for children with ASDs begins with assessing their current interests and skills and attempting to assess their potential interest in activities with which they have limited experience (e.g., *Activity Assessment Manual*, 1990; *FACTR: Functional Assessment of Characteristics for Therapeutic Recreation*, 1988).

Self-Selected Leisure Preferences

As with all other children, youngsters with ASDs prefer some activities more than others, but in children on the spectrum, these preferences are often exaggerated. A good starting point involves exposing the student in school or child at home to a variety of leisure activity options in various settings: 1) indoors at home or school or 2) outdoors in the backyard, park, or playground. By providing opportunities for a child to participate in various activities when alone or with other children, you can also determine the likelihood that the activity will promote socialization. For each activity, you must identify the materials necessary (e.g., card game, box for collecting specimens) and keep track of the amount of time the child independently engages in the activity.

Leisure Activities Requiring Support

For some activities (e.g., playing with blocks), a child may require no assistance and may play independently. For others (e.g., using a Spirograph), a child may need assistance initiating an activity but once underway needs no further help.

Leisure Activities Requiring Learning New Skills

Finally, there may be activities in which a child is clearly interested but lacks the skills to engage in those pursuits (e.g., a board game). Once an inventory of self-selected indoor and outdoor activities has been obtained along with the degree of independence in each, it is helpful to observe the child's social engagement during those activities. Does he or she prefer to play alone or interact with peers or engage in cooperative play (e.g., imaginary play with dolls or cars)?

Consider Other Activities a Child Might Find Engaging But Has Never Experienced

New activities that are similar to self-selected activities provide a good starting point.

LEISURE ACTIVITY OPTIONS

Indoor Leisure Activities

Indoor Activities for Younger Children or Older Children with Limited Cognitive and Language Skills

There are a variety of leisure indoor activities for children with ASDs that vary with age and functioning level. Examples are listed in this section.

Megabloks

The Imagination Bucket contains 600 brightly colored construction blocks and pieces that are easily manipulated by small hands. These are definitely favorites of children with ASDs.

Coloring

Simple coloring books, including simple line drawings of familiar animals, buildings, and places, are preferred. Coloring books that include items that are divided in numerous small areas should be avoided. Crayons that can be easily held by younger children should be used. If a child has poor coordination, an occupational therapist can help with slip-on grips to slide over crayons to make them easier to hold (http://www.otideas.com/Items/PencilGrips.htm). School supply stores often sell these supplies as well.

Painting (or Fingerpainting for Younger Children)

Safe paints in a limited number of primary colors that can be poured into plastic cups or receptacles are preferable. Most hobby stores have kits that include paint and cups. Large sheets of heavy paper are preferred so they don't tear or wrinkle when pressed by the child's hands. Newspapers to place under the fingerpainting paper should be spread on the table. The child can wear a plastic apron to minimize concern about spilling paint on clothing. An old terrycloth towel should be kept nearby for messes. Some parents find it useful to place a plastic cloth on the floor beneath the table in case of spills.

Easy Board Games (2–3 Players)

My First Board Game consists of four simple board games for young children: The Colorful Peacock, Going to the Zoo, The Fire Brigade Game, and Farmyard Animals. The games progress in required skill level. No reading or number skills are required. The Very Hungry Caterpillar Game is based on the classic children's book. It challenges children to identify colors and shapes. Kids can play either cooperatively (a "winnerless" game) or competitively. Goose is Loose is a fabric board game especially suitable for younger children.

Easy Card Games (2–3 Players)

Go Fish, Crazy Eights, and Old Maid are good for younger children or older youngsters with more cognitive limitations. A parent teaches the basic rules to a child with an ASD. Once the child has learned to take turns and understands the rules, a sibling or peer can be included as well.

Puzzles (4–10 Pieces; Wooden or Cardboard)

Start with puzzles in which the shapes of entire animals or objects match with the pieces to place in the puzzle board. Puzzle pieces with handles are often easier for younger children to use. As a child masters puzzles at this level, begin using four-piece puzzles in which diagrams of each piece are printed within the appropriate place on the puzzle board so the child only has to match the piece in his or her hand with the place on the puzzle. The next step involves doing puzzles without the matching diagrams, usually 4–5 piece puzzles. As children gain more skill with these puzzles they can graduate to more complex puzzles. Puzzles are good to do because a child gains a sense of accomplishment after completing the puzzle.

Pretend Toy Activities

Preferred pretend activities involve toy people corresponding to family members and implied activities, such as farms, houses, doctors' offices, parks, or other venues the child is likely to encounter in real life. Activities that involve only things, such as vehicles (e.g., cars, trucks or tractors, airplanes, rocket ships) or buildings, are less desirable. Encouraging the child to play house with prompts to include various family members in his play can promote taking perspectives and conversing about each family member's actions. Before a routine doctor visit, it is a good idea to have a child pretend he or she is going to the doctor and talk through what people will be there and what will happen during the visit.

Indoor Activities for Older Children or High-Functioning 4–6 Year Olds

Ring Toss Games

Ring toss sets include 4–5 pegs with score numbers and colored rings. Each participating child "wins" points depending on the pin on which his or her rings land when tossed. It is a simple game requiring minimal language and entry-level perceptual motor skills.

Board Games (Up to 4 Players)

Magnetic board games, such as Magnetic Fun Board, consist of four magnetic games in one: Powder Pete magnetic drawing, Inch Worm maze, Tic-Tac-Toe, and Doodle Balls. Geomag Magnetic Challenge Game (magnetic sticks and a board in which to insert them), Snakes and Ladders fabric board game, and Chutes and Ladders can be enjoyable games for children who have learned to take turns.

Card Games (Up to 4 Players)

Animal Rummy, Hearts, and Crazy Eights for younger children in this age group and Rook for older children are often appropriate. The dinosaur card game includes several classic children's card games, including dinosaur matching (for younger children) and more advanced games for older children. The cards feature brightly colored images of dinosaurs that are appealing to children.

Doodle Pro (Fisher-Price)

Doodle Pro provides children with practice using a stylus to create images on a doodle pad, which can be easily erased to start a new drawing. Children can be taught to take turns making drawings, which promotes reciprocal play.

Little People Sets (Fisher-Price)

Little People Sets can be used to teach role playing and taking others' perspectives. Some can be structured so they have a specific sequence of steps, whereas others are intentionally unstructured to encourage creative play.

View-Master (Fisher-Price)

Using the View-Master can be a very popular activity for children with ASDs. It comes with a large variety of reels featuring different topics, such as story characters, popular cartoons, and marine and wildlife, and some include sound effects.

Making Collages

Children who have difficulty drawing or coloring within lines often enjoy creating collages, which requires less eye–hand coordination. Photographs of animals, people, or places can be cut out of magazines and fixed to construction paper with glue sticks to create interesting groups of images about specific topics (e.g., farm animals, things that fly in the sky, winter activities). Although collages need not be organized in any particular way, after a child has gained skills in pasting and placing images on paper, he or she can be encouraged to arrange photos in specific sequences like a cartoon that tells a story.

Painting with Brushes, Tempera

Older children with reasonably good eye–hand coordination may enjoy painting with tempera on heavy construction paper. Usually watercolor painting is too demanding for most children with ASDs, though some may graduate to watercolors after gaining experience with tempera.

Collecting Stamps, Stickers, Trading Cards, Leaves, Rocks

Collecting, sorting, organizing, and displaying items are among the most popular leisure activities for children with ASDs. This often begins with collecting stickers (e.g., cars, sports figures, story characters) or actual objects (e.g., leaves, rocks). In planning, collecting, and displaying items, parents need to provide the child with an appropriate photo album or series of small boxes into which the collected items can be stored. Children with ASDs may choose to categorize collected items very differently from they way adults may classify them, which is often an interesting way to gain insights into the way they see the world. Stamp collecting is usually limited to higher-functioning older children with Asperger syndrome or PDD-NOS.

Cooking and Meal Preparation with Adults

Cooking with adults serves multiple purposes, including promoting socialization and communication as well as gaining functional skills for everyday living. Meal preparation usually begins with sandwiches and beverages, such as spreading mayonnaise on bread and placing luncheon meat on top. Higher-functioning children who can read can participate by helping select recipes from children's cookbooks, gathering items needed for the recipe, and actually helping prepare the dish. This has the advantage of helping the child acquire executive function skills in planning, including making a shopping list, going to the store and selecting the items, and then actually preparing the meal. It is an especially good activity because there is a natural consequence: The child can enjoy eating or drinking what he or she has helped prepare.

Outdoor Activities and Places

Outdoor activities are often especially appealing to youngsters with ASDs because they involve gross motor activities and involve fewer language demands. Activities are arranged by age and cognitive skill level.

Outdoor Leisure Activities for Younger Children (4–7 Years Old) or Older Children (8 and Up) with Fewer Cognitive and Language Skills

Playground Play

Swinging, riding on Merry-Go-Rounds, and climbing on monkey bars are good, parallel free-play activities that place minimal social demands on a child. As children learn to play alongside siblings or peers, they can be taught to take turns, which helps them develop skills at reciprocal interactions.

Tetherball

In this activity a ball is suspended from a pole by a nylon rope. The ball is inflated and then hit back and forth by the child with an ASD and siblings or peers. Inexpensive sets can be purchased for $20. Professional sets can be much more costly but are unnecessary for younger children. Tetherball is a very good activity because it requires limited motor skills and implicitly requires taking turns. It can be exciting and very enjoyable for a younger child with an ASD.

Jumping Rope

A sibling and parent can swing a jump rope slowly while a child with an ASD jumps. This teaches perceptual motor coordination but may be too difficult for many younger children.

Trampolines

These bouncy surfaces come in different sizes and may come with handles that can be held to prevent falling off the trampoline. They are often a favorite activity for youngsters with ASDs. Trampolines require close parental monitoring for safety.

Swimming

Many children with ASDs don't like to submerge their head under water. Wading pools are often a good way to introduce swimming to children with ASDs. Discovering that splashing in the water, tossing a ball, squirting water on their siblings with an Airhead

Figure 10.1. Craig, who has an autism spectrum disorder (ASD), especially enjoys outdoor recreation activities like swimming. Though many youngsters are initially apprehensive about having their head under water, with gradual practice and encouragement, most children with ASDs enjoy water sports.

Aqua Zooka, and lying down on a float are enjoyable activities sets the stage for actually swimming (see Figure 10.1). Eventually most children discover, sometimes by accident, that getting their head wet can be fun, too. It is often easier for children with ASDs to participate in swimming lessons taught by a teacher experienced with students with disabilities than learning from their own parents. Swimming usually places minimal social demands on the child and is a healthy physical activity that can be enjoyed regardless of the season, at least in areas with YMCAs, JCCs, and other recreation centers. One mother said she loved how her son's self-esteem grew during their time at swimming lessons, and it allowed him to socialize with other kids at his lessons which only had a few kids.

Hiking

Walking along creeks, rivers, around lakes, and along wooded trails with parents and peers can be a terrific leisure activity for youngsters with ASDs starting at a very early age and extending into high school. A mom reported that the family enjoyed hiking at a regional park because the trails made it fairly easy to keep track of their son with an ASD and keep him safe and that only a few places were close to the water.

Before embarking on a hiking trip, prepare a list of supplies you will want to take with you, such as mosquito spray, sunscreen, cortisone ointment for itches, a cap or hat to ward off the hot sun's rays, a thermos filled with juice, several bottles of water, dried fruit for snacks, a child-sized backpack, heavy socks, and comfortable shoes with cleats. If you plan to do spring and fall hiking, bring gloves or mittens and a scarf. Above all, require that your child wear a whistle around his or her neck on a sturdy cord. Teach him or her how to blow the whistle in case he or she wanders off and isn't able to see you.

The activity can be made more enjoyable by reading a book to the child about things he or she is likely to encounter, such as frogs, snails, birds, wildflowers, leaves of various types of plants, rocks, and other collectables before going for the hike. Because children with ASDs enjoy organizing activities, collected specimens can be brought home for sorting into categories and for later discussions. Hiking is similar to a playground and swimming in that it is a minimally socially demanding activity but provides opportunities for talking and interacting along the trail. It is often a good idea to first expose your child with an ASD to hiking by trekking a relatively short (e.g., 1 mile) loop trail that returns to the same beginning point. Once your child is comfortable hiking for longer periods, trails requiring more skills that cover longer distances can be added.

Tee-Ball

Children with ASDs often have underdeveloped eye–hand coordination and may avoid sports activities. Tee-ball is a good activity that can be practiced at first with parents and siblings and later as part of an organized team with neighborhood peers. It not only develops motor skills but teaches following rules, taking turns, and coordinating activities with those of others, all important skills for children with ASDs to learn.

Riding a Tricycle or Scooter

Nearly all children with ASDs can master riding a tricycle, and some learn to ride a scooter by the time they are 4–5 years old. Both are good outdoor activities that encourage exercise and strengthen balance and motor skills. They also teach the need for following safety rules (e.g., wearing a helmet), staying on the sidewalk, stopping at the curb, and not riding too fast.

Figure 10.2. Ten-year-old Michael is playing Wiffle ball, which is an especially suitable activity for a boy with autism his age. Michael has good gross motor skills, but has less developed fine motor coordination required for many indoor games and activities.

Outdoor Leisure Activities for Older Children (8 Years and Older) with More Limited Skills or High-Functioning 4–7 Year Olds

Wiffle Ball

The Wiffle Ball was designed to take the place of baseball, stickball, and softball for boys and girls in backyards and playgrounds. It is made of a tough rubbery plastic and is lightweight and cannot be thrown or hit any great distance. It is a safe substitute for more demanding games, such as softball or badminton (see Figure 10.2).

Badminton

Badminton is a popular game among higher-functioning older children with good eye–hand coordination. The rackets are lightweight and less likely to hurt someone if they are inadvertently struck by the racket. The shuttlecocks are lightweight with rubbery heads that are entirely safe. Because of the drag on the plastic "feathers" at the rear of the shuttlecock, it rapidly slows when crossing the net, which makes it easier to hit than a table tennis ball, for example. My grandson Michael, who is 10 years old and has high-functioning autism, plays badminton with his older brother and sister and is able to comfortably hold his own.

Bowling

It is often a good idea to teach the basic idea and skill involved in bowling by using an indoor bowling game, such as Carrom Table Top BOWL-A-MANIA Game, that includes a hardboard play surface with printed color graphics and a durable polyurethane finish. The game includes 10 hardwood pins, an easy-to-use pin locator, and a score pad. After the child understands the goal of knocking down the pins and taking turns, a trip to the bowling alley with family exposes him or her to the actual game. Children's bowling balls (e.g., 6 pounds) can be purchased or rented.

Hiking

As noted above regarding younger children, hiking can be an excellent outdoor activity for youngsters with ASDs, especially verbal children who are interested in science and nature. Follow the same preparation procedures as with younger children, including safety considerations. Prior to a hiking trip, reading a book with the child about the area in which the hike is planned can create interest in and an expectation about what will be experienced. If you are planning to walk along a river with rock formations, a visit to the science museum focusing on exhibits about rocks and fossils before hiking will make the outing more enjoyable. Take a book out of the library about wildflowers in your area and common fauna (e.g., frogs, toads, lizards, birds, squirrels, chipmunks) and look at the pictures together. Tell the child that you are going to make a list of each animal the child sees during the hike. While you are hiking plan to stop every 20 minutes or so for a drink of water or juice and once an hour for a snack. You can use these breaks to talk about what your child has seen so far during the hike. Older children may be able to take photographs of things they find interesting on their outing, which can be downloaded on a computer and printed for a photo album. On returning from the hike, review the list of animals and see if you can find photographs in a nature book and discuss which ones the child saw on his or her hike. One successful hike begets another and another.

Gymnastics, Martial Arts, and Dance Lessons

Many children with ASDs find participating in these physical movement activities relaxing and preferable to leisure activities that involve more talking and socializing. Children who are especially tactilely defensive may initially resist martial arts classes, but they often come to enjoy them when they realize they are in control of the physical contact. All three of these activities improve motor coordination, which can be especially problematic for children with Asperger syndrome. In addition to classes at private schools, most YMCAs, YWCAs, JCCs, and other community youth organizations, as well as public schools offer after-school and weekend gymnastics, martial arts, and dance classes for young people.

Frisbee and Disc Golf

Foam Frisbees can be purchased for younger children, and as they gain skills throwing and catching these colorful plastic discs the firmer and heavier plastic versions can be used. For older children, evening Frisbee games using the Aerobie Skylighter or Nite Ize Flashflight can be especially enjoyable because these illuminated Frisbees appeal to the youngsters' visual orientation. Children who gain greater skills tossing Frisbees may enjoy disc golf, in which Frisbees are thrown into netted targets that are arranged around the backyard or in a park. Points are earned for each successful target entry. This is an advanced skill that may be too difficult for children under 8 or 9 years of age.

Miniature Golf

Miniature golf is another terrific family activity in which to include a child with an ASD. There are miniature golf courses in nearly every state in the United States and throughout the United Kingdom. Before taking your child with an ASD to a miniature golf course, it is wise to visit the site yourself to make certain the course is at an appropriate difficulty level. Some are professional courses used in national and international competitions that may be too difficult. A brief discussion with the course manager regarding your child may alert you to any times that would be more appropriate than others to visit to avoid crowds.

Therapeutic Horseback Riding

Horseback riding can be a wonderful activity for some children with ASDs. Horses are large and can be frightening to some children, but others are attracted to these graceful animals and express affection for them. Noreen, the mother of a 6-year-old girl with an ASD, said she found horseback riding very beneficial for her daughter. She gets to brush the horses and feed them. Horseback riding has also built her confidence. Just visiting the farm with all the cats, dogs, pigs, miniature horses, and so forth is an event in itself.

Riding can improve balance and coordination, increase motor skills, increase range of motion, and promote a positive outlook and sense of belonging. The rhythm of the horse's movements helps strengthen spine and pelvic muscles and improves posture and coordination. The unique relationship that often develops between a horse and rider can lead to an increase in self-confidence, patience, and self-esteem. There are nearly 100 Internet sites listing therapeutic horseback riding services for children with disabilities in the United States (see http://dmoz.org/Sports/Equestrian/Handicapped_and_Therapeutic_Riding/United_States/). Many of them accommodate children with ASDs. It is important that parents visit the facility before enrolling their child to make certain they are satisfied with the animal their child would be riding, the stable's hygiene and the horses' care, the qualifications of riding instructors, and assurances for the children's safety.

Bicycle Riding

Nearly all children can learn to ride bicycles (see Figure 10.3). The first step is safety, fitting the child with an appropriate and approved helmet and making certain the bicycle is in good working condition and is equipped with front and rear reflectors and an easily operated bell. For the latest information on helmet safety, check the Consumer Product Safety Commission web site (http://www.cpsc.gov/businfo/regsumbicyclehelmets.pdf). Most families start with small bikes with training wheels and have an adult hold his or her hand on the back of the rider's seat. As the child gains confidence, the adult releases his or her grip on the seat but keeps within distance so the bike can be stopped if necessary. It is best to practice riding in a vacant parking lot so you don't need to be concerned about your child careening off the sidewalk into the street. Once the child is able to pedal, balance, make turns, and brake on command, lessons can switch to the sidewalk near home. The training wheels are lifted slightly to provide some support and then

Figure 10.3 Elliot, who is 6 years old and attends a regular education class this year, takes great pride in having learned to ride a bicycle. While his ASD limits his language and some social skills, he excels at gross motor activities.

eventually are removed. A novel approach has been developed by an organization called Lose the Training Wheels™ that teaches bicycle riding using adapted bicycles taught within a summer camp format. By using adapted wheels, all children, even those with significant disabilities, can ride almost immediately. The adapted wheels are removed once the child is able to pedal, steer, and balance. Camps are offered throughout the country when a group of children who are seeking training has been constituted. (See http://www.losethetrainingwheels.org for further information.)

Family bicycling can be an enjoyable consequence of learning to ride a bicycle. Going for rides during evenings and on weekends provides exercise, an enjoyable outdoor experience, and an opportunity for socialization with family members and friends. Primary emphasis must be placed on choosing a bicycle pathway that is completely free of vehicular traffic and other risks, such as teenagers rapidly riding by on rollerblades or skateboards.

Backyard Camping

Backyard camping is an enjoyable family activity in which other children can join in after the first successful outing with parents and siblings. A day or two before setting up your tent, read the children a book about camping, such as *When We Go Camping* by Marriet Ruurs and Andrew Kiss (2004). Talk with your children about exactly what you will be doing, such as cooking dinner outdoors and sleeping in sleeping bags. Next you will need to assemble some supplies. Many camping stores sell inexpensive children's tents that instantly assemble, called pop-up tents. You don't have to stake them into the ground. Set up the tent on a Friday afternoon so the kids can play in it and feel comfortable inside the tent. Parents may want to set up an inflatable mattress inside the tent for comfort. If your children don't have sleeping bags, very inexpensive gear can be purchased at discount superstores. Next, purchase an inexpensive battery-operated lantern and a flashlight for each child. Set up a small charcoal cooker about 8 feet from the tent. Place paving tiles on the grass first and the charcoal cooker on top to avoid damaging the lawn.

Around 7 p.m., prepare a "hobo dinner" of some of your child's favorite vegetables and chopped pieces of precooked chicken breast with some chopped onion and wrap the food in foil. Place the wrapped food on the charcoal for a few minutes until the vegetables are cooked and the ingredients are warm but not too hot. Place the mixture in taco shells or tortilla wraps and serve. Some families prepare Sloppy Joes in the kitchen and reheat them on the campfire, which are served the same way. Milk or juice from the refrigerator can be served and dessert can be fresh fruit or gelatin pudding. Singing campfire songs (see http://www.scoutsongs.com/categories for suggestions) is always a favorite after-supper activity, and so is roasting marshmallows. Roasting marshmallows and making s'mores is an enjoyable activity for children, but great care must be taken to ensure the child isn't accidentally burned. Parents must explain safe behavior around the fire and provide constant supervision. If you have doubts about your child's ability to be safe near the fire, then exclude this activity from your outing.

If your neighborhood is an urban area and has few nature sounds, check out a nature CD from the library and play it to create outdoor ambiance for your backyard campsite. Suggest the children be very quiet and try to identify the sounds they hear as the sun is going down and night approaches. They may hear mourning doves, crickets, frogs, dogs, owls, or insects. Invite your child's favorite stuffed animal to join in your backyard campground, which your child with an ASD is likely to find reassuring, along with your child's blanket. As the night sky darkens, discuss what the children are seeing in the sky (e.g., moon, stars, planes) and search for patterns and imaginary pictures that the stars make in the sky. Because children with ASDs are very visually oriented, they are often quite good at recognizing constellations. If you are backyard camping in August, you may see the Perseid meteor showers, which a child with an ASD will find amazing.

When it's time for sleep, encourage the children to use the bathroom indoors and brush their teeth. Then help them into their sleeping bags and make certain each has a stuffed animal and blanket and give each a small flashlight. Be sure to collect all paper plates and leftover food and place in a closed rubbish container before turning in. You don't want to attract unwelcome visitors during the night. One last thing, zip the tent opening, otherwise your child with an ASD may wake up in the middle of the night snuggled up with the neighbor's cat, which may scare the daylights out of the child. It may take awhile for the children to fall asleep, so don't be surprised if you hear whispering well beyond their usual bedtime. If you are very lucky, the children will sleep the entire night without waking you up and asking to go indoors to their own beds. But even if they drag you out of your sleeping bag at 12:30 a.m. and want to go indoors, it's not the end of the world. Usually by the second or third backyard camping expedition their anxiety and excess excitement has dissipated, and it's pure fun. The more the child with an ASD is involved in helping plan for the next backyard camping "trip" the more he or she will enjoy it. For more ideas about backyard camping, see http://www.backyardcampout.org/.

Visiting a Friend's House

Helping your child feel comfortable spending time with his or her friends' families begins by visiting for short periods while adults chat over coffee and the children play nearby. After a few such visits, tell your child you're going to go home for a few minutes and to continue playing with Sheila (a friend) until you return to pick him or her up. If your child feels comfortable with Sheila's parent, staying away for 15–30 minutes should be long enough to determine whether your child is ready for a more extended stay without your presence. These play dates usually work better if a specific activity is planned, such as playing a preferred board or card game. Before the next daytime visit, tell your child in advance what game he or she and Sheila will be playing. Drop him or her off with Sheila's parent around 10 a.m. and say, "Okay, I'll see you after lunch," and leave. In most instances, the child will be happy to see you leave because that means he or she can play with Sheila without adult interference. Lunch is usually an enjoyable activity with a friend, which is a good end point for the visit.

If parents drop off their child during the evening before going out to dinner or to a movie, it could be a prelude to a sleepover. Bring along your child's pajamas and say, "Daddy and Mommy will pick you up before bedtime. Sheila's mom will help you with your pajamas so you won't have to change for bed when we get home." By staying out longer on subsequent occasions, most children will eventually feel sufficiently comfortable to fall asleep at their friend's house. The next step is a planned sleepover, which in most instances will be uneventful. This same strategy can be used with grandparents and other relatives, usually requiring fewer steps because the child is more familiar with them and generally feels safe with them. Making time spent with friends and relatives "work" depends on careful planning and providing an appropriate activity the child enjoys. Before going to Grandma's house, for example, ask the child what game or other activity he or she would like to play with Grandma. If your child is able to choose an appropriate activity, it is more likely the visit will go well because he or she has some say in what will happen after arriving at Grandma's house.

Going to a Children's Museum, Aquarium, or Planetarium

Taking a child with an ASD to a museum, aquarium, or planetarium can be made more successful with careful planning and preparing the child for what he or she will experience. Most museums have brochures and many provide online photos and diagrams of the museum and the setting. A good starting place is to convert some of the images into a visual schedule. For example, the first image might be a photo of the front steps of the museum. The next image might show people purchasing tickets. Print out images of 5–6 exhibits that you suspect may be interesting to your child (e.g., mummies, armor, decorative costumes, paintings). Lay them on a table and say, "We're going to the museum. What should we see first?" Give the child time to look at the pictures and to select the first he or she finds most interesting. Place them in the child's visual schedule album. Commend your child's effort and ask what else he or she should see. Encourage your child to select 3–6 images, depending on the child's age and verbal and intellectual ability. Place them sequentially in the schedule. Then say, "After the jewelry (the last exhibit), we'll have a snack" and point to the image of the museum restaurant and place that last in the visual schedule. This same strategy can be used at the aquarium, planetarium, library, or the zoo. The important ingredients that make the outing successful are 1) having clear expectations, 2) permitting the child to have a choice in what to do and see, and 3) converting those expectations and choices into a visual schedule.

As noted earlier, many museums aren't well suited to the interests of children with ASDs, but science museums and art museums increasingly provide special exhibit areas designed specifically for children. If you plan to take your child to a natural history museum, consider one that provides dioramas of precise depictions of geographical locations and anatomically correct mounting of specimens. These dioramas are windows into a world of animals, their behavior, and their habitats, which can be more captivating to young children. By encouraging the child to select which dioramas he or she wishes to see before leaving home, the child will be more likely to remain interested throughout the visit.

Aquariums are also good places to take children, but they pose challenges. The display rooms are often darkened, which may be disturbing to your child. Explain to the child in advance that the rooms will be darkened, and if possible download a photo of an aquarium exhibit showing a semidarkened room for the child to see. Comment on how much fun the aquarium will be. A second issue is that aquariums often have unusual odors that the child may dislike. By keeping the first visit short, if the child is bothered by the darkened rooms or odors, you can leave before the child becomes overly upset. Finally, some exhibits may be designed in ways that make it difficult to see the fish or other living specimens among coral, rocks, or underwater plants. It is best to avoid these exhibits because the child will be unable see anything interesting in them.

Planetariums can be terrific experiences for some older children, but others may become alarmed when the room darkens. Again, preparation can make all of the difference. Several days before the planetarium visit, take your child with an ASD outdoors on a clear, cloudless night and sit down in comfortable chairs and look at the moon and stars together. A night when the moon is nearly full is usually easier for the child because the moon's additional illumination on trees and nearby houses provides a visual frame of reference. If the child is old enough, show him or her a star chart of the constellations and select an easy one to identify and help the child find the star pattern. Usually the Big Dipper and Orion are easiest for most children to see. After 15–30 minutes or so of backyard stargazing, the child is less likely to be disturbed when the planetarium show begins and the room darkens. It is a good idea to select a short planetarium show, especially in the beginning. Sit near the exit so if problems arise it is easy to leave.

Going to the Zoo

As zoos have increasingly incorporated authentic terrains, seeing animals has become more difficult for children, especially those with ASDs. On a first visit to a large zoo, such as the San Diego Zoo or the Minnesota Zoo, it is wise to study the layout of the zoo before leaving home. Zoos often feature trails that can be walked or toured by monorail. It is often best to begin with the animal farm or petting zoo and perhaps two smaller areas featuring small- and medium-sized animals, such as lemurs, small cats, and foxes. The Minnesota Zoo features a raptor program in which hawks and other birds of prey fly over the visitors and land on a zookeeper's arm. Although this is a marvelous thing for older children to watch, seeing a hawk or falcon swoop overhead can be alarming to a child with an ASD and may be better to avoid. As with museum visits, preparing a visual schedule of the order in which animals will be seen can make the trip more enjoyable to your child with an ASD.

Going to Water Parks

Kammy, the mother of a 5-year-old, reports, "As a family, we take 3–4 trips to the Wisconsin Dells water parks per year. Elliott loves all the activity and practices so many valuable skills—turn taking, waiting in line patiently, observational learning (watching what kids do on certain equipment and practicing himself), and, of course, learning to use elevators appropriately." Another mother reports, "My child loves water places, especially the wave pool, and roller coasters—neither are a regular day outing, of course, but when we look for things to do as a family, plays, movies, and tent camping don't work from an interest or safety perspective." The larger theme parks with wider ranges of rides, particularly thrill rides, are often more difficult for children with ASDs. However, many theme parks classify rides as "thrill," "family," and "kids," which make it possible to plan in advance of a trip which rides are most appropriate for your child. Plan to take frequent breaks in quiet areas away from the noise.

Going to the Library

I often recommend to parents that a trip to the library is one of the best "first" community recreation or leisure outings for their children. It has several advantages: 1) It is quiet, 2) it is child friendly, 3) there is an opportunity for the child to choose a book or DVD to check out, 4) many libraries provide times when a librarian reads a book to a group of children gathered around seated on the floor, which is a nonthreatening social learning situation, and 5) the visit can be short, which prevents problems. On your first trip to the library, introduce your child to the librarian and explain to the librarian that your child has an ASD, and ask the librarian if he or she has any questions. Ask for suggestions for books or DVDs that might be especially appropriate.

Attending Sporting Events

Some children with ASDs find attending sporting events exciting even if they don't fully understand the game. Any sporting event that is expensive to attend should be avoided, however, because there is a good chance you may have to leave midway through the game. I never recommend taking a child with an ASD to a professional football, basketball, or hockey game. Although seats for the least desirable tickets can occasionally be purchased for \$5, many tickets for professional sports events can cost up to \$150 or more. High school games are usually ideal because the crowds are smaller, they are usually less noisy, the child is more likely to see familiar people at the game, and it costs little to attend. If your child becomes bored or overwhelmed midway through the game, leaving early is much less of a problem. Preparing for attending a sporting event involves the same steps as other activities but can be supplemented by watching a similar game on television, so the child has a realistic sense for what he or she will be experiencing.

SUMMARY

At the beginning of this chapter, I noted that Margaret Mead wrote that cultivation of human capacities and leisure are intertwined. For children with ASDs to lead rich and fulfilling lives, they must acquire skills in varied leisure activities, some isolated and others involving family members and peers. Beginning in early childhood, parents and teachers can play important roles in assessing interests and ways of extending the range of a child's leisure skills, including indoor and outdoor activities. Few children with ASDs achieve the skill level of Jason McElwain, the 17-year-old high school senior of the Greece Athena high school basketball team in Rochester, New York, who scored 20 points in 4 minutes to lead his team to victory in their season finale game (CBS News, 2006). But all children with ASDs can develop skills that enrich their lives and prepare them for a more independent and fulfilling adolescence and adulthood.

11

The Art of Living Together

Community Participation

Living together is an art that most of us learn as we are growing up with family, friends, classmates, and others in our communities. But attaining those skills is not an automatic process for children with ASDs. Most children with ASDs enjoy participating in community outings, going swimming, visiting the library, going to the zoo, or spending time at a friend's house but initially lack the skills to do so. Helping youngsters with ASDs learn the necessary skills to participate in their communities lays the foundation for a fuller and richer life that will extend into adulthood.

CHILD-FRIENDLY COMMUNITY SETTINGS

Many features of child-friendly community settings are the same for all young children, including those with ASDs.

- Child-friendly places are first and foremost safe. Parents need not be concerned about their child's physical or emotional well-being while in such settings.

- Child-friendly settings make allowances for children's physical size differences by providing appropriate furnishings (e.g., tables, chairs, booster seats), access steps or ramps, and surface coverings to prevent injuries.

- Child-friendly places are designed with children's interests and preferences in mind, providing the kinds of activities that are engaging to them.

- Child-friendly places understand that children are noisy and messy. They also take into consideration that children may be noisy and create messes for many adult settings, which is part of being a child. They may have sound attenuating ceilings or draperies to reduce the echo of children's voices, and use surfaces that are washable.

- Child-friendly places are welcoming. They make parents with young children feel welcome. There are several excellent resources for all parents on how to identify and access child friendly places: The Child Friendly Initiative (http://www.childfriendly.org), Kinder Start's Child Friendly Places (http://www.kinderstart.com/kfp.php), and Child Friendly Travel.com (http://www.childfriendlytravel.com).

But successful community participation by children with ASDs requires more careful planning than is involved in including typical children in the community. It requires identifying appropriate settings, preparing the people in those settings for your child, preparing your child for a particular setting, and planning for an appropriate length of each visit.

IDENTIFYING APPROPRIATE SETTINGS

Community situations must have certain physical properties to be conducive to effective participation by children with ASDs. Although each child's needs are somewhat different, the following are some of the most common features of supportive environments for children with ASDs. Not every child is equally impacted by a given factor, but they are considerations parents might weigh when planning community outings for their child. In the example shown in Figure 11.1, Melody's parents have listed eight places they are considering taking her for community activities. For each place, they have rated the degree to which that setting is appropriate or may present problems for Melody. They have rated each factor on a scale (1 = Unfavorable, 2 = Acceptable, and 3 = Preferable). Each

	Crowd	Sound	Lights	Temperature	Tempo	Appropriate activity	Fright	Structure	Wait	Depart	Total score	Rank
Friend's house	3	3	3	3	2	3	3	1	2	2	25	2
Children's museum	2	2	3	3	1	2	2	2	1	2	20	4
State fair	1	1	2	2	1	3	2	1	1	1	15	6
Restaurant	2	2	3	3	2	1	3	2	1	1	20	4
Library	3	3	3	3	2	2	3	3	2	3	27	1
Mall	1	1	2	2	1	2	2	1	1	2	15	6
Swimming	2	1	3	3	1	3	2	1	3	3	22	3
Zoo	1	2	3	2	1	3	1	2	2	2	19	5

Figure 11.1. Community outing options for Melody. Melody's parents have rated various possible places in the community that she might visit, according to factors described in the text (e.g. degree of crowding, sound level, etc.). For each factor, Melody's parents rate it as being Preferable (3), Acceptable (2), or Unfavorable (1). They add the numbers in each row to obtain a total score, and then the last column ranks each community setting from that with the highest score, "Going to the Library," which is most likely to be successful, to those with the lowest scores, "State Fair" and "Shopping Mall," which are likely to be least successful.

will be briefly discussed along with reasons they can be relevant to a child's success in the community.

Crowding

Most children with ASDs feel uncomfortable in crowds, especially groups of strangers. Situations that involve being jostled, pushed, or otherwise being in close proximity to strangers are the most troubling. Wedding receptions and other stand-up gatherings in which adults mill about chatting are usually problematic for children with ASDs. Similarly, entering the foyer of an athletic stadium or concert venue can be dreadful for many youngsters with autism because there are crowds of people elbowing one another, people are standing in crowded lines, and people are shouting nearby as they sell programs and concessions. Sounds resonate off hard surfaces creating an unwelcome cacophony. Some children with ASDs find a quiet corner in which to retreat when they are taken by the parents into such situations.

Sound Level

As noted in Chapter 9, there is some evidence that children with autism may be more sensitive to high-frequency, loud sounds than their typical peers. Situations in which music, announcements from loud speakers, whistles, and other unpredictable loud sounds, such as popping balloons, are often problematic for many children with ASDs. For example, youngsters with ASDs often like to attend the circus but may find the noise level intolerable. Some find it necessary to wear sound-dampening earplugs because of the annoying din.

Bright/Flashing Lights

Though usually less of a problem, some situations that involve bright blinking, flashing, or twirling lights are disturbing to children with ASDs. Some restaurants that specialize in children's birthday parties often feature twirling or blinking bright lights when a child's birthday is announced, which may be alarming to some children. Fairground midways are often areas with unpredictable, dazzling, bright, and twirling lights, for example on Ferris wheels, which may overwhelm many youngsters with ASDs.

Temperature

Children with ASDs are often troubled by hot, humid places, which can serve as settings for behavioral outbursts. Many families enjoy visiting a conservatory on a Sunday afternoon and taking in the exotic foliage and flowering plants. But doing so from June to August can be a mistake for many children with autism because some greenhouses may have temperatures exceeding 80 °F with high humidity. Feeling trapped among adults who are meandering slowly along winding paths with overhanging plants can precipitate panicky outbursts. It may be better to save visits to such places for cooler weather and at less crowded times.

Tempo

Some situations, such as a backyard picnic, are low-key, slow-paced, and leisurely. Others are frenetic, such as going on a series of rides at a carnival. As a general rule of thumb, children with ASDs do poorly in high-tempo, hectic situations. They cannot process information rapidly enough to cope with changing events going on around them, and they quickly feel overwhelmed. They usually prefer fewer highly stimulating activities and at a slower pace. If parents are considering sports activities for their children, they might consider tee-ball, Wiffle ball, miniature golf, or hiking (see Figure 11.2). Basketball and soccer are great sports, but they are fast-paced and involve a lot of shouting and body contact, which are often difficult for youngsters with ASDs to tolerate. Children with ASDs may try valiantly to participate in such athletic activities, and even enjoy the idea of playing soccer, but once on the field they quickly feel besieged.

Appropriate Activities

Some situations provide few, if any, age-appropriate activities geared for the cognitive level and emotional characteristics of a child with autism. Although most children's museums and science museums provide engaging activities for youngsters, many other exhibition settings offer few such opportunities. Art, archeology, and natural history museums may not interest many children with autism, whereas a planetarium or aquarium may captivate them. Some art museums have special sections set aside for children with opportunities for painting and creating constructions that are based on current exhibits, which can be very enjoyable for many youngsters with ASDs. Each setting has to be evaluated to determine whether those features are available.

Frightening Features

Some situations are inherently frightening to children: disappearing escalators, horror films, ferocious zoo animals, loud vehicles (e.g., at auto races), roller coasters, the roar of a jet plane taking off, or the sound of ocean surf. Occasionally, parents plan to take their typical children on an outing, such as a snowmobile ride, but that is often a mistake for a child with autism who may find the roar of the snowmobile engine alarming. When visiting the zoo, start by visiting areas with small mammals (e.g., otters, foxes, small primates), birds, reptiles (e.g., snakes), and amphibians (e.g., frogs, salamanders). If the child tolerates a visit to smaller zoo animals, try visiting intermediate-sized animals, such as wolves, goats, or wallabies on the next visit. Only after enjoying seeing intermediate-sized animals is it wise to expose the child to the large predators, elephants, and giraffes.

Degree of Structure

Some activities are naturally structured, such as playing checkers or having lunch at a fast-food restaurant; however, many other situations are unstructured. Wandering from room to room in a museum, driving to a vacation spot in the family automobile, or going on a shopping trip to the mall are all unstructured from the child's perspective. There is a beginning, but there is no clear middle or end. There may be numerous starts and stops along the way; however, the child can't tell when this interminable series of events will come to an end. Unstructured situations are confusing to most children with ASDs, and may lead to challenging behavior. If one must involve a child with an ASD in such activities, the use of visual schedules indicating, in advance, specific sub-steps along the way that are visually represented may make these unstructured situations more tolerable. In choosing settings for community outings, parents are encouraged to begin with those that provide more structure. Alternatively, parents can impose structure by telling the child in advance which three areas of the children's museum they will visit before stopping for lunch and a treat.

Waiting

Waiting in line is nearly always difficult for children with ASDs. Families often research which stores, restaurants, and other places have long lines. They avoid those with the longest lines, or if they are unavoidable, they go at hours when queues will be the shortest. Planning ahead can help. A family decided to visit Disney World on spring break. After parking their car, they approached the entry gate and realized there were 15–20 people in line ahead of them. That meant their daughter with PDD-NOS was going to have to wait 10–20 minutes in the hot sun before she could enter the entertainment area. Before leaving home it is important to tell the child that there will be a line at the site and that he or she will have to wait to get into the park. That helps prepare him or her. Older children who are more cognitively capable often enjoy playing a handheld electronic game while they are waiting. For other children, before leaving the hotel an apple (or pear) and an orange (or tangerine) can be cut up into bite-sized pieces and placed in a plastic sandwich bag. The fruit pieces are mixed so the juice from the orange or tangerine comes in contact with the apple or pear, which will keep them from turning brown. As every third or fourth person ahead of the family in line passes through the gate, a parent can say, "You're doing a great job waiting," and give the child a piece of fruit and say, "Just a few more minutes." When selecting places for community outings, it is worth deciding in advance whether the wait in line is worth it. Many parents decide that if it involves a long wait, it isn't worth the resulting outburst from their child with an ASD.

Easy Departure

Before leaving on an outing, it is helpful that you consider how you will depart from the venue expeditiously if it is necessary. In other words, what is your exit strategy? Many children with ASDs find themselves in situations that seem intolerable, and they begin to have a meltdown. They begin crying and become increasingly distraught. Parents know from experience that if they don't leave shortly, it is likely a full-blown outburst will ensue. Leaving a fast-food restaurant is usually easy, but leaving in the middle of a movie when accompanied by the child's brother and sister is much more difficult. If the child's siblings are too young to remain in the theater without an older person in attendance, a teenage neighbor or an adult friend can be invited along to the movie and can remain behind with siblings if the child has to leave. By identifying places that can be left easily if necessary, parents avoid the painful experience of having to carry their child, kicking and screaming through a crowded theater, museum, or restaurant to make their exit.

PREPARING PEOPLE IN THE SETTING FOR YOUR CHILD

Some parents of high-functioning children with ASDs prefer that their child's disability status not be known to people in the surrounding community to avoid being stigmatized. Although there may be advantages to that approach, often neighbors, recreation center staff, and others realize the youngster is different, but may not say so to the child's parents. They may speculate among themselves as to "what is wrong with the child," but never tell you. But when a problem later erupts while the child is in the community, parents may discover that those in the community misunderstood or misinterpreted the nature of the child's disability, which can create problems. Generally, the greater the awareness of those in the surrounding community who frequently interact with your child and are aware of your child's strengths and weaknesses, the better it is for your child.

Securing Community Support

Children with ASDs who are entering new community settings require understanding and support from people in that environment in order to be successful. It is helpful if friends, neighbors, librarians, and staff at the nearby recreation center who regularly interact with your child are prepared for his or her characteristics and behavior. Many people outside of human services settings may have never encountered a child with autism, and often what they have read in magazines or have seen on television doesn't adequately prepare them to assist your student or child in succeeding. A good place to begin is by preparing a brief introduction to your child that can be shared with people in the community who are most likely to interact with your child. Include a photograph of your child and a description about ways in which he or she is like typical children, and some things people may notice that may look unusual. A short explanation of the reasons he or she does odd things will help people in your community more correctly interpret your child's behavior:

This is our son Blake. He's 5 years old and is in kindergarten. Blake has autism, which makes him a little different from most kids his age. Autism is a brain development disorder that affects language and how children interact with people. He likes the usual things other kids enjoy, like playing video games, playing catch with his dad, and building Legos with his brother. You will notice some differences in Blake, too. He doesn't talk very much. He understands a lot of what people say to him, but it takes longer for him to react to a question, so you may think he isn't paying attention, but he usually is. If you are patient and repeat your question, he usually answers. He seldom looks at strangers' faces, but after he gets to know you he may do so. He doesn't mean to be rude. It's just that he finds people's faces confusing.

Blake does some things that may look odd to you. When he is excited, sometimes he flaps his hands or makes screeching sounds. That just means he's thrilled about something. Blake has very definite ideas about the way he does things. He expects everything will always be done exactly the same way. If there is a change in routine he becomes upset easily and may cry. It's not the end of the world, but sometimes he acts as though it is. He can't help it. It is just part of autism. Occasionally he has meltdowns. He just loses it, crying and carrying on as though something awful has happened. He's usually upset because something he expected to happen didn't happen the way he thought it should. He may cry for awhile, but he'll get over it. Blake functions best if you are consistent in the way you interact with him. If you follow pretty much the same routine each time you see him, he will know what to expect and act appropriately and is less likely to have problems. If you say his name first when addressing him, and then ask your question, or ask him to do something, he is likely to react appropriately. For example, "Blake, would you like a treat?" or "Blake, put this on the table, please." He has trouble understanding long sentences, so keeping it short and to the point helps. Raising your voice doesn't help, and it might scare him, so that's not a good idea. Thanks so much for helping Blake. We really appreciate your assistance. If you have questions, call us at (123) 456-7890 or rebbecaj19@eNet.Com. We live at 9876 Oak Lane, Middletown.

Sincerely,

Becky and Rob Jacobsen

Transactional Supports

A "sink or swim" approach to involving your child in community activities is unlikely to be successful. If your child is abruptly introduced into many community settings, he or she may sink rather than swim. People in the community need to help him or her learn how to negotiate his or her way through the maze of confusing and, at times, frightening situations he or she will encounter. Some key members of the community need to be identified who are willing to play a supportive role in the way they interact with your child. In the SCERTS® model (Prizant, Wetherby, Rubin, Laurent, & Rydell, 2005a, 2005b) of intervention for children with ASDs, adjustments made in the way people interact with a child with autism that promote his or her independence and competence are called *transactional supports*. This implies that those surrounding the child must interact differently with him or her in order to make his or her community adjustment more successful. It also means that activities must be designed, and in a sense, engineered to maximize the chances of the child's successful interaction with his or her environment.

Communicative Intent

Helping those who interact with your child focus on what he or she intended to communicate, not just the specific words he or she used, can be especially helpful. If 9-year-old Lisa is asked what she did at school, she may reply, "Penguins have feathers." She is attempting to respond to the question by telling the speaker something she learned in school. At times children with ASDs respond with delayed echolalia to questions because they can't recall the correct words necessary to respond appropriately. Among the more common responses are television ads and song lyrics. Kyle is asked what he did at Scouts, and after a pause he replies, "Apply directly where it hurts" from a television advertisement. Kyle didn't know how to explain that the Scout troop practiced making bandages for treating injuries. It can be a problem if people in the community who interact with children with ASDs interpret such responses as indicating that the child isn't making sense. Instead, it is helpful if the person can rephrase the question and add prompts. For example, instead of the person asking, "What did you do in school today?" the questioner can ask, "Did you talk about animals in school today?" or "Did you paint in school today?" This way the questioner is more likely to receive a more appropriate answer.

Help Adults Understand that a Child's Failing to Comply Is Not Intentional

When children are asked to do something inconsistent with their rigid routines, they frequently fail to do as asked. That doesn't mean they are being defiant, it means that what they were asked to do just doesn't seem right to them. If the librarian asks William to put the book he's finished reading in the container of books to be reshelved, he may instead put the book back in the bookshelf in the wrong place. He isn't being obstinate, but it is likely that he was taught at home to always put his books away after reading them. When the swimming instructor says to the children in her class, "Okay, everyone dunk your head underwater," Robin may refuse to do so because the only time she dunks her head in water is when her hair is being washed, which she dislikes. Explaining to staff members in such a community setting the reasons why your child isn't complying can help them think of other ways to garner the child's cooperation. For example, before making the foregoing request, the instructor might say, "We're *not* going to wash your hair. We're going dunk our heads under water to get them wet," and it is more likely Robin may follow the direction.

Providing Supplementary Cues

When negotiating new community situations, it helps for your child to have additional supportive cues. When going to the library, a visual schedule representing the steps in selecting books to be checked out, putting away books you decide not to check out, and having books scanned by the librarian will help avoid the problem William encountered above. A series of laminated photos (so they don't get wet) held in a keyring can be clipped to your child's swimsuit, functioning as a visual schedule of the steps in swimming. Showing the swimming instructors how to prompt your child to look at his or her visual schedule will assist them in better understanding your child and using the same strategy with other activities, such as showering, drying with a towel, and getting dressed to go home. By using a combination of manual gestures together with spoken requests, children will be more likely to follow spoken instructions of those they encounter in the community.

Slower Communication

Because children with ASDs are slow at processing information, busy nurses in the doctor's office or recreation center staff members teaching tee-ball may speak too rapidly and seem impatient. Although children may not understand everything someone has said to them, they can often detect when an adult is annoyed with them. Suggesting to community-support people to speak more slowly and avoid rushing your child will help them be more successful in working with your child. By using shorter phrases or sentences and supplementing the sentences with visual cues (e.g., gestures, pictures), they will find their communication efforts are usually more effective.

PREPARING YOUR CHILD FOR THE SETTING

Whenever possible, children with ASDs should be prepared for what to expect when entering new situations and activities. By keeping surprises to a minimum, it is less likely that a visit to a neighbor's house or hike along the creek will end in an emotional outburst.

Tell Your Child When, Who, and What

Children with ASDs have difficulty accepting new settings, especially those with unfamiliar sounds and smells, such as an indoor swimming pool; or situations that appear frightening, such as entering a semidarkened planetarium chamber. Preparing your child for what to expect and providing them with brief exposure to the situation, when possible, before embarking on your first outing can prevent problems such as a meltdown.

When the Situation Will Begin

Tell your child when the event is going to occur. For many youngsters with ASDs, it is more helpful to tell them, "We're going to go to Kevin's house after dinner," rather than "at 7 o'clock." Time specified by the clock is often not very meaningful to children with ASDs and may provoke repetitive questions: "Is it time yet?"

Who Will Be Present

By telling your students who will be present during a school activity, they are more likely to accept the situation. By saying, "We're going to music with Dawn, Jacob, and Abigail" the child understands what to expect. "We're going for a walk with Penny and her mom" prepares the child for the social context of the event.

What Will Be Done

"We're going to walk along the creek and collect rocks" tells the child three things: 1) he or she is going for a walk, 2) the walk will be along the creek, and 3) he or she is going to collect rocks. The child doesn't need to fear that he or she might be called upon to engage in an activity he or she finds disturbing, such as going swimming in the creek. By saying, "We're going to Grandma's house, and we'll have ice cream on the way home," you are telling the child what he or she will be doing and the consequence (i.e., an ice cream treat).

When the Activity Will End

"We'll come home after we pick up the laundry" specifies a meaningful endpoint. "Put away your crayons when the timer rings" tells the child that a specific cue will tell him or her when the activity is over. "We'll have a snack as soon as you have finished your spelling words (pointing to a visual schedule)" not only sets a concrete end point, but it specifies a reward to be provided when the activity is completed.

Visiting the Setting

Sometimes it is a good idea to bring your student or child to a new setting for a short period of time before an activity actually begins so he or she becomes desensitized to novel cues. Find a time when there will be few people present, with a low noise level, and few distractions. Bring the child to the new situation for 5–10 minutes and then leave after he or she has had an opportunity to see and hear what he or she will experience during the actual activity. The following two hypothetical scenarios illustrate the strategy:

Consider an 8-year-old with Asperger syndrome named Bruce. He is apprehensive about swimming lessons. His father says, "After breakfast we're going to the YMCA. You can see the pool, but you won't go swimming. We'll look around for a minute, then we'll come home." This provides an opportunity for Bruce to enter the YMCA building when there are few children present, be greeted by the swimming instructor, walk into the swimming pool area and look around, and then leave. Bruce has an opportunity to experience the hollow sound of the room and the odd smell of the chlorinated water in the air and to see someone standing in the shallow end of the pool. The situation isn't frightening, which will make it easier for him when he has his first lesson the following week.

Linda says she doesn't want to go camping because she's afraid of lions and tigers in the woods. Her mother tries to explain that there are no lions and tigers in the woods near the lake where they go fishing, but Linda is not reassured. Linda's father sets up a small pop-up tent in the backyard behind the house. Linda's mother makes chicken salad sandwiches, which are Linda's favorite, and then cuts them into quarters and packs them in a backpack, along with a thermos of lemonade. Linda's father says, "Linda, you bring the backpack" and points to it. Linda brings the backpack to the tent, and her father places a lantern on the floor of the tent and lights it as it is getting dark. He suggests Linda and her brother, Sam, pretend they are camping. They sit in a circle and play a card game, and then open the backpack and enjoy the sandwiches and lemonade. After 30 minutes, they turn off the lantern and return to the house as Linda's father says, "That was fun. It was just like camping."

A few days later, Linda and Sam's father takes them for a walk in a wooded area not far from their house where there is a small pond. He points out squirrels and birds and says, "That robin has a very pretty song." He encourages Linda to look at the bird through binoculars. "Listen to that squirrel scolding his neighbor," Sam remarks. "There are only small animals here, no big animals here," Linda's father concludes. When they return from their walk, Linda's mother reads her a book about a family's camping trip that includes pictures of a family sitting by the campfire roasting marshmallows on sticks and eating them. Linda's mom says, "That looks like fun!" The following week when Linda's family drives to the lake to go camping, Linda's fear has largely subsided because she has experienced fun elements of camping, and heard a story about enjoyable activities during camping.

START SMALL FOR SHORT TIME INTERVALS

When I visit a major art museum the first time, especially one about which I've heard wonderful comments, I often feel compelled to take in as many of the exhibits as possible. That is usually a mistake. The collections of many museums are far too vast to actually visit all in a single trip. The result is that I feel rushed, a bit overwhelmed, and I have limited enjoyment of the museum visit. The strategy I've found more agreeable involves selecting five or six of the dozens of possible exhibit areas, and focus on them. By deciding in advance which areas are of greatest interest, I avoid the feeling of pressure to move quickly on to the next room in the museum. If I've visited the last gallery on my planned list and still feel refreshed, I may visit another gallery but seldom more than that. As I depart through the museum exit, I often find myself pleasantly reflecting on which works I enjoyed most, and which artists I'd like to learn more about, rather than feeling frazzled. The same strategy works well with children with ASDs. Less is often more.

Start Small

The same approach applies to taking children with ASDs into the community as well as to museums. After deciding on a setting, such as the zoo, select three or four exhibits that are most appropriate (e.g., monkeys, zebras, kangaroos, pandas). Tell the child in advance which animals he or she will be seeing. Provide him or her with a visual schedule with images of each of the animals that will be seen. Review the schedule with him or her before leaving home. After the image of the last animal on the visual schedule, add a photograph of the reward that will be provided at the conclusion of the visit (e.g., a popsicle). Plan for no more than 30–45 minutes on the first outing. If the initial visit goes well, with no behavioral outbursts, add 1–2 additional exhibit areas during the next visit. In most instances, children with ASDs begin to tire after 45–60 minutes, so it is wise to limit a typical community outing to that duration. More stimulating activities involving faster tempos should be for shorter durations (e.g., 20–30 minutes).

Consider Less Costly Venues

Parents may feel that it isn't worth driving across town to the science museum, paying for admission and for parking, to only visit a fraction of the museum's exhibits. But the reality is that no one will enjoy the outing if the child with an ASD begins fussing and crying or has a meltdown after an hour of being reluctantly led from exhibit to exhibit. At the end of the encounter, everyone will be distraught, and what had been intended to be a pleasant family outing may disintegrate into an emotional fiasco. For some families, it is better to select community activities that involve little financial outlay so they won't feel that the cost has been too great for a short foray into the community, which is generally more enjoyable.

Coping with Long Outings

If families plan to take children with ASDs to theme parks or vacation locations that involve much longer time periods, it is wise to break the half-day or daylong visit into a series of shorter periods with frequent rests. The greater the crowding, the noisier the location, the longer the lines, the more difficult it will be for a child with an ASD, which will mean each series of planned activities will need to be shorter (e.g., no more than 30–45 minutes) followed by a quiet time. By identifying quiet respite locations along the route of the planned series of rides and exhibits, parents can prepare the child with an ASD and his siblings for the way the day's activities will be scheduled. Many commercial theme parks provide online maps indicating the location of rides and exhibits that can be used to plan the best way to divide a 3–4 hour visit into a series of shorter activities interspersed with snacks and quiet down time. By contacting the theme park that a family is considering attending and requesting information about "quiet sites" distributed throughout a given park, parents can more adequately plan their visit. Some parents take turns playing quietly with the child with an ASD while the other parent takes siblings on additional rides or exhibit visits before the entire family resumes their day's sojourn.

INCORPORATE SIBLINGS AND PEERS

Many children with ASDs are fortunate enough to have typical siblings as playmates. Children who have had early intervention services that include learning imitation often begin modeling their siblings' behavior during play.

Activities for Preschool-Age Children and Siblings

Younger children with ASDs who participate in community outings with their brothers or sisters usually engage in parallel play rather than interactive play. Taking the child with an ASD and his sibling to a park to swing, slide, and climb on the monkey bars can provide a wonderful opportunity for the child to learn important play skills. It can also be used as a vehicle for learning to take turns swinging, pushing their sibling who is swinging, and learning to play catch.

As children grow a little older (4–5 years of age), many children with ASDs attempt interactive or reciprocal play. Camping is a good activity because it provides the opportunity to learn beginning cooperative skills (e.g., collecting sticks for building a fire). Although it is helpful to involve siblings in activities with their sister or brother with an ASD, it is also important that they not be burdened with caring for their sibling.

Peer Play Dates

Selecting peers for play dates requires matching the children's characteristics. Little girls are often more socially-oriented than boys of the same age, but some boys are terrific playmates as well. As a result, it may be a good idea to speak with parents of girls in the neighborhood who are about the same age as the child with an ASD about their willingness to permit their daughter to come to the home of the child with an ASD for play dates. Planned, structured activities usually are more effective than leaving the children to their own devices to create play activities. Parent-led activities, such as making cookies or doing an art project, ensure that both children are involved in aspects of the endeavor. Such activities can be used to teach turn-taking. Once a child with an ASD is comfortable playing with a neighbor child within his or her own home, it may be appropriate for him or her to play with the peer in the peer's home. Parents can drink coffee and chat nearby while the children play to ensure that any problems that may arise are quickly resolved. Often after 1–2 such visits, the mother of the child with an ASD can usually leave her child with the peer's parent for an hour or so before returning to retrieve him or her. That increases the child's independence and comfort playing with other children without his parent being present.

Activities for Older Children with Autism Spectrum Disorders and Their Peers

Older, high-functioning children with ASDs are encouraged to participate in community outings with peers, such as going swimming together at a recreation center or having a snack at a fast-food restaurant. The steps involved in a given community activity are practiced first with a parent or older sibling to make certain the child with an ASD has the component skills to participate in the same activity with a peer. A parent accompanies the two 11–15-year-olds to ensure their safety as well as being able to intervene and resolve any problems that might arise. Finding peers who are also interested in video games, computers, or similar music can provide a vehicle for promoting interactions. As with any other adolescent, teenagers with ASDs often want their parents to "leave them alone" with their friends; however, until the child's safety and the limits for a given activity have been established, that is usually unwise. Many teenagers with ASDs visit their friends' homes while the peer's parents are home to provide supervision.

Sustaining Peer Relationships

The greatest problem higher-functioning youngsters face in sustaining relationships with peers revolve around pragmatic language and social skill deficits. They often find it difficult to coordinate their comments with those of peers and may be insensitive to peers' preferences and emotions. Providing practice through social skills groups, listening carefully to a speaker's comments, and responding accordingly can be helpful. A youth with an ASD may repeatedly talk about a topic that is uninteresting to a peer. Teaching a teenager to discriminate peers' gestures and facial expressions can help him or her tell when his or her peer is bored with his or her remarks and wishes to change the subject. Social activities within the community that revolve around specific activities (e.g., taking photographs) are more effective than those involving unstructured interactions (e.g., "hanging out" together). A high-functioning youngster who gets together with a typical peer to create a multimedia computer presentation on a topic of mutual interest provides the opportunity for cooperating, compromising, and engaging in creative activity.

SUMMARY

Children with ASDs can learn to participate in and enjoy a wide array of community settings with proper preparation. Identifying community settings with optimal features can make outings more successful. That involves surveying physical and social features of settings, preparing those in the community with whom the child frequently interacts to understand the child, and preparing the child for those settings. Incorporating siblings and peers into community outings adds to the richness of the child's experiences and strengthens his or her social skills, which increases his or her ability to lead enjoyable and more meaningful lives as an adolescent and young adult.

References

Abramson, R.K., Ravan, S.A., Wright, H.H., Wieduwilt, K., Wolpert, C.M., Donnelly, S.A., et al. (2005). The relationship between restrictive and repetitive behaviors in individuals with autism and obsessive-compulsive symptoms in parents. *Child Psychiatry and Human Development, 36*, 155–165.

Activity assessment manual. (1990). Ravensdale, WA: Idyll Arbor, Inc.

Afaghi, A., O'Connor, H., & Chow, C.M. (2007). High-glycemic-index carbohydrate meals shorten sleep onset. *American Journal of Clinical Nutrition, 85*, 426–430.

Afzal, M.A., Ozoemena, L.C., O'Hare, A., Kidger, K.A., Bentley, M.L., & Minor, P.D. (2006). Absence of detectable measles virus genome sequence in blood of autistic children who have had their MMR vaccination during the routine childhood immunization schedule of the UK. *Journal of Medical Virology, 78*, 623–630.

American Dental Association. (2002). Baby's first teeth. *Journal of the American Dental Association, 133*, 5.

American Psychiatric Association. (1994). *Diagnostic and statistical manual of mental disorders* (4th ed.). Washington, DC: Author.

Aristotle. (350 BCE). *Politics: A treatise on government. Book 3, Part VI* (B. Jowett, Trans.). Retrieved June 6, 2007, from http://classics.mit.edu/Aristotle/politics.3.three.html (Original work published 1914)

Ayres, A.J. (1979). *Sensory integration and the child.* Los Angeles: Western Psychological Services.

Baker, J. (2003). *The social skills picture book teaching play, emotion, and communication to children with autism.* Arlington, TX: Future Horizons.

Baranek, G.T., Foster, L.G., & Berkson, G. (1997). Tactile defensiveness and stereotyped behavior. *American Journal of Occupational Therapy, 51*, 91–95.

Baron-Cohen, S. (2002). *Mind reading: An interactive guide to human emotions.* London: Jessica Kingsley Publishers.

Baron-Cohen, S., Allen, J., & Gillberg, C. (1992). Can autism be detected at 18 months? The needle, the haystack, and the CHAT. *The British Journal of Psychiatry, 161*, 839–843.

Bettelheim, B. (1967). *The empty fortress: Infantile autism and the birth of the self.* New York: Free Press.

Boddaert, N., Chabane, N., Belin, P., Bourgeois, M., Royer, V., Barthelemy, C., et al. (2004). Perceptions of complex sounds in autism: Abnormal auditory cortical processing in children. *American Journal of Psychiatry, 161,* 2117–2120.

Bodfish, J.W., Symons, F.J., & Lewis, M.H. (1999). *Repetitive Behavior Scale–Revised.* Morganton, NC: Western Carolina Center.

Bodfish, J.W., Symons, F.J., Parker, D.E., & Lewis, M.H. (2000). Varieties of repetitive behavior in autism. *Journal of Autism and Developmental Disorders, 30,* 237–243.

Bolton, P.F., Pickles, A., Murphy, M., & Rutter, M.J. (1998). Autism, affective and other psychiatric disorders: Patterns of familial aggregation. *Psychological Medicine, 28,* 385–395.

Bondy, A., & Frost, L. (2001). *A picture's worth: PECS and other visual communication strategies in autism.* Bethesda, MD: Woodbine House.

Bonnel, A., Mottron, L., Peretz, I., Trudel, M., Gallun, E., & Bonnel, A.M. (2003). Enhanced pitch sensitivity in individuals with autism: A signal detection analysis. *Journal of Cognitive Neuroscience, 15,* 226–235.

Bopp, K.D., Brown, K.E., & Mirenda, P. (2004). Speech-language pathologists' roles in the delivery of positive behavior support for individuals with developmental disabilities. *American Journal of Speech-Language Pathology, 13,* 5–19.

Bowlby, J. (1988). *A secure base: Parent–child attachment and healthy human development.* London: Routledge.

Califiero, J.M. (2005). *Meaningful exchanges for people with autism: An introduction to augmentative and alternative communication.* Bethesda, MD: Woodbine House.

Capucilli, A.S., & Stott, D. (2000a). *The potty book for boys.* Hauppauge, NY: Barron's Educational Series.

Capucilli, A.S., & Stott, D. (2000b). *The potty book for girls.* Hauppauge, NY: Barron's Educational Series.

Carr, E.G., Levin, L., McConnachie, G., Carlson, J.I., Kemp, D.C., Smith, C.E., et al. (1999). Comprehensive multi-situational intervention for problem behavior in the community: Long-term maintenance and social validation. *Journal of Positive Behavior Interventions, 1,* 5–25.

Carr, E.G., Reeve, C.E., & Magito-McLaughlin, D. (1995). Contextual influences on problem behavior in people with developmental disabilities. In L.K. Koegel, R.L. Koegel, & G. Dunlap (Eds.), *Positive behavioral support: Including people with difficult behavior in the community* (pp. 403–423). Baltimore: Paul H. Brookes Publishing Co.

CBS News Early Show. (2006, February 23). Autistic teen hoop dreams come true [Television broadcast]. New York: CBS.

Centers for Disease Control and Prevention. (2004). Prevalence of no leisure-time physical activity—35 states and the District of Columbia, 1988–2002 [Electronic version]. *Morbidity and Mortality Weekly Report, 53,* 82–86.

Charlop-Christy, M.H., Loc, L., & Freeman, K.A. (2000). A comparison of video modeling with in-vivo modeling for teaching children with autism. *Journal of Autism and Developmental Disorders, 30,* 537–552.

Constantino, J.N., Lajonchere, C., Lutz, M., Gray, T., Abbacchi, A., McKenna, A., et al. (2006). Autistic social impairment in the siblings of children with pervasive developmental disorders. *American Journal of Psychiatry, 163,* 294–296.

Coyne, P., Nyberg, C., & Vandenburg, M.L. (1998). *Developing leisure-time skills for persons with autism.* Arlington, TX: Future Horizons.

Dan, B., & Boyd, S.G. (2006). A neurophysiological perspective on sleep and its maturation. *Developmental Medicine and Child Neurology, 48,* 773–779.

Davis, K., Parker, K., & Montgomery, G. (2004). Sleep in infants and young children, Part One: Normal sleep. *Journal of Pediatric Health Care, 18,* 65–71.

Dawson, G., & Watling, R. (2000). Interventions to facilitate auditory, visual, and motor integration in autism: A review of the evidence. *Journal of Autism and Developmental Disorders, 30,* 415–421.

Deer, B. (n.d.). *The Lancet scandal.* Retrieved June 1, 2007, from http://briandeer.com/mmr-lancet.htm

Demichelli, V., Jefferson, T., Rivetti, A., & Price, D. (2005). *Vaccines for measles, mumps and rubella in children.* London: Wiley.

DiLavore, P. C., Lord, C., & Rutter, M. (1995). The Pre-Linguisic Autism Diagnostic Observation Schedule. *Journal of Autism and Developmental Disorders, 25*(4), 355–379.

Dunn, W. (1999). *The sensory profile manual.* San Antonio, TX: The Psychological Corporation.

Eliot, T.S. (1950). *The cocktail party*. Orlando, FL: Harcourt, Inc.

Ellis, E.M., Ala'i-Rosales, S.S., Glenn, S.S., Rosales-Ruiz, J., & Greenspoon, J. (2006). The effects of graduated exposure, modeling, and contingent social attention on tolerance to skin care products with two children with autism. *Research in Developmental Disabilities, 57,* 585–598.

Erman, M. (2004). Clinical update: Management of insomnia in the primary care practice. *Current Perspectives in Insomnia, 2.* Retrieved March 16, 2007, from http://www.medscape.com/viewprogram/3310

Evans, D.W., Canavera, K., Kleinpeter, F.L., Maccubin, E., & Taga, K. (2005). The fears, phobias, and anxieties of children with autism spectrum disorders and Down syndrome: Comparisons with developmentally and chronologically age matched children. *Child Psychiatry and Human Development, 36,* 3–26.

FACTR: Functional assessment of characteristics for therapeutic recreation. (1988). Ravensdale, WA: Idyll Arbor, Inc.

FirstSigns. (n.d.). Research in autism spectrum and other disorders. Retrieved September 19, 2007, from http://www.firstsigns.org/index.html

Folstein, S., & Rutter, M. (1977). Infantile autism: A genetic study of 21 twin pairs. *Journal of Clinical Child Psychology and Psychiatry, 18,* 297–321.

Fouse, B., & Wheeler, M. (1997). *A treasure chest of behavioral strategies for individuals with autism.* Arlington, TX: Future Horizons.

Frost, R. (1920). *Mountain interval.* New York: Henry Holt and Company.

Fuller, P.M., Gooley, J.J., & Saper, C.B. (2006). Neurobiology of the sleep–wake cycle: Sleep architecture, circadian regulation, and regulatory feedback. *Journal of Biological Rhythms, 21,* 482–493.

Galmmeltoft, L., & Nordenhof, M.S. (2007). *Autism, play, and social interaction.* London: Jessica Kingsley Publishers.

Geir, D.A., & Geir, M.R. (2003). An assessment of the impact of thimerosal on childhood neurodevelopmental disorders. *Pediatric Rehabilitation, 6,* 97–102.

Geir, D.A., & Geier, M.R. (2004). A comparative evaluation of the effects of measles, mumps, and rubella immunization and mercury doses from thimerosal-containing childhood vaccines on the population prevalence of autism. *Medical Science Monitor, 10,* PI33–PI39.

Gernsbacher, M.A., Dawson, M., & Goldsmith, H.H. (2005). Three reasons not to believe in an autism epidemic. *Psychological Science, 14,* 55–58.

Giannotti, F., Cortesi, F., Cerquiglini, A., & Bernabel, P. (2006). An open-label study of controlled-release melatonin in treatment of sleep disorders in children with autism. *Journal of Autism and Developmental Disorders, 36,* 741–752.

Gilliam, J.E. (2006). *Giliam Autism Rating Scale–2 (GARS-2)* (2nd ed.). Austin, TX: PRO-ED.

Glascoe, F.P. (1997). *Parents' Evaluation of Developmental Status (PEDS).* Nashville: Ellsworth and Vandermeer Press.

Goldstein, H. (1999, December). *Communication intervention for children with autism: A review of treatment efficacy.* Paper presented at the first workshop of the Committee on Educational Interventions for Children with Autism, National Research Council, Tallahassee, FL.

Grant, C.M., Boucher, J., Riggs, K.J., & Grayson, A. (2005). Moral understanding in children with autism. *Autism, 9,* 317–331.

Gurney, J.G., McPheeters, M.L., & Davis, M.M. (2006). Parental report of health conditions and health care use among children with and without autism: National survey of children's health. *Archives of Pediatrics and Adolescent Medicine, 160,* 825–830.

Hecht, B. (1957). *Charlie: The improbable life and times of Charles MacCarthur.* New York: Harper Brothers Publishers.

Hellings, J.A. (2002). Treatment of co-morbid disorders in autism: Which regimens are effective and for whom? *Medscape General Medicine,* 2(1). Retrieved March 22, 2007, from http://www.medscape.com/viewarticle/430507

Hoban, T.F. (2004). *Sleep and its disorders in children: Seminars in neurology.* Retrieved March 17, 2007, from http://www.medscape.com/viewarticle/491438

Hodgdon, L.A. (1995). *Visual strategies for improving communication: Practical supports for school and home.* Troy, MI: Quirk Roberts Publishing.

Hollander, E., King, A., Delaney, K., Smith, C.J., & Silverman, J.M. (2003). Obsessive-compulsive behaviors in parents of multiplex autism families. *Psychiatry Research, 117,* 11–16.

Honda, H., Shimizu, Y., & Rutter, M. (2005). No effect of MMR withdrawal on the incidence of autism: A total population study. *Journal of Child Psychology and Psychiatry and Applied Disciplines, 46,* 572–579.

Horner, R.H., Dunlap, G., Koegel, R.L., Carr, E.G., Sailor, W., Anderson, J., et al. (1990). Toward a technology of "nonaversive" behavioral support. *Journal of the Association for Persons with Severe Handicaps, 15,* 125–132.

Horton, R. (2004). The lessons of MMR. *The Lancet, 363,* 747–749.

Issue. (n.d.). *The American Heritage Dictionary of the English Language, Fourth Edition.* Retrieved December 3, 2007, from http://dictionary.reference.com/browse/issue

Itard, J.M.G. (1801). *The wild boy of Aveyron* (G. Humphrey & M. Humphrey, Trans.). New York: Appleton-Century-Crofts. (Original work published 1962)

Jang, M. (2003). *Breakthroughs in the evaluation and treatment of autism.* Retrieved June 11, 2007, from http://www.miriamjangmd.com/DAN-protocol.html

Joyce, B.A., Keck, J.F., & Gerkensmeyer, J. (2001). Evaluation of pain management interventions for neonatal circumcision pain. *Journal of Pediatric Health Care, 15,* 105–114.

Just, M.A., Cherkassky, V.L., Keller, T.A., Kana, R.K., & Minshew, N.J. (2006). Functional and anatomical cortical underconnectivity in autism: Evidence from an FMRI study of an executive function task and corpus callosum morphometry. *Cerebral Cortex, 17,* 951–961.

Kahng, S., Iwata, B.A., & Lewin, A.B. (2002). Behavioral treatment of self-injury, 1964–2000. *American Journal on Mental Retardation, 107,* 212–221.

Kanner, L. (1943). Autistic disturbance of affective contact. *Nervous Child, 2,* 217–250.

Kaye, J.A., del Mar Melero-Montes, M., & Jick, H. (2001). Mumps, measles, and rubella vaccine and the incidence of autism recorded by general practitioners: A time trend analysis. *British Medical Journal, 322,* 460–463.

Kennedy, C.H., & Meyer, K.A. (1996). Sleep deprivation, allergy symptoms, and negatively reinforced problem behavior. *Journal of Applied Behavior Analysis, 29,* 133–135.

Kennedy, C.H., & Thompson, T. (2000). Health conditions contributing to problem behavior among people with mental retardation and developmental disabilities. In M.L. Wehmeyer & J.R. Patton (Eds.), *Mental retardation in the 21st century* (pp. 211–231). Austin, TX: PRO-ED.

Kennedy, F. (n.d.) "Freedom is like taking a bath—you have to keep doing it every day!" *About Women's History.* Retrieved June 12, 2007, from http://womenshistory.about.com/library/qu/blqustan.htm.

Khaifa, S., Bruneau, N., Roge, B., Georgieff, N., Veuillet, E., Adrien, J.L., et al. (2004). Increased perception of loudness in autism. *Hearing Research, 198,* 87–92.

Kientz, M.A., & Dunn, W. (1997). A comparison of the performance of children with and without autism on the Sensory Profile. *American Journal of Occupational Therapy, 5,* 530–537.

Klein, K.C., & Diehl, E.B. (2004). Relationship between MMR vaccine and autism. *The Annals of Pharmacotherapy, 38,* 1297–1330.

Kolevzon, A., Mathewson, K.A., & Hollander, E. (2006). Selective serotonin reuptake inhibitors in autism: A review of efficacy. *Journal of Clinical Psychiatry, 67,* 407–414.

Kolko, D.J., Anderson, L., & Campbell, M. (1980). Sensory preference and over-selective responding in autistic children. *Journal of Autism and Developmental Disorders, 10,* 259–271.

Kroger, K.A., Schultz, J.R., & Newsom, C. (2007). A comparison of two group-delivered social skills programs for young children with autism. *Journal of Autism and Developmental Disorders, 37*, 808–817.

Laidler, J.R. (2005). U.S. Department of Education data on "autism" are not reliable for tracking autism prevalence. *Pediatrics, 116*, e120–e124.

Lauritsen, M., & Ewald, H. (2001). The genetics of autism. *Acta Psychiatrica Scandinavica, 103*, 411–427.

LeBlanc, L.A., Coates, A.M., Daneshvar, S., Charlop-Christy, M.H., Morris, C., & Lancaster, B.M. (2003). Using video modeling and reinforcement to teach perspective-taking skills to children with autism. *Journal of Applied Behavior Analysis, 36*, 253–257.

Levin, L., & Carr, E.G. (2001). Food selectivity and problem behavior in children with developmental disabilities: Analysis and intervention. *Behavior Modification, 25*, 443–470.

Lord, C., Risi, S., Lambrecht, L., Cook, E.H., Leventhal, B.L., DiLavore, P.C., Pickles, A., & Rutter, M. (2000). The Autism Diagnostic Observation Schedule–Generic (ADOS): A standard measure of social and communication deficits associated with the spectrum of autism. *Journal of Autism and Developmental Disorders, 30*, 205–223.

Lord, C., Rutter, M.D, DiLavore, Ph.D., & Risi, S. (1989). *Autism Diagnostic Observation Schedule (ADOS)*. Los Angeles: Western Psychological Services.

Lord, C., Rutter, M., Goode, S., Heemsbergen, J., Jordan, H., Mawhood, L., et al. (1989). Autism diagnostic observation schedule: A standardized observation of communicative and social behavior. *Journal of Autism and Developmental Disorders, 19*, 185–212.

Lord, C., Storoschuk, S., Rutter, M., & Pickles, A. (1993). Using the ADI-R to diagnose autism in preschool children. *Infant Mental Health Journal, 14*, 234–252.

Lord, C.E., & McGee, J.G. (2001). *Educating children with autism* (pp. 98–100). Committee on Educational Interventions for Children with Autism, Division of Behavioral and Social Sciences and Education, National Research Council. Washington, DC: National Academies Press.

Lovaas, O.I. (1987). Behavioral treatment and normal educational and intellectual functioning in young autistic children. *Journal of Consulting and Clinical Psychology, 55*, 3–9.

Lovaas, O.I., & Schreibman, L. (1971). Stimulus overselectivity of autistic children in a two-stimulus situation. *Behaviour Research and Therapy, 9*, 305–310.

MacDonald, G. (1877). *The Marquis of Lossie*. Retrieved June 7, 2007, from http://www.gutenberg.org/dirs/etext04/mloss10.txt

Markov, D., & Goldman, M. (2006). Normal sleep and circadian rhythms: Neurobiologic mechanisms underlying sleep and wakefulness. *Psychiatric Clinics of North America, 29*, 841–853.

Markus, C.R., Jonkman, L.M., Lammers, J.H., Deutz, N.E., Messer, M.H., & Rigtering, N. (2005). Evening intake of alpha-lactalbumin increases plasma tryptophan availability and improves morning alertness and brain measures of attention. *American Journal of Clinical Nutrition, 81*, 1026–1033.

Martson, S. (1990). The magic of encouragement. *The Columbia world of quotations.* Retrieved June 6, 2007, from www.bartleby.com/66/

McClannahan, L.E., & Krantz, P.J. (1999). *Activity schedules for children with autism: Teaching independent behavior.* Bethesda, MD: Woodbine House.

McClannahan, L., & Krantz, P. (2005). *Teaching conversation to children with autism: Scripts and script fading.* Bethesda, MD: Woodbine House.

Mead, M. (1967). *The changing cultural patterns of work and leisure.* Washington, DC: U.S. Department of Labor, Manpower Administration.

Mercer, L., Creighton, S., Holden, J.J., & Lewis, M.E. (2006). Parental perspectives on the causes of an autism spectrum disorder in their children. *Journal of Genetic Counseling, 15,* 41–50.

Miles, J.H., Takahashi, T.N., Bagby, S., Sahota, P.K., Vaslow, D.F., Wang, C.H., et al. (2005). Essential versus complex autism: Definition of fundamental prognostic subtypes. *American Journal of Medical Genetics Part A, 135*(2), 171–180.

Morin, A.K., Jarvis, C.I., & Lynch, A.M. (2007). *Therapeutic options for sleep-maintenance and sleep-onset insomnia.* Retrieved March 18, 2007, from http://www.medscape.com/viewarticle/552873.

National Autistic Society UK. (n.d.).*Checklist for Autism in Toddlers.* Retrieved June 2, 2007, from http://www.nas.org.uk/nas/jsp/polopoly.jsp?d=128&a=2226

National Digestive Diseases Information Clearinghouse. (n.d.). *Lactose intolerance.* Retrieved March 1, 2006, from http://digestive.niddk.nih.gov/ddiseases/pubs/lactoseintolerance/

National Institute of Child Health and Human Development. (2007). *Lactose intolerance.* Retrieved June 12, 2007, from http://www.nichd.nih.gov/health/topics/lactose_intolerance.cfm

National Institutes of Health. (2006). *Lactose intolerance* (NIH Publication No. 06-2751). Washington, DC: U.S. Government Printing Office.

Niedecker, L. (2002). *Collected works.* Berkley: The University of California Press.

Nikopoulos, C.K., & Keenan, M. (2007). Using video modeling to teach complex social sequences to children with autism. *Journal of Autism and Developmental Disorders, 37,* 678–693.

Nikopoulos, C., Keenan, M., & Hobbs, S. (2007). *Video modeling and behaviour analysis: A guide for teaching social skills to children with autism.* London: Jessica Kingsley Publishers.

O'Neill, R.E., Horner, R.H., Albin, R.W., Sprague, J.R., Storey, K., & Newton, J.S. (1997). *Functional assessment and program development for problem behavior* (2nd ed.). Pacific Grove, CA: Brooks/Cole.

O'Riordan, M., & Passetti, F. (2006). Discrimination in autism within different sensory modalities. *Journal of Autism and Developmental Disorders, 36,* 665–675.

Oliver, M. (1992). *New and selected poems.* Boston: Beacon Press.

Oram Cardy, J.E., Flagg, E.J., Roberts, W., Brian, J., & Roberts, T.P. (2005). Magnetoencephalography identifies rapid temporal processing deficit in autism and language impairment. *NeuroReport, 16,* 329–332.

Ozonoff, S., & Rogers, S.J. (2006). Annotation: What do we know about sensory dysfunction in autism? A critical review of the empirical evidence. *Child Psychology and Psychiatry, 46,* 1255–1268.

Palmer, R.F., Blanchard, S., Jean, C.R., & Mandell, D.S. (2005). School district resources and identification of children with autistic disorder. *American Journal of Public Health, 95,* 125–130.

Parker, S.K., Schwartz, B., Todd, J., & Pickering, L.K. (2004). Thimerosal-containing vaccines and autistic spectrum disorder: A critical review of published original data. *Pediatrics, 114,* 793–804.

Parpia, N. (2007b). *Potty training chart & stickers by Potty Scotty (for boys).* Pearland, TX: Mom Innovations.

Parpia, N. (2007a). *Potty training chart & stickers by Potty Patty (for girls).* Pearland, TX: Mom Innovations.

Partington, J.W. (2006.) *The assessment of basic language and learning skills–revised.* Pleasant Hill, CA: Behavior Analysts, Inc.

Patterson, J. (1993). *Potty time.* New York: Grosset & Dunlap.

Piazza, C.C., Patel, M.R., Santana, C.M., Goh, H.L., Delia, M.D., & Lancaster, B.M. (2002). An evaluation of simultaneous and sequential presentation of preferred and nonpreferred food to treat food selectivity. *Journal of Applied Behavior Analysis, 35,* 259–270.

Ploog, B.O., & Kim, N. (2006). Assessment of stimulus overselectivity with tactile compound stimuli in children with autism. *Journal of Autism and Developmental Disorders, 37,* 1514–1524.

Polimeni, M.A., Richdale, A.L., & Francis, A.J. (2005). A survey of sleep problems in autism, Asperger's disorder and typically developing children. *Journal of Intellectual Disability Research, 49,* 260–268.

Prizant, B.M., Wetherby, A.M., Rubin, E., Laurent, A.C., & Rydell, P.J. (2005a). *The SCERTS® Model: A comprehensive educational approach for children with autism spectrum disorders. Vol. I: Assessment.* Baltimore: Paul H. Brookes Publishing Co.

Prizant, B.M., Wetherby, A.M., Rubin, E., Laurent, A.C., & Rydell, P.J. (2005b). *The SCERTS® Model: A comprehensive educational approach for children with autism spectrum disorders. Vol. II: Intervention.* Baltimore: Paul H. Brookes Publishing Co.

Quill, K.A. (2000). *Do-watch-listen-say: Social and communication intervention for children with autism.* Baltimore: Paul H. Brookes Publishing Co.

Rhefeldt, R.A., Kinney, E.M., Root, S., & Stromer, R. (2004). Creating activity schedules using Microsoft PowerPoint. *Journal of Applied Behavior Analysis, 37,* 115–128.

Rice, C. (2007). Prevalence of autism spectrum disorders: Autism and developmental disabilities monitoring network, 14 sites, United States, 2002 [Electronic version]. *Morbidity and Mortality Weekly Report, 56,* 12–28.

Ritvo, E., Freeman, B., Mason-Brothers, A., Mo, A., & Ritvo, A. (1985). Concordance for the syndrome of autism in 40 pairs of afflicted twins. *American Journal of Psychiatry, 142,* 74–77.

Robins, D., Fein, D., Barton, M., & Green, J. (2001). The Modified Checklist for Autism in Toddlers: An initial study investigating the early detection of autism and pervasive developmental disorders. *Journal of Autism and Developmental Disorders, 31,* 131–144.

Rogers, S.J., Hepburn, S., & Wehner, E. (2003). Parent reports of sensory symptoms in toddlers with autism and those with other developmental disorders. *Journal of Autism and Developmental Disorders, 33,* 631–642.

Rosten, L. (1968). *The joys of Yiddish.* New York: Pocket Books.

Russell, A.J., Mataix-Cols, D., Anson, M., & Murphy, D.G.M. (2005). Obsessions and compulsions in Asperger syndrome in high-functioning autism. *British Journal of Psychiatry, 186,* 525–528.

Rutter, M., Bailey, A., Lord, C., & Berument, S.K. (2003). *Social Communication Questionnaire (SCQ).* Los Angeles: Western Psychological Services.

Rutter, M., LeCouteur, A., & Lord, C. (2002). *Autism Diagnostic Interview–Revised (ADI-R).* Los Angeles: Western Psychological Services.

Ruurs, M, & Kiss, A. (2004). *When we go camping.* Ontario, Canada: Tundra Books.

Sacks, O. (1998). *The man who mistook his wife for a hat: And other clinical tales (5th ed.).* New York: Touchstone.

Sallows, G.O., & Graupner, T.D. (2005). Intensive behavioral treatment for children with autism: 4-year outcome and predictors. *American Journal on Mental Retardation, 110,* 417–438.

Sandman, C.A., Barron, J.L., & Coman, H. (1990). An orally administered opiate blocker, naltrexone, attenuates self-injurious behavior. *American Journal on Mental Retardation, 95,* 93–102.

Santosh, P.J., Baird, G., Pityaratstian, N., Tavare, E., & Gringras, P. (2006). Impact of co-morbid autism spectrum disorders on stimulant response in children with attention deficit hyperactivity disorder: A retrospective and prospective effectiveness study. *Child: Care, Health and Development, 32,* 575–583.

Scarr, S. (1984). *Mother care/other care.* New York: Basic Books.

Scholper, E., Reichler, J., & Renner, B. (1988). *Childhood Autism Rating Scale (CARS).* Los Angeles: Western Psychological Services.

Schreck, K.A., & Mulick, J.A. (2000). Parental report of sleep problems in children with autism. *Journal of Autism and Developmental Disorders, 30,* 127–135.

Schreck, K.A., & Williams, K. (2005). Food preferences and factors influencing food selectivity for children with autism spectrum disorders. *Research in Developmental Disabilities, 27,* 353–363.

Schreibman, L., Koegel, R.L., & Craig, M.S. (1977). Reducing stimulus overselectivity in autistic children. *Journal of Abnormal Child Psychology, 5,* 425–436.

Shattuck, P.T. (2006). The contribution of diagnostic substitution to the growing administrative prevalence of autism in U.S. special education. *Pediatrics, 117,* 1028–1037.

Skellern, C., McDowell, M., & Schluter, P. (2005). Diagnosis of autistic spectrum disorders in Queensland: Variations in practice. *Journal of Paediatric and Child Health, 41,* 413–418.

Smeeth, L., Cook, C., Fombonne, E., Heavey, L., Rodrigues, L.C., Smith, P.G., et al. (2004). MMR vaccination and pervasive developmental disorders: A case control study. *The Lancet, 364,* 963–969.

Symons, F.J., Fox, N.D., & Thompson, T. (1998). Functional communication training and naltrexone treatment of self-injurious behavior: An experimental case report. *Journal of Applied Research in Intellectual Disabilities, 11*, 273–292.

Szymborska, W. (1993). *View with a grain of sand.* New York: Harcourt Brace and Company.

Taylor, B., Miller, E., Farrington, C.P., Petropoulos, M.C., Favot-Mayaud, I., Li, J., et al. (1999). Autism and measles, mumps, and rubella vaccine: No epidemiological evidence for a causal association. *The Lancet, 353*, 2026–2029.

Thompson, T. (2007). *Making sense of autism.* Baltimore: Paul H. Brookes Publishing Co.

Thompson, T., & Carey, A. (1980). Structured normalization: Intellectual and adaptive behavior changes in a residential setting. *Mental Retardation, 18*, 193–197.

Thompson, T., Hackenberg, T., Cerutti, D., Baker, D., & Axtell, S. (1994). Opioid antagonist effects on self-injury: Response form and location as determinants of medication effects. *American Journal on Mental Retardation, 99*, 85–102.

Toth, K., Dawson, G., Meltzoff, A.N., Greeson, J., & Fein, D. (2007). Early social, imitation, play, and language abilities of young non-autistic siblings of children with autism. *Journal of Autism and Developmental Disorders, 37*, 145–157.

Tse, J., Strulovitch, J., Tagalakis, V., Meng, L., & Fombonne, E. (in press). Social skills training for adolescents with Asperger syndrome and high-functioning autism. *Journal of Autism and Developmental Disorders.*

U.S. Census Bureau. (2007). *The 2007 statistical abstract: The national data book.* Retrieved April 22, 2007, from http://www.census.gov/compendia/statab/arts_entertainment_recreation/recreation_and_leisure_activities/

Wakefield, A.J., Murch, S.H., Anthony, A., Linnell, J., Casson, D.M., et al. (1998). Ileal-lymphoid-nodular hyperplasia, non-specific colitis, and pervasive developmental disorder in children. *The Lancet, 351*, 637–641.

Watanabe, M., & Sturmey, P. (2003). The effect of choice-making opportunities during activity schedules on task engagement of adults with autism. *Journal of Autism and Developmental Disorders, 33*, 535–538.

Weiss, M.J., & Harris, S.L. (2001). *Reaching out, joining in: Teaching social skills to young children with autism.* Bethesda, MD: Woodbine House.

Wheeler, M. (1998). *Toilet training for individuals with autism and related disorders.* Arlington, TX: Future Horizons.

Woods, D.W., Miltenberger, R.G., & Lumley, V.A. (1996). Sequential application of major habit reversal components to treat motor tics in children. *Journal of Applied Behavior Analysis, 29*, 483–493.

Yerys, B.E., Hepburn, S.L., Pennington, B.F., & Rogers, S.J. (2007). Executive function in preschoolers with autism: Evidence consistent with a secondary deficit. *Journal of Autism and Developmental Disorders, 37*, 1068–1079.

Zandt, F., Prior, M., & Kyrios, M. (2006). Repetitive behavior in children with high-functioning autism and obsessive-compulsive disorder. *Journal of Autism and Developmental Disorders, 37*, 251–259.

Zarcone, J.R., Lindauer, S.E., Morse, P.S., Crosland, K.A., Valdovinos, M.G., McKerhar, T.L., et al. (2004). Effects of risperidone on aberrant behavior of persons with developmental disabilities: I. A double-blind crossover study using multiple measures. *American Journal on Mental Retardation, 106*, 525–538.

Index

Page references to figures are indicated by *f*.